FROM THIS DAY FORTH

FROM THIS DAY FORTH

The Joy of Marriage

Brenton G. Yorgason / Terry R. Baker / Wesley R. Burr

BOOKCRAFT
Salt Lake City, Utah

Library of Congress Catalog Card Number: 82-70016
ISBN O-88494-450-6

First Printing, 1982

Lithographed in the United States of America
PUBLISHERS PRESS
Salt Lake City, Utah

*This book is dedicated to all
couples who have found their
marriage meaningful and who
share with us the hope and dream
and prayer that, with guidance
from the Holy Spirit, an eternally
rewarding relationship is in store*

Contents

Acknowledgments

We express particular gratitude to the following couples (listed alphabetically) who in this book have shared growing moments in their marriages. This they have done so that you, the reader, may take heart, knowing that the pleasures and pains of marriage are shared by others.

Tom and Marilyn Alexander
Rulon and Sandee Barlow
Dick and Jessie Bastian
Floyd and Kathy Bird
Steve and Sheryle Dixon
Steve and Mary Jane Grow
Robert and Carolee Harmon
Wes and Diane Homolik
Ronald and Ann Jamison
Reed and Sue Jensen
Allen and Cheryl Johnson
Dave and AnnEtta Merrill
Ray and Charlotte Neal
John and Susanne Olsen
John and Sybil Rees
Eric and Sandra Steppan
Steve and Wendy Stewart
Greg and Ann Sumner
Robert and Sylvia Taylor
Richard and Sharlene Thomas
Meridith and Loraine Willis

Marriage is ordained of God.
(D&C 49:15.)

1

There is no earthly happiness
exceeding that of a reciprocal
satisfaction in the marriage
state. (Giles.)

A Covenant Beginning

An eternal marriage, much like a large and beautiful forest, cannot be fully appreciated by simply looking at a few of the trees or by walking through it on any given day. The purpose of this chapter, and ultimately of this book, is to allow you to examine this marital forest in each of its seasons from a broad spiritual and intellectual point of view. As you do this, you will focus on questions such as: What are the purposes of life? What, within an eternal perspective, gives life its meaning and purpose? And then, finding the answers to these questions, you can consider what marriage *is* and *ought to be*, and why it is the foundation for eternal exaltation.

To fully comprehend your personal forest, perhaps it would be well for you to reach back in time and consider, if you will, what has transpired since you were begotten in spirit form by your Heavenly Father. Your spirit body resembled the earthly body you now have (1 Nephi 11:11; Ether 3:16). Even so, your spirit body did not have the physical elements of flesh and bone, but was made of matter "more fine or pure" (D&C 131:7) than the matter you understand at present here upon the earth.

Your personal pre-earthly experience allowed you to learn many things as well as to learn about and know joy. While this *did* occur, you could not experience a "fullness of joy" in that condition (D&C 93:33-4). Before this could happen, you had to (a) obtain a physical body, and (b) gain the knowledge and skills available by living in an environment where good and evil were competing with each other (2 Nephi 2:23). The core of your true timber surfaced when you responded by desiring a physical body and meeting the challenge of dealing with the opposition that presented itself here in mortality.

There are several aspects of the pre-earthly condition that will help you understand the central, permanent role of marriage. The individuals you were born to in your pre-earth life were a married couple (D&C 131:1-4), and their purpose centered around helping you, and other intelligent beings like you, to progress and grow. This they did by providing for you your spirit body, teaching you, creating an earth for you to progress upon, and laying additional foundations for you which would create an environment for your further progress.

And so this plan, the plan of salvation, was introduced and then implemented. An earth was created, you were placed, with others, upon it, and consistent with the plan, evil was allowed to enter into the world. You were given your "free agency," or freedom to respond to the good and evil forces as you desired, and judging by some of the literature you read, you seem to be responding appropriately to the forces of good, or the influence of the Holy Ghost, which if persisted in will ultimately allow you in your post-earth life to become a god or a goddess. When you progress to that point, you will then unite with your eternal mate in giving birth to your own spirit children and thereby repeat the cycle of life and eternal progression. As this occurs, you will, for the first time, begin to understand the joy and glory available to you and your companion and your eternal offspring (D&C 76:89-98).

To achieve this fulfilling condition, you must first take the preliminary steps of faith in Jesus Christ, repentance, baptism by the proper authority, and reception of the gift of the Holy Ghost. You must then be endowed with power within a holy temple and there be sealed in celestial marriage by the proper authority. And then, by remaining worthy of the temple blessings, you will be able to overcome all things. This is the *only way* you will be able to attain this unbelievably great destiny, for celestial marriage is the *key* to the entire plan.

Thus you see that marriage is much more than a convenient social arrangement or a civil contract. It is a sacred and eternal covenant that existed before the foundations of this earth were laid. It is an "order of the priesthood" (D&C 131:2) that is everlasting. It is a holy ordinance that plays a vital role in helping you and your spouse gain exaltation and eternal life.

Today and Always

It was a cold but beautiful December morning. I had longed for this day all my life, and now it had finally arrived. I was so excited my heart was beating a mile a minute.

My husband was a convert to the LDS church, and we had worked for seven years for this day. Now it was time to take our two little boys to the Manti Temple to be sealed for time and all eternity.

It was the most wonderful and peaceful feeling as we entered the temple for the first time. I will never forget all the family and friends that took time out to be with us on this special day.

The Spirit of the Lord was so strong in that beautiful sealing room. When they brought our two sons in to be sealed to us all dressed in white, and their tiny hands rested on ours, I just couldn't hold back the tears. Our little family all together kneeling at the altar was the happiest and most rewarding moment in all of my life, for I knew that at last we were becoming an eternal family unit.

*I felt like this was a new beginning for us. Our marriage
took on a new meaning as we now had something to strive
for and work for together.*

*Even though we, like everyone, still have our daily trials
and tribulations, we are strengthened by the knowledge that
our love can now be eternal and that we, through our righteousness, can truly become a family for eternity.*

Specific LDS Teachings About Marriage

In addition to teaching that marriage is a lofty, sacred order,
the Lord has also given a number of specific teachings about
marriage. Each of these teachings provides a piece to an overall
puzzle, and when they are all taken together, they identify the
bounds the Lord has set for marriage.

THE POWER TO SEAL IS NECESSARY

Even as the Lord gave to Peter the keys of the kingdom of
heaven, the binding power (Matthew 17:19), so also have these
keys been given in this dispensation. These keys are the "keys of
the priesthood," and they are the power that seals marriages.
When couples are sealed by the power and keys of the priesthood and then continue worthy to have their sealing ratified (or
approved) by the Holy Spirit of Promise (D&C 132:7), their
marriage then

> shall be of full force when they are out of the world; and they shall
> pass by the angels, and the gods, which are set there, to their
> exaltation and glory in all things, as hath been sealed upon their
> heads, which glory shall be a fulness and a continuation of the
> seeds forever and ever. (D&C 132:19.)

MARRIAGES ARE TO BE ETERNAL

The Savior has indicated clearly that marriages should last
forever. This he taught in response to the taunting Pharisees:

> And he answered and said unto them, Have ye not read, that
> he which made them at the beginning made them male and female,
> And said, For this cause shall a man leave father and mother,
> and shall cleave to his wife: and they twain shall be one flesh?

> Wherefore they are no more twain, but one flesh. What therefore God hath joined together let not man put asunder.
>
> They say unto him, Why did Moses then command to give a writing of divorcement, and to put her away?
>
> He saith unto them, Moses because of the hardness of your hearts suffered you to put away your wives: but from the beginning it was not so. (Matthew 19:4-8.)

This scripture reveals that the Lord's highest law is for his children to live in a system where divorce, annulment, and desertion are unknown. Even so, he recognizes that in some historical periods the people cannot live this very demanding law. When this occurs, he holds this idea as something to strive toward while allowing the people to live lesser laws that are consistent with their level of progress. Thus the Lord values stability, but apparently he recognizes that it is not always possible.

MARRIAGE IS FOR BEARING CHILDREN

Parenthood is one of the most underlying purposes of marriage, and all Latter-day Saints should strive to be parents. By righteously complying with the command to multiply and replenish the earth if physically possible, a couple then prepares for the blessing of bearing additional children by procreating spirit bodies after the resurrection.

The process of being a parent is not a matter that you should take lightly. It is at the very heart of LDS theology. President Spencer W. Kimball has provided some additional information and advice about this issue:

> "Be fruitful, and multiply and replenish the earth." The Lord does not waste words. He meant what he said. You did not come on earth just to "eat, drink, and be merry." You came knowing full well your responsibilities. You came to get for yourself a mortal body that could become perfected, immortalized, and you understood that you were to act in partnership with God in providing bodies for other spirits equally anxious to come to earth for righteous purposes. And so you will not postpone parenthood. There will be rationalists who will name to you numerous reasons for postponement. Of course, it will be harder to get your college degrees or your financial start with a family, but strength like yours will be undaunted in the face of difficult obstacles. Have your family as the Lord intended. Of course it is expensive, but

you will find a way, and besides, it is often those children who grow up with responsibility and hardships who carry on the world's work.

. . . Do not limit your family as the world does. I am wondering now where I might have been had my parents decided arbitrarily that one or two children would be enough, or that three or four would be all they could support, or that even five would be the limit; for I was the sixth of eleven children. Don't think you will love the later ones less or have fewer material things for them. Perhaps, like Jacob, you might love the eleventh one most. Young people, have your family, love them, sacrifice for them, teach them righteousness, and you will be blessed and happy all the days of your eternal lives. (Spencer W. Kimball, *Marriage* [Salt Lake City: Deseret Book Company, 1978], pages 22-23; hereinafter cited as *Marriage*.)

MARRIED COUPLES ARE TO TEACH THEIR CHILDREN

In addition to the opportunity and responsibility of bearing children, the Lord has revealed that married couples should rear their children properly. This is the Lord's most emphatic statement about this matter:

And again, inasmuch as parents have children in Zion, or in any of her stakes which are organized, that teach them not to understand the doctrine of repentance, faith in Christ the Son of the living God, and of baptism and the gift of the Holy Ghost by the laying on of the hands, when eight years old, the sin be upon the heads of the parents.

And they shall also teach their children to pray, and to walk uprightly before the Lord. (D&C 68:25, 28.)

As a child I always remember how gentle and shy my father was. Private is a very inadequate word to describe him. I knew very little of his feelings or of his childhood.

And then I moved from Australia to the United States. It was then that I began to appreciate the quiet, gentle presence of my father. For ten years I ached to sit at his side and feel of his love. And then it happened. Father came for Christmas.

As we gathered our children around him, he reflected with sheer happiness a Christmas that brought him a small wooden horse-drawn fire truck. The truck cost his parents two shillings (about 20¢), which was considered a small for-tune for them at that time. The money had been saved by my German grandmother, one penny at a time over a period of a year.

He told of each small detail of the toy, one wheel that didn't quite turn properly, and the beautiful brass bells on top, and the tiny ladder that hooked and unhooked to the side of the engine.

He told it all with a smile and a look that took each of us back to that Christmas long ago that was most memorable for us all. That Christmas with Father was the last time I saw him, and now I regret deeply that there are so many things that I do not know about him.

MARRIAGE PREVENTS LONELINESS

While bearing and rearing children are the central reasons for marriage, there are many others. The Lord indicated that another reason is that "it is not good that the man [or the woman] should be alone" (Genesis 2:18; Moses 3:18). Marriage prevents loneliness and provides an opportunity to learn unselfishness and to work as a team in bringing about righteousness. This is a simple truth, but one which has far-reaching implications.

THE PRIESTHOOD IS TO PRESIDE

There are several scriptures which teach that the husband is to preside in the home. At the time of the Fall, Eve was told that her husband should "rule over" her (Genesis 3:16; Moses 4:22). Later, Paul wrote to the Ephesian Saints:

> Wives, submit yourselves unto your own husbands as unto the Lord. For the husband is the head of the wife, even as Christ is the head of the church; and he is the savior of the body. Therefore, as the church is subject unto Christ, so let the wives be to their own husbands in every thing. Husbands, love your wives, even as Christ also loved the church, and gave himself for it. (Ephesians 5:22-25.)

The analogy of husbands presiding over wives as Christ presides over the Church provides some clues about *how* husbands should preside. They should preside in righteousness and with a gentle warmth. They should lead with persuasion rather than with force, with long-suffering rather than with a quick temper, with gentleness rather than with toughness, with meekness rather than with an all-knowing attitude, with love unfeigned rather than love merely verbalized, and with kindness rather than with abrasiveness (Matthew 5-7; D&C 121:36-43). *Presiding does not mean that the husband gets his way more than others, or that he must always have the final say. It means that he directs the process in the home.* That is the key phrase in what it means to preside. He guides the process of making decisions and getting proper things done.

MARRIAGE IS NECESSARY FOR EXALTATION

The scriptures clearly teach that we are not exalted as individuals. We are exalted only as couples. Section 132 of the Doctrine and Covenants discusses the process of becoming gods, with the entire discussion involving what *couples* do rather than what individuals do. The main verses are 19 to 24, where the Lord states that "they shall pass by the angels . . . to their exaltation," and "then shall they be gods," and "then shall they be above all." In the preceding section the Lord explicitly teaches that marriage is necessary for exaltation:

> In the celestial glory there are three heavens or degrees; and in order to obtain the highest, a man must enter into this order of the priesthood [meaning the new and everlasting covenant of marriage]; and if he does not, he cannot obtain it. He may enter into the other, but that is the end of his kingdom; he cannot have an increase. (D&C 131:1-4.)

This doctrine can perhaps be best understood by referring to the couplet that was coined by President Lorenzo Snow: "As man now is, God once was; and as God now is, man may become." In reality, the authors feel this can be clarified to conclude with, ". . . as God now is, *couples* may become."

SEXUAL INTERCOURSE SHOULD BE CONFINED TO MARRIAGE

The Lord has provided a number of clear and straightforward instructions about sexual interaction. He has explicitly forbidden adultery (Exodus 20:14; D&C 42:23-26). He has also indicated that his children should not "do anything like unto it" (D&C 59:6). In the Sermon on the Mount and in his instructions to the Nephites he provided some additional details:

> Behold, it is written by them of old time, that thou shalt not commit adultery; but I say unto you, that whosoever looketh on a woman to lust after her, hath committed adultery already in his heart. Behold, I give unto you a commandment, that ye suffer none of these things to enter into your heart. (3 Nephi 12:27-29.)

There are also several scriptures that teach that deviations from commandments in the sexual area are extremely serious. One of these is Alma's timely chastisement of his son, Corianton:

> Now this is what I have against thee; thou didst go on unto boasting in thy strength and thy wisdom.
>
> And this is not all, my son. Thou didst do that which was grievous unto me; for thou didst forsake the ministry, and did go over into the land of Siron, among the borders of the Lamanites, after the harlot Isabel.
>
> Yea, she did steal away the hearts of many; but this was no excuse for thee, my son. Thou shouldst have tended to the ministry wherewith thou wast entrusted.
>
> Know ye not, my son, that these things are an abomination in the sight of the Lord; yea, most abominable above all sins save it be the shedding of innocent blood or denying the Holy Ghost? (Alma 39:2-5.)

You should not get the impression that the Lord is only interested in the negative side, in telling you what you should *not* do. His teachings indicate that he thinks that sexual interaction is beautiful, wholesome, lovely, and necessary in marriage. He commands his children to multiply and replenish the earth, and the husband and wife should cleave unto each other and become "one flesh" (Genesis 2:24). Sexual behavior in its proper place is a highly valued and precious part of life. But as Mormon indicated, chastity and virtue are "most dear and precious above all things" (Moroni 9:9), and Jacob conveyed the word that "I the Lord God delight in . . . chastity" (Jacob 2:28).

MARRIAGE IS ORDAINED OF GOD

Paul indicated that "marriage is honourable" (Hebrews 13:4), and latter-day revelation indicates that "marriage is ordained of

God" (D&C 49:15). Marriage is more than a convenient social institution that has evolved from and is consistent with today's economic and social structure. It is an institution that is ordained —or in other words commissioned, desired, and appointed—by God.

Some people in our modern society suggest that marriage is not really necessary. One recent book, in fact, is titled *Is Marriage Necessary?* (Lawrence Casler [New York: Human Sciences Press, 1973]). As a result there are more and more people choosing to live their adult lives as a "single." It is fairly easy to understand why some people who do not have the restored gospel would choose this style of life. Many of them do not understand the purpose of life, the purposes of marriage, and the beauties that can come from a peaceful, loving home. They have been reared in a society that teaches them that "God is dead" and that the greatest satisfactions come from material posessions. It is important that those who know about the restored gospel reject these short-sighted beliefs and practices. As you reject this apostate creed, you will recognize even more that marriage is a beautiful arrangement that can help you attain the greatest joys and satisfactions. It is ordained of God for noble and lofty reasons, and you should seek rather than avoid it.

MARRIAGE IS A SACRED COVENANT

Historically, the marital institution has been viewed in a number of different ways, and even now it is regarded differently by different groups in our contemporary society. Some consider it a legal arrangement or civil contract governed by secular institutions that make and enforce laws. Others see it as a personal commitment that is more personal and of higher order than the mere "piece of paper" that happens to create legal obligations. The Lord has said that his style of marriage is an "order of the priesthood" (D&C 131:2), and this makes it a sacred order. All LDS temple sealings of husband and wife are civil contracts, and they are also personal commitments; but most importantly they are also sacred arrangements—sacred covenants.

THE WEDDING MUST BE PERFORMED ON THE EARTH

Several revelations indicate that marriages are not performed in heaven. They must be done on the earth (Matthew 22:30; D&C 132:16). There will be marriage in heaven, but there will be no weddings. This means that each Latter-day Saint should select a partner and marry while he or she has the opportunity in mortality.

This teaching raises a question about those who do not have the opportunity to marry in this life. For example, what will happen to men who lose their lives in the military service before they have the opportunity to marry? Or what about women who would like to marry but never have the opportunity? Will they lose the blessings of marriage forever? Several prophets have discussed this issue, and they indicate that a just Lord will certainly provide this blessing for those who genuinely do not have the opportunity to marry in this life. President Joseph Fielding Smith answered the question in the following manner:

> If this privilege is granted to us to work vicariously for the dead who lived during past ages, surely the Lord will not deprive those who are now living and who are less fortunate, and because of no fault of their own, fail to receive these great blessings upon which, through faithfulness, exaltation is based and offered to the dead. The case of Alvin Smith is in point. He died before the restoration of the gospel, but after the coming of Moroni, yet the Prophet saw him in [a] vision partaking of the blessings of exaltation. . . .
>
> Therefore, through the mercy and justice of the Lord, any young woman who maintains her virtue and accepts . . . the gospel will receive the fulness of the glory and exaltation of the celestial kingdom. The great gift of eternal life will be given her. This gift the Lord has described, shall be a "fulness and a continuation of the seeds forever and ever." All the gifts of exaltation will be hers, because she has been true and faithful, and what was denied her here will be given to her hereafter. . . .
>
> In the great plan of salvation nothing has been overlooked. The gospel of Jesus Christ is the most beautiful thing in the world. It embraces every soul whose heart is right and who diligently seeks him and desires to obey his laws and covenants. Therefore, if a person is for any cause denied the privilege of complying with any of the covenants, the Lord will judge him or her by the intent of

the heart. (Joseph Fielding Smith, *Answers to Gospel Questions,*
comp. Joseph Fielding Smith, Jr., 5 vols. [Salt Lake City: Deseret
Book Company, 1957-66], 2:35-37.)

MARRIAGE SHOULD BE A LOVING RELATIONSHIP

Paul counseled husbands to "love your wives even as Christ
also loved the church" (Ephesians 5:25). Jacob also taught that
marriage is better when "husbands love their wives and . . .
wives love their husbands" (Jacob 3:7). Thus love is an important part of marriage, and when individuals marry in the Lord's
prescribed manner, it should not be for simply a "convenience"
relationship. Some marry because a spouse is a needed com-
modity for their progression and advancement. They "need" a
spouse for their profession, or in order to be given responsible
positions in the Church. Although these may be some of the
reasons to marry, Latter-day Saints should especially love their
mate and realize that love is an important dimension of a Celestial marriage.

TEMPLE MARRIAGE IS A STYLE OF LIFE, AS WELL AS AN EVENT

Some feel that the event of a marriage in the temple is an
assurance of their exaltation. An unfortunate example of this was
shared with one of the authors:

A devoted Latter-day-Saint girl fell in love with a not-so-
devoted LDS boy. The young man wanted to marry, but the girl
insisted she would never be married anywhere except within a
temple. To this the boy finally and begrudgingly agreed, and he
proceeded to go through the necessary steps to obtain a temple
recommend. The date was set, arrangements were made, and the
night before the ordinance was to be performed the boy's fra-
ternity brothers gave a bachelor's party from which he appeared
at the temple the next morning with red eyes and a slight hang-
over. Even though the girl was aware of the incident, the marriage was performed, and the girl felt she had accomplished her
goal.

What the girl apparently did not understand is that the marriage ceremony in the temple is an important event that begins a
style of life. It does not automatically qualify the couple for

exaltation. Section 132 of the Doctrine and Covenants is quite clear about this:

> And as pertaining to the new and everlasting covenant, it was instituted for the fulness of my glory; and he that receiveth a fulness thereof must and shall abide the law, or he shall be damned, saith the Lord God.
>
> And verily I say unto you, that the conditions of this law are these: All covenants, contracts, bonds, obligations, oaths, vows, performances, connections, associations, or expectations, that are not made and entered into and sealed by the Holy Spirit of promise, of him who is anointed . . . whom I have appointed on the earth to hold this power . . . are of no efficacy, virtue, or force in and after the resurrection from the dead; for all contracts that are not made unto this end have an end when men are dead. (D&C 132:6-7.)

Elder Bruce R. McConkie of the Council of the Twelve gives us the following clarification of what it means to be sealed by the Holy Spirit of Promise:

> To seal is to *ratify*, to *justify*, or to *approve.* Thus an act which is sealed by the Holy Spirit of Promise is one which is ratified by the Holy Ghost; it is one which is approved by the Lord; and the person who has taken the obligation upon himself is justified by the spirit in the thing he has done. (*Mormon Doctrine,* 2nd ed. [Salt Lake City: Bookcraft, Inc., 1966], page 361.)

The girl whose goal was a temple marriage apparently obtained it, but she had not yet achieved the more important goal of a Celestial marriage that was approved and ratified by the Holy Spirit of Promise and by the Lord.

Freedom Within the New and Everlasting Covenant of Marriage

A MARITAL STEWARDSHIP

The teachings in the previous few pages describe the boundaries the Lord has set for marriage. Since the Lord is the same yesterday, today, and forever (D&C 20:12), these characteristics of marriage do not change as social conditions change and new innovations or life-styles are accepted in the world. New technologies and social inventions will change most social institutions, such as governments, economic systems, and educational institutions, but they will not change the basic characteristics of the new and everlasting covenant of marriage.

It is important to realize also that the "boundaries" the Lord has set for marriage do not rigidly define every aspect of married life. He has provided the above guidelines and specific limits that define the basic nature of marriage, but his boundaries allow for considerable flexibility in marital relationships. Therefore, couples have some freedom in deciding what they want their marriage to be like.

One way to look at this is to view marriage as a *stewardship*. The Lord has identified some basic boundaries of this stewardship by giving instructions, such as avoiding adultery, loving each other, being presided over by the priesthood, etc. Then, within these boundaries, couples have the freedom and the responsibility to govern their own marital stewardship.

AREAS IN WHICH COUPLES MAY MAKE CHOICES

What, then, are some of the aspects of marriage in which there is room for individual variation—within the bounds the Lord has set? One of these areas is the amount of independence a husband and wife have in their marriage relationship. This independence is not a dichotomy in which they are either independent or not independent. It is a continuum having two extremes, with many different levels or degrees, as shown on the accompanying continuum.

Amount of Independence

0	1	2	3	4	5	6	7	8	9	10
None	*Very, very little*		*A small amount*			*Quite a bit*		*A great deal*		*Total independence*

It would seem that no couple would ever want to be at either extreme of independence in marriage. If each spouse had complete independence, it would not be a marriage at all. They do not even have that much freedom with a missionary companion or a roommate in a dorm. At the opposite extreme, no one would want to be so closely tied to his or her spouse as to have no freedom at all. Some couples, however, may desire a relationship such as the Robinsons' (below), which is illustrative of a marriage with relatively little freedom:

The Robinsons

"We have a saying in our marriage: No secrets. We have none, and we love it! We share everything with each other; our thoughts, our disappointments, our temptations: everything. I like to know where she is going when she leaves, and I always let her know what I'm doing. If I'm going to be home late, I always call her as soon as I know my plans. Marriage to us means *really* being one."

The Robinsons are at level two or three in the above continuum. They have very little independence, and they prefer this in their marriage. Others may desire more independence. This desire for more elbow room is not inconsistent with the gospel ideals, as illustrated by the Cannings. They know the Robinsons and, in fact, socialize with them each month as they attend the temple together, spend evenings enjoying special cultural events together, etc. Even so, the Cannings are quite different in the area of independence:

The Cannings

"I'm a fairly private person. I love to be alone to think, to read, to meditate, and to plan. We do a lot of things together in our marriage and with the kids, but it is also important to us that we be individuals and have our individuality. This means that we need some separate areas of our lives that aren't really shared. We feel this type of relationship creates something special that could be obtained no other way, and it is created in the trust and respect we have for each other. I think that I am a better wife and John is a better husband than we would be if we were like the Robinsons. Their style is perfect for them, but if we lived that way, it would drive us up the wall."

The Cannings' marriage is about a seven on the Amount of Independence continuum. They have a great deal of independence, and for them it is healthy and suitable. And so you could ask:

Which marriage is better?
Which couple is more righteous?

The answer probably is *neither*. This is evidently an area in which the gospel allows for differences. Both couples can retain their own styles and be equally happy and successful. In fact, with their personality differences, they probably need to have their own styles to be happy and have joy. If the couples were to switch lives, they would all suffer and possibly fail as a result.

Another area in which couples can differ is in how fast a pace they choose to live. Some couples desire a fast pace; they are always on the run. They like to fill every minute with something. They have a lot of energy, and they find it fulfilling to use it. Other couples prefer a slower pace in which they have more time to relax and as a consequence have few demands.

This difference can be seen in various regions of the United States. The pace of life has traditionally been slower in the South and in rural areas, and it is faster in the North and West and in urban areas. Some of these regional differences seem to be disappearing, but couples still may differ from each other, and they may also desire different paces at different stages of their lives. For example, life is usually much more hectic when the children are small than when a couple reaches the "empty nest" stage of marriage.

This, too, is shown here on a continuum.

Pace of Life

0	1	2	3	4	5	6	7	8	9	10
Very slow pace		*Slow pace*			*Moderate pace*			*Fast pace*		*Very fast pace*

Again, are the couples who live a fast pace more apt to be keeping the commandments than those who live a slower-paced life? Or could the opposite be true? As to the extremes, both are bad. Couples who try to "run faster than they can" are unwise stewards, and they would be better off moving at a slower pace. On the other hand, living an extremely slow life is inconsistent with the admonition to "be anxiously engaged in a good cause, and do many things of their own free will, and bring to pass much righteousness" (D&C 58:27). This still leaves considerable room for differences in individuals and couples. As you consider the perils of being extremists, you should be cautious in placing your marriage relationship below a two or above a nine, but if it feels natural and right you should feel *good* about placing yourselves at any of the middle points along the continuum.

Two Wholes Equal "One"

My wife and I began our marriage by merrily skipping along with the belief that togetherness in all things brought oneness! For years I would reluctantly escort my wife to the symphony. Once there, I would spend the entire evening grumbling through my beard from boredom. In return, she would traipse off with me to football games and there fidget and yawn as though she were staring at an empty field.

Eventually, after years of mutually hurt feelings and constantly strained tempers, we began to simply refuse to attend events we found personally dull. After the initial shock of this passed, we began to really enjoy our separate interests alone or with friends. While we continued to share mutually rewarding activities (such as dining out, attending movies, and our regular visits to the temple), we developed a special respect for our "alone" activities. We each found relaxation and regeneration from our "alone" times, and as the dust of defensiveness settled, we actually began sharing these fulfilling feelings (and new things viewed or learned) with each other.

Perhaps the greatest relief we each sense from this pattern is that we are truly beyond trying to hang guilt on one another for simply being our own distinct individual selves. We now thoroughly enjoy each other without feeling threatened by our differences. It's great! For us, two wholes make a wonderful one!

There are many other dimensions or areas of life in which you have some freedom *within* the bounds the Lord has set. The following list identifies many of these areas. As you read them, you will no doubt feel strongly about some of these dimensions and not care much about others. In considering these areas, you should remember that some preferences are determined by the person you married. On the other hand, you may feel strongly about some of them regardless of the person you married. Also, in some of the following areas you have considerable freedom to choose your style of life, while in other areas the counsel of prophets or others such as your parents and friends places some restrictions, and thus you have less freedom. In each area there is *some* freedom for individual differences, *and each of you would do well to examine this list to determine what you want your marriage to be like.*

Areas Permitting Flexibility in Marriage

1. How much intellectual stimulation should we provide each other?
2. How much privacy should each spouse have? How much of our life is not known by our spouse?
3. How much affection is expressed physically? How much touching, embracing, kissing, snuggling, etc.?
4. How much affection is expressed verbally? How frequently should we do such things as saying, "I love you," and writing poetry, affectionate comments, tender phrases, etc.?
5. How much time is spent with close friends?
6. What proportion of our friends should be friends of both of us or of only one of us?
7. How much will personal development be emphasized in the marriage? For the husband? For the wife?
8. How much time should be devoted to Church callings? How much would be too little for us?
9. How much do we want to travel?
10. How will the "power" or control in the relationship be arranged? Will the husband be highly dominant? Should the husband and wife have equal power? Should one have control in some areas and the other in other areas, and if so, which, where?

11. How much friendship or companionship should exist in the relationship?
12. How much will the relationship change over the years? Will it always be evolving or will it be fairly static?
13. How important should the physically intimate part of our lives be, compared to other parts?
14. How much should we be independent of or dependent on each other?
15. When we disagree on something, how shall we handle the disagreement?
16. How important is it to each partner for us to get ahead or be highly successful financially or socially?

In summary, the authors hope it has become evident that there are some characteristics that all marriages should have, and there are also many areas where you may choose a unique style of life. You can be different from others without jeopardizing the quality of your marriage relationship. This flexibility is not only healthy, it is *crucial* as you find the style of marriage that best suits you and your spouse.

Identifying Your Personal Goals in Marriage

Lighting a Fire

Some time ago my wife and I were asked to give a fireside to the young marrieds in our ward on the subject of "How to Make a Marriage Celestial."

As we began to prepare, we began to analyze our own marriage. In doing so, we came to the conclusion that we had been sliding along in our relationship without doing anything in particular to better it. As a consequence, we found many areas in which we had both been quietly dissatisfied. Being the priesthood holder, I felt I should take the bull by the horns and set some definite goals. As we made ready for our presentation, I developed a checklist of things we could do, and a timetable for getting them started. Now, several months later, we have found that not only are certain new "celestial habits" ingrained in our relationship, but our self-respect as well as our feelings of love and unity have increased a hundredfold. Another interesting outcome is that we gave a pretty good fireside presentation to boot!

Success in marriage is achieved as you set and then reach your goals. Your ultimate goal should be to enter into the presence of your heavenly parents and become like them. In order to achieve this ultimate goal of a celestial marriage, it is necessary to take hundreds of preliminary steps and set many intermediate goals. Therefore, if you are to achieve a successful marriage, you must identify your personal goals and then create a life-style that will allow you to attain those goals. If you were perfect—or at least close to being perfect—you could have goals like the following:

1. Always be charitable and kind.
2. Always communicate with patience, understanding, and empathy.
3. Always be unselfish, particularly with your time and desires.
4. Never allow your becoming tired, cross, or angry to be vented on your spouse.
5. Never raise your voice or speak unkind words.
6. Never even be tempted to do anything that would hurt feelings.
7. Be able to solve problems and differences quickly and effectively together.
8. Always encourage each other's personal growth.
9. Always respect each other's opinions and seek each other's counsel on all important decisions.
10. Achieve complete agreement about how each of you should perform your marital roles.
11. Completely keep all covenants made in the gospel, including being free from all sin, being chaste, virtuous, truthful, unselfish, strictly living all the commandments and devoting yourselves and all that you have or may have to the Lord's cause.

Unfortunately, you live this life in a less-than-perfect state. You enter mortality innocent and pure, but you eventually find yourself in a fallen state wherein you have many faults, failings, limitations, and imperfections.

What, then, should you do about your marital goals?

You must *first* recognize that the process of perfecting yourself and your marriage is a very long process. You cannot become perfect immediately or in a short time. It is as though you were on a ladder that reaches far into the sky. You can gradually climb the ladder, but you can't do it immediately or all in one step. You do it one step at a time, gradually rising higher and higher.

Second, you need to determine where you are on the long ladder that leads to perfection. Some are higher than others, and some are fairly close to the bottom. In fact, some people haven't even bothered to step on the bottom rung. It would behoove you to think long and hard about where you are on the ladder, and then set your personal goals so that they are steps you can reach.

Third, you need to have long-term *and* short-term goals. Your ultimate goal is perfection—being at the top of the ladder. To get there, you need to have some intermediate goals and some short-term goals. You need intermediate goals like getting married in the temple and teaching your children the gospel as you rear them. Your short-term goals need to be small steps that you can reach. As you think about your short-term marital goals, you need to realize that many of them, in fact all of them, are less-than-ideal while you move step by step up the ladder. In the short run, you may need to put up with some undesirable faults in yourself and your spouse. For example, you may have a very realistic goal of being spiteful or jealous less often. Or you may have the goal of using less physical violence when you have problems in your relationship. These are not very noble goals, but they are the kind you may need if you are to move a step up the ladder.

Thus each couple's marital goals are a unique set. They should be tailor-made for you as an individual and as a couple. It is foolish to have only ideal goals that are so far beyond your immediate reach that you never have any successes. You need to have long-term goals of exaltation and perfection, but also have some short-term goals. You *need to realize that where you are on the ladder right now is relatively unimportant. What is important is that you are working at the process of moving in a positive direction, one or two rungs at a time.*

Summary

The purpose of this chapter has been to place marriage in its eternal perspective — that is, at the very heart of the gospel. The chapter also discusses a number of specific Latter-day Saint teachings about what marriage should be. These teachings set some boundaries for an eternal view of marriage, and these boundaries are not negotiable. They are the same yesterday, today, and forever. As a couple, you should learn what they are and create a marriage that is consistent with these bounds which the Lord has set. Within these bounds, the chapter also discusses areas where you are free to make choices regarding your relationship. This shows that there is some structure to marriage and also some freedom for individual differences. This idea is essential if you are to understand and then accept your uniqueness as a couple and as individuals.

The final aim of the chapter has been to consider the importance and the timeliness with which you as a couple must discuss, and then establish, both long-term as well as short-term goals. Accomplishing this will set directions in your marriage. It will also prepare you for eternal progression as a couple. And it will establish a precedent in your relationship of communicating, discussing similarities and differences, and providing a growing environment as your celestial marriage is contemplated and then finally realized.

With this base established, you can now move through the later chapters with a perspective and foundation. You will study the many relevant aspects of marriage that will help you grow and improve and create this most lasting and most significant of all relationships.

. . . the Lord God hath given a
commandment that all men should
have charity, which charity is
love. And except they should
have charity they were nothing.
(2 Nephi 26:30.)

2

Fashioning Love with Love

As you reflect upon the many moments in your marriage, each of you will no doubt capture and relive a myriad of feelings as you think of your love for your spouse. Perhaps your most often pursued "butterfly of love" before marriage was the romantic love which captured your hearts. Even though you each thought at the time that this romantic love was eternal love, hopefully you can look back with a wink and a smile, knowing now that so many other things enter into love to form the eternal feelings of love you now share. That is not to toss out your romantic feelings for each other, for hopefully you still treasure these feelings and the moments of expressing them to each other. Instead, perhaps you could regard romantic love as an exciting and essential prelude to the complete and eternal love you are now experiencing.

Before exploring your love for each other as a couple, take a moment to back away from your relationship and consider love from a more general perspective. You can do this by tuning in on the words of the Lord which were recorded by Matthew (22:36-39) wherein the two great commandments are presented. These are to love and totally respect the Lord, and then to love your neighbor (your companion) as yourself.

This love of mankind is often referred to in the scriptures as *charity*, or the pure love of Christ (Moroni 7:47). Some of its synonyms are benevolence, compassion, generosity, love of God, and mercy.

Unfortunately, the world today is one where "the love of men shall wax cold, and iniquity shall abound" (D&C 45:27). We not only see examples of this in the warring of nations, but we can also see it clearly in our own neighborhoods as it seems that more and more of us have less and less patience for the mistakes and weaknesses of others. This tendency seems to have evolved as we have collectively turned inward, concerning ourselves only with our personal pleasures and needs.

Even so, as Latter-day Saints we know charity to be the foundation upon which all successful relationships (and therefore successful marriages) are built. Should you fail to acquire this trait and try to negotiate your marriage without it, it will be like trying to cross the ocean in a sailboat without a rudder. It is going to be almost impossible for you to weather the inevitable marital storms.

The underlying importance of charity was emphasized by Paul as he said: "And though I have the gift of prophecy, and understand all mysteries, and all knowledge; and though I have all faith, so that I could remove mountains, and have not charity, I am nothing." (1 Corinthians 13:2.) Nephi expressed similar sentiments when he proclaimed: ". . . the Lord God hath given a commandment that all men should have charity, which charity is love. And except they should have charity they were nothing." (2 Nephi 26:30.)

If you are a married couple who has the ability to do all else well, including such important things as Church activity, financial solvency, communication skills, etc., and yet *have not charity*, you are fast becoming "as sounding brass, or a tinkling cymbal" (1 Corinthians 13:1). In other words, your marriage is fast becoming empty, hollow, and incomplete. Expressed positively, *charity* should become the foundation upon which you strive to build your marriage, for without it none of the other attributes you have incorporated into your marriage will be of much worth to you.

Charity in Marriage

What does it mean to be charitable in your marriage? Being a charitable couple means more than holding hands and embracing often, although this is a beginning. If you combine the wisdom and understanding of Paul and Mormon, you will find a more complete picture of what charity should mean in an eternal relationship. In 1 Corinthians 15 and Moroni 7 these great men use many phrases to define *charity*. From the perspective of the present authors these characteristics of love can be divided into three main themes that can better help each of you understand how you can be more charitable toward your eternal companion. The themes are: (1) that you should be concerned about others rather than be selfish; (2) that you should be patient and enduring with yourselves and others; and (3) that you should be righteous in your hearts as well as in the way you behave.

BEING CONCERNED ABOUT OTHERS

Concern for others involves several separate behaviors. Five of these are: (1) seeketh not her own; (2) vaunteth not itself; (3) is not puffed up; (4) envieth not; and (5) is kind.

Simply stated, those of you who use these techniques care about each other, and your actions toward each other demonstrate this care. The opposite of these actions would be such behaviors as selfishness, conceit, egotism, uninvolvement, and being concerned only about yourself.

Modern prophets have said much about the importance of being concerned about others. Spencer W. Kimball has declared:

> The marriage that is based upon selfishness is almost certain to fail. . . . But the one who marries to give happiness as well as to

receive it, to give service as well as to receive it, and looks after the interests of the two and then the family as it comes will have a good chance that the marriage will be a happy one. . . .

Total unselfishness is sure to accomplish another factor in successful marriage. If each spouse is forever seeking the interests, comforts, and happiness of the other, the love found in courtship and cemented in marriage will grow into mighty proportions. (*Marriage and Divorce* [Salt Lake City: Deseret Book Company, 1976], pages 22-23; hereinafter cited as *Marriage and Divorce.*)

This type of charitable love in marriage is a sure sign of maturity among both partners. To be able to place a relationship above one's own desires and needs is to have moved from childhood to manhood and womanhood. It is recognized by many as one of the most basic steps in creating a celestial marriage.

The linkage between maturity and charity was implied by Paul at the end of his sermon on the meaning of charity when he said: "When I was a child, I spake as a child, I understood as a child, I thought as a child: but when I became a man, I put away childish things." (1 Corinthians 13:11.)

Could Paul have been saying that to be charitable one needs to grow up? Is it immature to be selfish and self-centered? Perhaps a couple need only to look at the behavior of their small children for the answers. Young children live in a self-centered world of their own "wants" while for the most part ignoring the needs of those around them. They want food when hungry, they want their diapers changed, they want the attention of parents, they want another child's toys. They are not yet experienced or mature enough to be able to empathize or to put themselves in someone else's shoes — to vicariously feel as another person feels. About the time most children start to develop this ability they get baptized and are then held accountable for their actions.

Even so, some Latter-day Saints develop empathy very slowly and marry with little ability to place themselves in the emotional shoes of their spouse. Some observed marital errors of immature partners include these *true* incidents:

Incident 1
A husband, against his wife's wishes, purchased a new four-wheel-drive pickup, even though they were behind on their

house payments. Rather than face the righteous wrath of his wife, he hid the pickup at a friend's house.

Incident 2

A wife surprised her husband when her family arrived for a family reunion at their home. She had not asked her husband for permission because she knew he would not approve. The husband retaliated by doing obnoxious things that upset both his wife and her family members.

Incident 3

A wife was so upset with her husband for never being at home or paying any attention to her that she took his new Buick, which she saw was getting far more attention and care than she was, and proceeded to drive it in a reckless manner around and around the apartment building parking lot. When her husband came out and tried to stop her she chased him around the parking lot in an attempt to run over him. As the police arrived she rammed into their cars and continued to chase until she came to rest, car and all, in the front room of one of the neighbors.

In each of these instances the married partners could greatly benefit from learning to effectively and maturely deal with their feelings, as well as to each respond to the feelings of the spouse.

The first two aspects of being concerned about others, "seeketh not her own" and "vaunteth not itself," are closely related to unselfishness in meaning and practical application. The third, "is not puffed up," is more closely related to pride as a person interacts with his spouse. In everyday actions it means such things as being more concerned about being "right" than caring about the feelings of one's companion. Or, when a person has a difference of opinion with his spouse, he only superficially listens enough to be able to formulate his counterattack. Or, when one spouse sends a message that could be interpreted in a negative way, the other takes great offense and allows his righteous indignation to head toward the boiling level. Carried further, it could also mean refusing to quickly forgive one's spouse for offending—or even not to forgive him at all and to harbor ill feelings over an extended period of time.

The opposite of pride or being puffed up is humility. To be humble in marriage is to be teachable and to admit that there just may be another solution to the problem than the solution one partner may have suggested. It is also to appreciate the subjective rightness of the partner's point of view even though one "knows" that it is incorrect when compared with one's own view. A humble person is also teachable enough to be willing to compromise even though he feels his plan is superior, and at times he will even give in and let the other person have his own way simply because the relationship is more important than the problem. To do these things is difficult for most people and requires self-mastery and great maturity.

The fourth aspect of charity, it "envieth not," is defined as a person's ability to overcome the common temptation to compare himself with others and to compete with them. This is a competitive world today, in which there is a great deal of emphasis placed on winning and being number one. It is seen not only in the athletic world but in the business world, in schools, and elsewhere — sometimes including one's own marriage. There are situations in which this competition can be healthy and exciting, but marriage is certainly not one of these situations.

Often when marriage partners compete with each other it is because one or each feels inferior to the other due to a lack of self-esteem. When this happens the spouse feels the need to criticize and otherwise try to put the other partner beneath his own perceived feelings of inferiority. That person thus uses his mate as a means of elevating himself — at the expense of his mate.

An example of this is provided in the following dialogue of a young couple who sought counseling after only a few months of marriage. The wife, who went to work each day, felt that it was unfair that she be forced to do all the housework while the husband just sat around the house giving orders. In this episode the wife is trying to get her husband to help:

H: What do you want? Do you want to tune the car while I come in and do the dishes?

W: Well, not really, but all it is that I'm asking is that —

H: It doesn't take any skill or training to do the housework, now, does it?

W: Not really. But I'm not asking you to do the dishes every night, I just want you to help every—

H: I never ask you to work on the car, do I?

W: No, but I just don't understand why we can't be more equal. I have to come home and hurry and fix your meal or you get angry with me, and you just sit there and watch TV. We work the same number of hours each day and I work just as hard as you do. Why can't you help me a little?

H: Well, what difference does it make? Who cares who makes the most money or who works the most hours each week? Housework is your responsibility because I gave you that assignment when we were married.

W: I still just don't understand why we can't be equal.

H: It's because you're a woman and I'm a man. You have your work and I have mine.

Could this husband be guilty of using his wife to build his own ego by making his marriage a contest in which he always has to win? Why was it necessary for him to always be in control and above his wife and her needs? How would developing attributes of *charity* have helped this marriage?

Research comparing competitive and cooperative groups sheds light on the possible effects of competitive and cooperative relationships in marriage. Deutsch summarizes some of these research findings as follows:

1. *Communication*

a) A cooperative process is characterized by open and honest communication of relevant information between the participants. Each is interested in informing, and being informed by, the other.

b) A competitive process is characterized by either lack of communication or misleading communication. It also gives rise to espionage or other techniques of obtaining information about the other that the other is unwilling to communicate. In addition to obtaining such information, each party is interested in providing discouraging or misleading information to the other.

2. *Perception*

    a)   A cooperative process tends to increase sensitivity to simi-
larities and common interest while minimizing the salience of differences. It stimulates a convergence and conformity of beliefs and
values.

    b)   A competitive process tends to increase sensitivity to dif-
ferences and threats while minimizing the awareness of similarities.
It stimulates the sense of complete oppositeness: "You are bad; I
am good."

3. *Attitudes toward one another*

    a)   A cooperative process leads to a trusting, friendly attitude,
and it increases the willingness to respond helpfully to the other's
needs and requests.

    b)   A competitive process leads to a suspicious, hostile atti-
tude, and it increases the readiness to exploit the other's requests.

4. *Task orientation*

    a)   A cooperative process enables the participants to approach
the mutually acknowledged problem in a way that utilizes their
special talents and enables them to substitute for one another in
their joint work, so that duplication of effort is reduced.

    b)   A competitive process stimulates the view that the solution
of a conflict can only be one that is imposed by one side or the
other. The enhancement of one's own power and the minimization
of the legitimacy of the other side's interests in the situation become
objectives. (Morton Deutsch, *The Resolution of Conflict* [New
Haven: Yale University Press, 1973], pages 29-30.)

From these findings it can easily be seen that competition in
relationships will lead to frustration and fighting and inability to
accomplish joint tasks. Cooperation, on the other hand, can lead
to successfully meeting goals together—which is the very key to
a couple's being happily married.

I Was There . . .

*I think that our ideas of what love is change with the pas-
sing of time. I have been able to see that love is being able to
place someone else's feelings, comforts, and needs above my
own. When I have given that kind of love and support un-
selfishly, I have been able to realize that I also helped myself,
even though at the time I didn't think I was. At the time I
thought I wanted something else for myself.*

The most difficult thing my husband and I have ever had to deal with was having our precious daughter killed in a highway accident. We both felt that we had been scalded to our very souls, we were hurt as deeply as it will ever be possible to be hurt. For many years previous to that time I had suffered physical pain from an ailment, but it was not even close to the physical and mental pain we both experienced at our daughter's loss.

When it happened I just wanted to go to my bedroom; go to bed and lie there alone in the dark and die as soon as possible. But I had to think of my husband and our remaining son, Von. He was eleven years old at the time, just six years younger than his sister, and had enjoyed a remarkably close relationship with her.

For months afterwards I literally had to force myself to clean the house, get myself cleaned up, put on some makeup, talk about something else. I fixed the meals as I always had. I walked and talked when I was dying inside. I never had it off my mind more than thirty seconds, yet I knew if I failed my husband and son at that point, it might ruin our family and make it so much harder for them.

To illustrate my mental anguish, let me mention an experience I had with our small riding lawn mower. During her growing up years, Viki had always kept up the lawns with the lawn mower, and would occasionally venture onto some of the neighbors' lawns too, if she thought they were in need of help. After she was gone, we had to take over her jobs about the home, and it was total misery. I didn't want my husband to have to suffer through cutting the lawn, so I went out and did it before he would return home from work. There was an exhaust on the mower placed in a very awkward position, and if the rider wasn't careful he would put his foot on the exhaust and receive a very bad burn. And this is exactly what happened. After I finished mowing and was changing my shoes, I saw that I had burned the top of my foot really badly over an area of about two inches square. I had been in so much pain in my heart and mind, that I didn't even feel the terrible burn on my foot, but could only see the huge blister raising up on the crest of my foot.

I am sure that for my own welfare it was best that I keep moving and working and trying to find something else to talk about with the two remaining members of my family. I know that if I had not had them, I would have given up and perhaps died or gone insane, and so I now see that I really helped myself by loving them so much that I put them first. Little did I realize that they were both doing the same for me. As a result we all learned that truly loving someone is giving of oneself and caring first for the welfare of another.

The fifth aspect of being concerned about one's partner is to show kindness to him. There are literally thousands of ways to do this. For husbands and wives it could mean refusing to be angry when the other is angry. Or it could mean making an effort to be more stimulating in conversation, being more attractive, or finding something new and sharing it with the other. Or it could be learning a new hobby such as chess or skiing just because the partner likes it, or giving compliments and encouragement, being affectionate, opening the door for the other, fixing a favorite dessert, or arranging a midweek lunch date. The list can be nearly endless.

For married couples, an important way of showing kindness is to observe what some have called the rituals of respect. These include remembering and properly honoring one's spouse on birthdays, Father's day, Mother's Day, anniversaries, Christmas, and other special days. The effort that it takes to make these events memorable is well worth it in the strength of the bonds that are created by doing so.

As you reflect back to your courting days, you will remember that in the courtship stage many young people go to great lengths in creating romantic rituals to show their love and devotion to the other partner. You may also recall that they seldom make proposals in ordinary ways. One creative young man arranged for the student card section to flash the "Will you marry me, Judy Cambell?" question at half-time at a college football game. As if this wasn't dramatic enough, the startled girl looked around to see where her boyfriend was, only to see everyone else looking up. They were looking at a hang glider soaring above the stadium. The glider gracefully descended upon the stadium and then landed right on the fifty-yard line. The pilot ran up the bleachers with all thirty-five thousand fans watching and presented the embarassed girl with the engagement ring. The newspaper later confirmed her excited acceptance.

Another young couple had just finished eating at a Chinese restaurant when the fortune cookies were brought out. As the girl opened her cookie she was greatly surprised to find that the enclosed note read, "Marilyn, will you marry me? I love you, Doug." Next the Chinese cook came out from the kitchen carrying a dozen long-stemmed roses which he presented to her on Doug's behalf.

One of the authors, while courting his wife-to-be, found a heart-shaped cheesecake on the inside window sill of his dorm room on Valentine's Day. What made this unusual was that the room was on the third floor. A ladder had been used to make the delivery early that morning.

These experiences all show effective means of demonstrating love and commitment in building romances. In addition, these innovative rituals of love can provide opportunities for couples, as the years pass, to further demonstrate their devotion to each other.

As important as it is to show these acts of kindness, it is just as important that there be an absence of unkind acts that may offset the kind ones. To tell a spouse "I love you" by arranging for a very special birthday party, or by washing the dishes for her, and then to nag at her the next day for not taking the garbage out or for forgetting an errand will not build the strong bonds of trust and affection that can come with *consistent* acts of kindness. For kindness and other acts of charity to have a lasting effect, they need to be performed in an environment in which unkind acts are very rare and quickly repented of.

Paul states this point well: "Owe no man anything, but to love one another: for he that loveth another hath fulfilled the law. . . . Love worketh no ill to his neighbor; therefore love is the fulfilling of the law." (Romans 13:8, 10.)

For love to be effective, it would appear that charitable acts must be done with an absence of uncharitable acts, or as Paul says, true love worketh no evil to his neighbor (or his spouse).

BEING PATIENT WITH OTHERS

Mormon and Paul mentioned patience with others as a dimension of charity and identified four parts of it. They are: (1) suffereth long; (2) is not easily provoked; (3) beareth all things; (4) endureth all things.

In fashioning a Christlike marriage relationship with your companion, you can gain many insights by taking a positive view of these four concepts. As you do, think of patience not as being passive but as being active. Patience is not simply "putting up with" or "tolerating." It is *concentrated strength*. It is the ability to be counted on by one's partner as well as others as a *constant* rather than an *unknown*. Mohammed once said that patience is the key to contentment. That is, when we love someone we are not easily brought to anger by that person, but rather we overlook weaknesses or differences by feeling safe, secure, and content in the depth of the relationship.

One of the mistakes couples ofttimes make in marriage is to lose the spirit of love (and of patience) as one partner begins to emotionally attack the other rather than to discuss a problem or situation which has arisen. Not only does this make the other partner defensive, but it also whittles away at the core of his self-esteem. When a person exercises patience in an awkward or unpleasant moment, this very act allows time to assess the situation, and he can then act toward the situation rather than react and attack his marriage partner.

Painting Patience

On one occasion, Tom was painting the house on a Saturday morning. We were planning to go to a football game in the afternoon, and both of us knew that we would have to leave at about 1:00 P.M. in order to go. Tom continued painting until about twelve noon, when he decided it was time to clean up. He had told me that we were nearly out of paint thinner and I went to get some. In the meantime, two of our children who were helping with the painting had managed to spill nearly a gallon of paint on the patio by knocking over the bucket twice. Tom used all the paint thinner in cleaning up the spills.

I returned at about twelve-thirty with the thinner, and it was clear by that time that Tom would never finish cleaning up in time to go. About ten minutes before it was time to go, I called and said we must leave in ten minutes. Tom was extremely frustrated, since he realized that he would never get everything cleaned up in time and that he could not leave dirty brushes since they would dry out during the game and would be extremely difficult to clean. He blew his stack, and in fact became angry when someone came to the door to see him just as he was trying to clean up himself. Finally, he angrily told me just to leave and go to the game without him.

Immediately, recognizing that he was angry because of frustration caused by his inability to get everything cleaned up on time, I backed down, asked how I could help, and cooled things down. We were slightly late for the game, but we went happy and enjoyed the game because I was willing to give in the whole way instead of standing up for my rights against Tom's anger born of frustration.

As you consider the other aspects of patience, keep in mind that all great marriages are the result of patient working and adjusting together. To suffer does not merely mean to endure pain and anguish, but, as Webster states, "to allow; permit; tolerate." Growth takes some suffering. Progress and improvement, whether in marriage or otherwise, demands some suffering. Surely then, you ought to invest and endure in your marriage to create beauty and joy and growth.

There are many ways to show patience in married life—to allow, permit, and tolerate. You have surely heard the advice to overlook the tube of toothpaste squeezed in the middle, or socks thrown in the middle of the bedroom, and you will agree that this is usually good advice. However, could you be just as patient if your mate were to become disabled? Or, could you tolerate your mate any longer if he or she were to commit adultery and beg your forgiveness? These misfortunes have happened to acquaintances of the authors, and in each instance the marriage was saved because patience and charity had been learned before the misfortune struck.

On the other hand, many marriages have dissolved because of such things as a husband who snores or slurps his food, or one who couldn't buy the type of house and car his wife wanted in the first two years of their marriage. Husbands have left wives because the women were ten pounds overweight, or had a couple of wrinkles, or had just reached forty.

The authors believe such couples should have paid attention to the old adage, "Go into marriage with both eyes wide open and afterwards keep both eyes half-closed." Many couples come into marriage so starry eyed that each partner refuses to see the the other's humanness. This may be all right if these human frailties do not affect the couple's salvation and the partners continue to ignore them for the rest of their marriage. When a person ceases to tolerate the humanness of his spouse, however, erosion of the relationship is sure to follow.

BECOMING TRULY RIGHTEOUS

President Spencer W. Kimball has shown that to be a loving person an individual must also be righteous.

> To be really happy in marriage, there must be a continued faithful observance of the commandments of the Lord. No one, single or married, was ever sublimely happy unless he was righteous. There are temporary satisfactions and camouflaged situations for the moment, but permanent, total happiness can come only through cleanliness and worthiness. One who has a pattern of religious life with deep religious convictions can never be happy in an inactive life. The conscience will continue to afflict unless it has been seared, in which case the marriage is already in jeopardy. A stinging conscience can make life most unbearable. Inactivity is destructive . . . in varying degrees. (*Marriage and Divorce*, pages 23-24.)

Paul and Mormon described this part of charity with five different behaviors: (1) thinketh no evil; (2) rejoiceth not in iniquity; (3) rejoiceth in truth; (4) doth not behave itself unseemly; (5) believeth all things.

Thinking no evil includes looking for the good in oneself and one's spouse. A person who thinks of good ways to behave is developing a pure mind. An evil person is morally corrupt and wicked. He neither edifies nor enlightens others, but instead chooses darkness and secrecy to cover his disobedient behaviors. He is destructive to faith, virtue, and good morals. He does not subject his behavior to principles. Instead he is a person who "behaves unseemly" and feels that laws are not applicable to himself. As a result he cannot be trusted, and without trust his love will wither and die.

Rejoicing not in iniquity but rejoicing in truth can help a marriage immensely. It can add beauty and depth. It can help add noble things to a couple's lives as they develop trust and unity. It can also help a couple avoid iniquity as they maintain a posture of obedience to God's commandments.

Believing all good things can also help a marriage. Through-out the scriptures, belief is a synonym for faith. Just as belief and faith are necessary for salvation (Hebrews 10:39; D&C 20:29), belief and faith in others are necessary to be a loving person. "Faith is not to have a perfect knowledge of things; therefore if ye have faith ye hope for things which are not seen, which are true" (Alma 32:21). It takes this type of faith in others to create the kind of trust that is needed in marriage. As you may have already come to appreciate, it is confidence in each other that sustains you throughout life's difficulties and binds you to each other.

Some people fear rejection by those they love and so are afraid to reveal who they really are. They hide their true feelings and retreat into themselves. This lack of faith or belief in oneself and others can continually put the skids under a person as he struggles to develop significant relationships. Unless a person learns to believe in others, he can never learn to be a charitable or a loving person.

HOW CAN YOU BECOME MORE CHARITABLE?

The first step in developing more charity in your marriage is to examine yourself, and to do this you must ask yourself the following questions about your personal behavior: "Am I as concerned about my spouse as about myself? Am I a patient and long-suffering person? Do I act kindly toward my spouse? Am I hopeful and optimistic? Do I endure things well? Am I gentle, meek, and humble (teachable) as I interact with my spouse? Am I envious of my spouse? Do I boast or act in a "puffed-up" manner? Am I easily provoked? And finally, do I think about evil things?"

If any of these behaviors are problems for you in your relationship with your companion, you can set some specific goals —preferably in writing—about what it is you need to change. You may want to discuss these goals with your partner, or you may want to discuss a particular behavioral tendency your partner has that you think should or could be acted upon as you move with your partner toward a fulfilling relationship.

As a commitment is made to change, you must then develop an exact plan for making the change. This plan must be stated in terms to include what you will do, for whom, and when the change will take place. You then need to record (probably in your personal journal) the progress you make in changing your behavior.

As you begin to have your own actions under control, you will find some very exciting and rewarding things happening in your marriage. It is clearly a law of human behavior that when you act in a certain way toward others, they have a tendency to reciprocate by acting in a similar way toward you. When you are harsh and defensive, others are usually harsh and defensive toward you. When you act with mercy and kindness, you usually receive mercy and kindness. This can be labeled the Law of Restoration in Human Interaction, since it is similar to the gospel law of restoration (Alma 41:13). You will have good restored to you for good, and evil for evil.

Therefore, one of the ways you can increase charitable behaviors in your marriage is to become a charitable companion by constantly thinking and performing acts of kindness.

Every Day

One of the most thoughtful things David does is to constantly tell me of his love and appreciation for me. He tells me he loves me . . . every day. Even when he's away he phones to tell me he loves and misses me each day.

David has never forgotten to thank me for fixing his meal, even when it's been a sandwich and a glass of milk. With that kind of thoughtfulness, he rarely gets just a sandwich. I feel like he deserves the best, so whatever it is, I try to make it very special, for I know it will be appreciated . . . because he tells me it is.

In addition to making the above changes, there is yet another way you can become a more charitable marriage partner. It involves how you respond to your partner's actions instead of how you treat your partner. It is one thing to act charitable when your spouse is cooperative and acting charitable. It is a horse of a different color, however, to return charity for a less than charitable action from your spouse. Those who truly pay the price in their marriages to master this technique are living a higher law and are becoming like the Savior.

The old law allowed an eye for an eye, and under it people tended to love their friends and to hate their enemies. The Savior taught a higher law which is one of the greatest paradoxes in all of human interaction. He has asked everyone to give back good for evil (Matthew 5), and yet, as with all of the Savior's teachings, the principle works to the giver's advantage.

While riding with a friend one day, one of the authors observed that this friend accidently moved the car into the next lane of traffic, thereby cutting another car off and causing the driver to swerve and slam on her brakes. The offended driver was furious and pulled alongside and yelled some very insulting remarks. It was obvious that this driver was overreacting to the incident and that she had no cause to be so rude. This seemed a perfect place to apply the law of restoration and return rudeness for rudeness. The friend, however, made a gesture to her indicating his complete apology and implying that he hoped she could still in some way have a good day. The lady was so shocked that all she could do was return his smile and drive away, embarrassed for her actions.

As a married couple, you can follow this example by not allowing yourselves to each become simply a reactor to your partner's actions. By learning to do this at this time in your marriage, you can short-circuit much of the contention that would otherwise (if it has not already done so) have appeared in your home.

A Taste of Heaven

As I was trying to make my home a "bit of heaven on earth," I often felt my efforts were neither noticed nor appreciated by John. Even though he would pass off a compliment every now and again, it was hard for me to believe or feel he really meant it.

Then one day I received a phone call from a woman in the ward. She called to say that she hoped someday her husband would be as proud of the way she cared for him and their home as mine was of me. I think that afternoon I floated around on cloud seventeen.

For some reason this was a turning point in my life, for I truly felt loved. I decided then and there that I would make a special effort to tell John how much I loved him and appreciated the many, many things he does for me and for our home. The payoff for becoming a "tellingly appreciative" wife is that John has become very vocal to me in his praise and appreciation.

This technique can also work in a relationship in which one partner is further along in his or her ability to follow the Savior's rules for interacting than is the other. The best way to teach this partner to be more charitable is to use the same techniques that were explained above. Joseph Smith taught these principles to the sisters in the Relief Society in 1842 when he said:

Nothing is so much calculated to lead people to forsake sin as to take them by the hand, and watch over them with tenderness. When persons manifest the least kindness and love to me, O what power it has over my mind, while the opposite course has a tendency to harrow up all the harsh feelings and depress the human mind. (*Teachings of the Prophet Joseph Smith,* comp. Joseph Fielding Smith [Salt Lake City: Deseret Book Company, 1938], page 240.)

Helping your spouse become more charitable can be done only as the Prophet Joseph has suggested—with love; by first putting your own life in order, and then by patiently applying the Savior's ideals for interacting.

Summary

While this discussion has been of a different nature, it is sincerely hoped that you have gained a new perspective in one of the most vital areas of a marriage relationship. As you fashion your eternal love with charity, you will be taking a gigantic step toward propelling your marriage into an eternally rewarding experience.

Perhaps you are now ready to drop back away from your feelings toward your partner and consider for a few moments your feelings toward yourself.

. . . and with all thy
getting get understanding.
(Proverbs 4:7.)

3

Much More
Than Small Talk

Communication is to marriage what sunshine is to a garden. It keeps it growing, giving it new energy and life.

Effective Communication

Effective communication is more than simply speaking clearly and listening well. It is much more complex and subtle. There are millions of little things that make a difference in how two people communicate, such as the time of day, the color of the room, their moods, their biorhythms, and the way they hold and move their bodies.

In many ways communicating is like being a pilot or a juggler. There are many things to keep in mind at the same time. A pilot has to keep track of altitude, air speed, fuel, temperature, distances, direction, terrain, time in the air, radio messages, weather, air pressure, flaps, and such seemingly irrelevant things as the air pressure in the tires and the blades on the windshield wipers. If a juggler is trying to juggle balls or hoops, he has to keep all of them going at the same time. That's the way it is with communication.

Perhaps the analogy of a pilot or a juggler isn't strong enough. Communication may be more like a circus. A circus that is bigger than the traditional "three-ring" circus — like, maybe, thirty rings, and something going on in all of them at the same time. One ring is for the words spoken. Another is for the feelings each person has and the ways these feelings surface as each person speaks. Another ring is how well both individuals are listening to the feedback they receive from each other. Another ring includes the nonverbal gestures and movements that contain so many messages, and another ring is for the physical surroundings such as tempo of music, noise level, and time of day, all performing high above the heads of those communicating. The rings go on and on, with all of the many aspects of communication that influence how well two people are able to share and receive messages and truly understand each other.

So, how can two or three chapters in this book help you communicate better with your partner? One way is to help you recognize what is going on in some of the "rings" of your communication circus. Another is to help you learn some additional skills that can help you watch more rings and get more joy out of it because you can learn how to do it better. So, what about the ring off to the far side. Let's call it "listening."

LISTENING

Most people know it is important to listen, but many who have this intellectual awareness do not have good listening habits. For example, how often are you thinking so much about what you are going to say that you don't really listen to what the other person is saying? How often are you so sure of yourself that your mind slams shut while someone else is trying to explain something? And how often do people say something that is important to them — only to have the next comment completely

ignore what was said? Oh that everyone could be like the wise
old owl!

> A wise old owl sat on an oak.
> The more he saw, the less he spoke.
> The less he spoke, the more he heard.
> Why can't we all be like that bird?
>
> (Author unknown.)

Thirty Sacred Minutes

*We found out, quite early in our marriage, that most of
the misunderstandings, confusion, and disappointments that
we experienced between us came about because of poor listening habits. We seemed oblivious to the warning given by
Zeno of Citium that "We have been given two ears and but a
single mouth, in order that we may hear more and talk less."
Through a simple bit of research we discovered that most
people don't listen very long without interrupting the person
who is speaking. Listening also takes some uninterrupted time
and a little concentration. Armed with these warnings about
how not to listen, we determined to spend some time away
from interruptions to listen to each other. For us this meant
waiting until everyone was asleep, taking a little stroll together, or jumping in the car and buying a soda pop and
then parking someplace. In this undisturbed environment,
we determined to try a little listening exercise consisting of
asking each other the following three questions:*

1.   What did you enjoy most today?

2.   What did you enjoy least today?

*3.   If you could do anything you wanted, what would
you really like to do?*

*The person asking the questions and listening to the
answer then had to repeat back (paraphrase) the answer he/
she heard. It was a great experience really listening and really
understanding. In fact, we not only started to listen more
carefully, we found out many things that were important to
each of us. Needless to say, our closeness increased and our
misunderstandings diminished. In fact, to this day we make*

time, sometimes thirty minutes an evening, to enjoy uninter-
rupted listening time together.

It may help your listening if you think about how important
it is to our Father in Heaven. As he introduced his son to Joseph
Smith, he commented, "This is My Beloved Son. Hear Him!"
(Joseph Smith—History 1:17). The Savior also taught that as we
get "ears to hear" we should hear as much as we can of his word,
listen to it as much as we can, try to understand it. Later, as he
gave revelations to Joseph Smith, he would frequently begin by
saying things like "Listen to the voice of . . . Jesus Christ," and
"Hearken and hear, O ye my people" (D&C 39 and 41). To
hearken means to give careful attention. The prophets also have
given more than a little attention to listening. Paul pleaded with
King Agrippa, "Wherefore I beseech thee to hear me patiently"
(Acts 26:3), and John commented, "Blessed [are] . . . they that
hear the words of this prophecy" (Revelation 1:3). When we
listen, it becomes Heavenly Father's most prominent method of
influencing us.

Real listening is one of the highest forms of human influence.
It is an art which is learned and which requires an emotional and
spiritual sensitivity that goes beyond words alone to the feelings
and real meanings of what is being said. By truly listening we are
saying to another, "You're a person of worth; I love you, respect
you, and want to understand you."

It is almost impossible to train a person to speak openly,
honestly, and constructively of his innermost feelings, wishes,
and needs unless he has acquired the faith that such expression
will meet with acceptance rather than with coolness or rejection.

CHECKING OUT

Another ring in your communication circus deals with situa-
tions in which
   —You think you understand the person, but you aren't sure.
   —You are finally getting a glimpse of what is going on, but
      you don't understand it well yet.
   —You are pretty sure you understand, but the other person
      doesn't think you do.

—You think you understand what is happening inside the
other person, but the other person doesn't seem to understand yet.

In these situations, the skill of *checking out* can be useful.
Checking out is the process of asking a question or saying something to find out if you are understanding correctly. In some
situations it is simple and easy. For example, you may hear
someone ask for something at the dinner table and not be sure
whether they said the water or the butter. A simple statement
like "You wanted the butter?" may be enough checking out. In
other situations, such as when you are trying to understand
complex and deeply felt emotions, checking things out takes
more time—and also more tact, delicacy, patience, and understanding.

There are three main ways to check out one's understanding
(see Sherod Miller et al., *Alive and Aware* [Minneapolis: Interpersonal Communication Programs, Inc., 1975]). They are: (1)
ask a simple question; (2) make a summary statement; and (3)
reflect or paraphrase. There are some do's and don'ts for each of
these.

Asking a simple question. Questions that ask *who, what,
when,* or *how* are usually the best type. For example:

Who did you say did it?
What did you mean when you said . . . ?
Where did you say you were?
When do you think I should . . . ?
How often did you say?

These questions are open-ended, and you usually get quite a
bit of information from asking them. If you want some more
specific information, you can ask more specific questions, such
as:

Did you say Harry should do that?
Was it five or six?
What did you think was the cause of . . . ?

When you are checking out, it is usually wise to avoid questions that ask "Why?" A *why* question usually leads to new

issues, new information, or exploration of something that hasn't been covered before. It seldom helps you verify what was just said.

This process of asking questions to check out might even be applied to the Savior's words, "Ask, and it shall be given unto you." (3 Nephi 14:7.) Certainly we don't always immediately and fully understand a scripture, an answer to prayer, etc.

Summarizing. Here you try to pull a number of things together and check them all out at once. You do it with a statement rather than a question, but you often imply that you'd like the other person to let you know if you've summarized it all correctly. Sometimes you may even make a summary statement and then add something like, "Have I got it straight?"

Summarizing places more responsibility on the person who is checking out, because that person is then restating the point or idea in his or her own words. It takes more time and energy, but it is sometimes more useful than a simple question, because a misunderstanding in the summary can be pinpointed and corrected. Also, if the summary is correct, the other person has more assurance that he or she has been understood.

It is usually wise to state the conclusion or summary in a tentative manner rather than state it as a firm conclusion. This makes it easier for the other person to either confirm it or to correct it. Some examples of summary statements are these:

"Then what is at the bottom of it is that I haven't shown as much consideration as I should, and this has gradually made you feel like I don't care about our relationship?"

"So you'd prefer bucket seats, and you want the green car if we can get the stripe down the side, but you'd rather have the blue one if we can't get the one with the stripe?"

"I gather that you wouldn't be too happy about having my mother stay with us all summer, but two weeks would be okay."

"When we add it all up, it looks like it would be better not to buy it. Is that where you are?"

Paraphrasing. This is the process of restating or reflecting what the other person has said. Sometimes this is done naturally. For example, if someone tells you his telephone number, you will often repeat it back to see if you have it right. In other situations it is not as natural, but it can be very helpful. When someone is expressing his reasons for doing something, sharing his feelings or opinions or wishes, you can learn a lot by paraphrasing what you think he has said. When someone is trying to understand a problem he is having or just getting something off his chest, you can be very helpful to him if you listen a lot and paraphrase a little.

Occasionally the other person's exact words can be used, but it is generally more helpful to use different words. It is also useful if the paraphrasing can get closer to the heart of the issue, the feeling, or problem rather than repeat the ideas exactly. This has the advantage of helping move the conversation along, as well as checking out. The following example illustrates this process:

"I feel like Mother is always watching me when she's here, and that inside she's shaking her head about how I do things. I've tried to not get stirred up inside, but there are times when I can just feel her eagle eye on me, and when she says something about how I ought to be doing things, I just get all tied up inside."

"You resent it when she criticizes you."

"That's right, and it's more than just a little too. Sometimes. . . ."

Many nonverbal messages are communicated when you paraphrase. If these messages have a connotation of condemnation or wrongness, the reflection will tend to make your spouse stop exploring feelings. If the nonverbalized messages convey an empathetic understanding and a warm concern, the reflection will tend to increase the exploration of feelings.

ISSUE VERSUS PERSONALITY

A third ring in your communication circus deals with separating the issue from the personalities of the individuals. It is not always possible to do this, but when issues can be depersonalized, it is usually easier to communicate. This point can be illustrated with several examples:

Separating Issue from Personality	*Mixing Issue with Personality*
"I'd like to have a discussion about the things we have been having for dinner lately."	"I think that your cooking is a problem."
"I think we have a problem with some of the things we have been eating."	"You're not buying the right food."
"Our being late all of the time is frustrating to me."	"You're always making us late."
"Are you satisfied with that painting job?"	"You're a sloppy painter."
"I'd like to get my way more."	"I think you're too bossy."
"I don't think my feelings and opinions are considered enough."	"You're inconsiderate."

It is easier to separate issues from personalities when the problems being discussed are fairly impersonal, such as deciding which color to paint a living room, where to take a vacation, or whether to subscribe to a magazine. Unfortunately, many of the issues in marital relationships are personal issues, and when such concerns are addressed it is more challenging and difficult to isolate the issue from the person.

It is most difficult to depersonalize an issue when the problem is part of an individual's personality. Even when this is the case, however, the problem will seldom involve his or her total personality, and it may be wise in such instances to separate from the individual as a whole the one aspect that is being discussed. Such problems must be dealt with delicately and sensitively if they are to be handled constructively. They are probably among the most difficult marital problems to solve, largely because of their personal nature.

TOUCHING

You may have learned early in childhood that a large part of your communication with others is nonverbal. You learned that you need to pay attention to the way people say things, and that such behaviors as a long sigh or a facial expression can help convey to you an understanding of what others *really* mean. You have also learned an elaborate set of gestures with your hands and face. These nonverbal skills become so important that you probably feel stifled and uncomfortable when you cannot see the other person or cannot use your hands to help express yourself. Those who don't believe this can try one of the following fun activities:

The Importance of Nonverbal Communication

Goal: To better realize how important the nonverbal part of communication is.

1. Sit on your hands and explain to your spouse something that is complex, such as an important emotional experience or how to drive to a friend's house.

or

Sit back-to-back (so your backs touch) and then talk about something that is important to both of you.
2. Then talk about how this disrupted your "natural" communication processes.

Touching almost always has meaning attached to it, and much of the time this meaning is universally understood. Sometimes, however, the meaning is unique to a particular subcultural group, a family, or a couple. You began developing a language of touch early in your life, and this language became very complex. Then as you began dating, you brought your habits of touching and not touching with you. In each relationship you gradually acquired an agreement about what different forms of touch mean. A touch on the back of the hand in one situation may mean "I love you—as a person you are very precious to me." In another situation it may mean "Let me have your attention."

Sometimes it is useful to discuss your language of touch. This is especially true in situations where certain types of physical touch or not touching mean one thing to one of you and something different to your spouse. In these situations, a discussion of these differences in "meaning" might mean the difference between understanding and misunderstanding.

Sometimes when you communicate through touch, the message you send is the one you intend to send. At other times, you send messages that are quite different from the ones you want to send. Also, the messages you receive may or may not be the ones your partner wants to send. The best way to make sure that the messages you want to send are the same as the ones that are received is to talk about this part of your communication.

THE OTHER PERSON IS RIGHT . . . TO HIM

Disagreements are inevitable in marriage. You were each reared in different families, and you have a number of differences as a result of the styles of your families. As President Spencer W. Kimball has observed:

> Two people coming from different backgrounds soon learn after the ceremony is performed that stark reality must be faced. There is no longer a life of fantasy or of make-believe; we must come out of the clouds and put our feet firmly on the earth. Responsibility must be assumed and new duties must be accepted. Some personal freedoms must be relinquished and many adjustments, unselfish adjustments, must be made.
>
> One comes to realize very soon after marriage that the spouse has weaknesses not previously revealed or discovered. The virtues that were constantly magnified during courtship now grow relatively smaller, and the weaknesses that seemed so small and insignificant during courtship now grow to sizeable proportions. (*Marriage and Divorce,* page 12.)

Some of these differences are so irrelevant to the relationship that they can be ignored. Others are so important that they *must* be resolved if the relationship is to continue. When you encounter differences, there is one aspect of these problems that is usually not verbalized, but it influences what happens when you try to manage them. This is whether or not you appreciate the *subjec-*

tive aspect of right and wrong; the fact that the other person is *right* in his or her own eyes.

A person may be wrong in an absolute sense. That is, his opinion would be indefensible if it were contested, or it would be unworkable if it were tried. It is therefore absolutely wrong. However, when a person believes that the opinion is correct, the opinion is correct *to that person*. In other words, the opinion is *subjectively* right, even though in an objective or absolute sense it may be wrong.

This distinction is not trivial.

It is very important in marriage.

It would be possible to try to resolve your differences by being highly concerned about the absolute correctness of your opinions and not being concerned about the subjective correctness; and some couples use this unwise approach. It is better to be sensitive to both the objective and the subjective correctness of the views whenever you try to resolve your differences or cope with problems. Why?

First, many differences in marital relationships are based on opinions, value judgments, or subjective interpretations. In these situations it is impossible to determine which of two conflicting opinions is really, in an absolute sense, correct.

Second, there seems to be something about human nature that makes many persons defensive and closed-minded when others ignore the fact that *they think they are right.* If you recognize and respect the subjective correctness, even though in an absolute sense you may turn out to be wrong, it generates more open-mindedness and less defensiveness. One way to approach this matter is to recognize that the world is perceived from the mind. You each see and understand and believe according to the information you have, your values, and your experiences. Your views are sensible and personal and precious. If you would recognize this, it would give a certain degree of integrity, respectability, and dignity that is subtly and almost imperceptibly taken away when subjective rightness is ignored.

A *third* advantage of recognizing subjective rightness is that it puts the person who is trying to change someone else's mind in a helpful rather than an authoritarian role.

A *fourth* reason couples may find it useful is that when you appreciate the subjective rightness, nobody is backed into a corner. Neither person has been completely right and the other completely wrong when a solution is found. Instead, it is a situation in which both persons are right in their own eyes. Each is trying to get the other to understand how he or she views the situation, and then they are working together to try to identify a solution that will be acceptable to both. Each spouse can try to communicate to the other that there might be a different way of looking at the situation rather than try to prove the other one wrong.

Thus, when you appreciate subjective rightness, your communication will probably be less *defensive*. You will both also tend to be more *adaptable* and *willing to listen* to the point of view of others. You will be more *open* to suggestions. Frequently the communication will be more *relaxed,* and the issues can be discussed in an atmosphere of respect for one another's opinions and respect for each other as individuals.

CREATE A FEELING OF BEING UNDERSTANDING

There is an important difference between understanding someone else and the other person having a "feeling" that you are being understanding. These two usually go together, but sometimes they don't. For example, a husband may understand that his wife wants to get out of the house at the end of the day after being confined with several young children. He may even realize that it is important to her. But if he has a strong desire to stay home and resists her request to take her out, she will probably think that he doesn't understand her. In this situation, he actually does understand her, but she doesn't have a feeling that he is understanding. With another couple the situation may be reversed. Consider the following example in which each is talking to himself:

Tom: With the merger coming up, I'll probably lose my job, and we used up most of our year's supply last time I was laid off. That operation put us so far in debt that I don't know what we'll do. There's no point in talking about it with Pam; she'll just say as she always does, "I'm sure you'll work things out." She just doesn't realize how bad off we are.

Pam: I heard about the merger, and I'll bet Tom is just worried sick about it. And all the bills we have don't make it any easier. He's so conscientious that I know it's just eating away at him inside. I'll bet that the best way for me to help him is to be supportive and encouraging, and let him know that I have confidence in him.

Pam understands Tom, but he doesn't realize that she does. He doesn't have a feeling of being understood.

These two skills are very different. The ability to understand the other person accurately is called *empathy*. It is a mental process that occurs in your head. You don't have to say anything or do anything except listen, observe, and occasionally check out your insights. The other skill is to be able to create a feeling in others that you understand them. It is much more complex because it involves interpersonal communication. You have to send the type of messages that will show you understand.

As you realize, it is important to empathize correctly in marital relationships, and most people *are* skillful empathizers. Many, however, fail to recognize that the other process is also important. In intimate relationships such as marriage, where most of the important things center around such things as emotions, personal beliefs, and the person as a whole, the ability to help the other person feel that you understand is extremely important.

The Mortally Wounded Octopus

And then there was the time my sweet husband decided that my life would never be fulfilled or complete until I had learned to ski. He must have had visions of us zipping down the glistening hill together at a pace of 80 m.p.h., although he forgot to ask me how I felt about it. In reality . . . well, you can still see the deep scars from my fingernails in the woodwork as he "assisted" me out of the front door. And you should have seen how he got me into the car! Neither I nor the car will ever be the same . . . and all for the sake of unity.

We finally arrived at the ski resort, and after a great deal of hard work I was goggled, zipped up to my nose, strapped into some tremendously long, skinny wooden sticks, handed some things that resembled gloves, and given a couple of sharp poky things to use (I suppose) if attacked by bears. So there I was, looking like a clone of the abominable snowman. And then I saw it . . . the chair lift! I broke out in a cold sweat, and found out only later, much later, that getting on was a real snap compared to trying to get off the crazy thing. I cried all the way to the top, which seemed to take four and a half days. It was at this point that my sweet unifying husband became visibly irritated. Enough said.

As I leaned forward to remove my person from the chair, I invented a new technique for dismounting —"the roller-skating giraffe technique." Going down the hill, I had only two thoughts. "If only I can come out of this in one piece — or at least several large pieces!", and "Hey, there surely are lots of people with outfits like that one — and that one — and that one." It turned out to be the same few people taking spills time after time.

After taking two and a half hours to traverse down a twenty-minute slope, I had mastered the technique of skiing off into powder to soften my falls, and it was at this point that I mastered an entirely new technique, "the mortally wounded octopus" technique, where arms and legs fly off in every direction. It was at the conclusion of one such contortion that I finally did what any other red-blooded American woman would have done — I cried!

It was at this moment that my all-too-unifying husband became visibly furious. "Okay," I told him, "I know you probably hate me, and that you aren't having any fun, so why don't you just go ahead by yourself? Go on! Just leave me here to die!" And of course I just cried all the more. And can you believe it? The next time I dried my tears enough to look up, there he was whizzing down the mountain . . . alone!

I had the rest of the entire day to sit in the car, eat my "alone" lunch, rub my poor twice-its-normal-size knee, and reminisce about the day we gained unity in our marriage.

Sometimes in marriage a feeling of being understood is more important than the understanding itself. Consider, for example, the following situation:

Bill: Jane is so understanding. When things aren't going well she takes the time to help me work things out and get back on the track. When I was having problems with Jeff, I brought it up one night and she stayed home from her meeting so we could talk it through. She understood the situation really well for only getting it secondhand, and had several ideas that really helped.

Jane: Bill and I talked the other night about a problem he was having on the job. Bill was really upset. I don't know the guy that made the mess, and I'm not sure what Bill is going to do about it. He may have to pay a fine or might even lose his job, I don't know. I tried to get the whole thing straight, but I don't think I ever did. About all I could do was listen and try to understand.

In this marriage, Jane didn't understand very much of what was going on inside Bill, but the way she behaved created a *feeling* that she was an understanding person, and this helped a great deal. The following list of behaviors identifies some things you may want to do and not do to create a feeling that you are "understanding."

Do	*Avoid Doing*
Take the time to let your partner know you understand when you do.	Put your spouse down for feelings he or she has that you don't understand. (They are

Do	Avoid Doing
Take the time to listen to your spouse, especially whenever he or she is emotionally upset about something.	genuine experiences for that person.)
Try hard to see things from the other person's point of view rather than your own.	Criticize the person's feelings. Some feelings are irrational, but they are nevertheless real.
Be patient until you know a lot about a situation.	Do something else (like reading or doing housework) while listening to the other person.
Try to get all the facts about something before making up your mind.	Jump to conclusions. Assume the other person knows you understand him.
Realize that your spouse lives in a different world and may see things differently.	
Check out how well you understand by repeating it back or questioning.	

PAY ATTENTION TO YOUR ENVIRONMENT

Another ring in your communication circus is your environment. It influences what is going on, and you need to adjust to it. The following three items are some of the things to consider.

Time of day. Many people are better communicators at some times of the day than at other times. Most people find that it is difficult to be congenial communicators just before the evening meal. (James H. S. Bossard and Eleanor S. Boll, *Sociology of Child Development* [New York: Harper, 1954].) In the typical home, dinner time is a period of fairly hectic activity. One or both parents are arriving home from the job, and people are hungry and tired. Also, after having to perform on the job all day, it is not uncommon to be tense and to need to unwind and rest. This is also a time of preparing the evening meal and is very busy. The net effect is that this is often a difficult time to communicate about something that is problematic, irritating, or serious.

The time of day also influences communication, because some people wake up more slowly than others. Some people are not really fully awake until ten or eleven in the morning, and they find it difficult to communicate about serious situations before then. Others wake up early and quickly, and the morning is the best time for them to tackle their problems. Some people are the most proficient in discussing things after ten or eleven at night, and others are so exhausted by that time that they can't even keep their heads up, let alone communicate.

Each couple has to discover which time of day is the best and worst for them. They can then try to resolve issues or make decisions at the good times and avoid the bad times.

Non-family pressures. All couples experience outside pressures that interfere with the kind of communication that is necessary when major decisions have to be made, differences have to be resolved, or problems have to be coped with.

It may be that the wise way to deal with external pressures is to be sensitive to them when they occur and to try to avoid facing issues that could be put off for a few days or a couple of weeks. This suggestion is, of course, contrary to the advice heard occasionally that married couples should "never let the sun set on a problem." It is therefore proposed here that occasionally the most effective thing a couple can do is let several days pass before dealing with certain problems. This is not arguing that couples should avoid facing problems indefinitely.

Physical setting. Architects and designers have long recognized that the physical setting influences the way people behave. Bright colors, such as reds, oranges, and purples, excite and arouse people. Beiges, greens, and blues relax people. Hard surfaces, such as tile, brick, ceramic, and marble, create different moods than soft surfaces, such as carpeting, draperies, and pillows. These effects can be used in homes to create different types of moods in different places or situations. Soft light, low calm music, and a fire in the fireplace are some common ways to create an atmosphere of calmness and peace.

In addition to these obvious examples, other things such as relaxing evening wear, slippers, reading material, and soft furniture also promote relaxation, calmness, and serenity. It is, of course, not always desirable to have a calm setting for discussions about important, sensitive, or problematic issues, but many times it is desirable to do what can be done to create a pleasant setting for serious discussions. For many people, trying to resolve an important issue while driving in downtown traffic in a compact car could create obstacles to effective communication, and such situations can usually be avoided if they are sensitive to the role of physical factors.

Summary

This chapter began with a general principle about communication. The principle is that the better our communication, the better our marriage. The rest of the chapter discussed skills you can use as couples to have effective communication. Some of the skills dealt with verbal communication and some with nonverbal communication. A few of them dealt with both verbal and nonverbal ways of communicating. While this chapter establishes the need for mature communicating and then sets forth some specific skills you can acquire, still at best it is a launching pad into even deeper communication which is so crucial to understand in preparing for an eternal relationship.

Men are, that they might have joy.
(2 Nephi 2:25.)

4

Communicating Your Feelings

You can appreciate the fact that people don't become very emotional in their relationships with the milkman, postman, or metermaid. They're a *little more* emotionally involved with their home teachers, bishop, boss, and neighbors. But with one's spouse, it is as different as night and day, as emotions then run very deep. Feelings are the substance of a marriage. Two people marry because they are in love. Each cares about the other with his whole being, and they share excitement and happiness, grief and depression, fulfillment and joy.

What does this mean for your marriage? It means that it is important for you to learn how to understand your emotions as well as your spouse's emotions; and then learn how to create the kinds of emotions you want (love, joy, happiness, security, peace, etc.), while decreasing as much as possible the emotions that you don't want (jealousy, depression, discouragement, rejection, sadness, etc.). However, before getting into how this is done, explore for a minute just how important the emotional side of life is . . . or should be.

How Important Are Emotions?

Some worldly cultures teach that the emotional side of life should be ignored, hidden, and avoided. For example, have you ever heard somebody say, "Don't feel that way," or "Boys shouldn't cry," or "Be tough" (which means, "Don't show or recognize your emotions")? Some scholars have called this set of beliefs the "John Wayne neurosis." It is the belief that the man should be the strong, silent type who doesn't show his emotions. He doesn't become discouraged, or if he does, he shouldn't show it. He should be a little awkward when people are tender and gentle and serene. He shouldn't show any emotion when a story or movie has a sad scene, and if he gets a lump in his throat, he should swallow or stiffen his back so he isn't "moved" by the situation. Oh, he can be sad at funerals, and even cry *then*—if it is someone who is close to him; but by and large he is to be "in control" and be the tough one that others lean on, the one who will think things through and be the leader rather than someone who is soft and emotional. Unfortunately some of these beliefs have crept unawares into the belief system of many Latter-day Saints.

One way to get a proper view of emotions is to gain an understanding of the scriptural view of emotions. We three authors did this when we were preparing to write this book, and (we hate to admit it) we were astounded! We had studied the scriptures all of our lives, but we had never looked at them from that particular approach. Our procedure was to begin reading the scriptures to look for references to *emotions,* and we started writing notes about the references that cited emotional experiences. Very quickly we had page after page of notes. We had so many that we were very surprised, and we learned what we feel is a very important lesson. *The scriptural view of the emotional part of man is very different from the modern worldly view.* We concluded that this is another area where the Apostasy has changed the beliefs in the world. We learned that men in the scriptures tended to experience emotions a great deal, and they recognized it, talked about it, shared it with others, and viewed their emotional experiences as an important part of their lives — very different from the "John Wayne neurosis" that predominates in the modern world. The following list of references illustrates how pervasively the scriptures refer to emotions or feelings. And remember, this list is just a very small selection — it is just to illustrate the point. Those who want to do what we did ought to do some reading from the same approach: read to see how prevalent the emotions are in the scriptures. Just for fun, try reading the book of Jacob in the Book of Mormon in this way.

Scriptural Emotions — A Sample

2 Nephi 32:8	it *grieveth* me
Jacob 2:9	*burdeneth* my soul
Jacob 2:28	for I, the Lord God, *delight* in
Jacob 2:35	*broken the hearts* of your tender wives
Jacob 4:3	learn with *joy*
Romans 12:15	do *rejoice,* and *weep* with them that weep
Enos 1:4	and my soul *hungered*
Enos 1:9	I began to feel a *desire* for the welfare of my brethren
D&C 63:32	I, the Lord, am *angry* with the wicked
Mark 1:41	and Jesus, *moved* with *compassion,* put forth his hand
D&C 4:5	and *faith, hope, charity* and *love*
D&C 87:6	to feel the *wrath,* and *indignation,* and *chastening*
Deuteronomy 28:47	with *gladness* of heart
Psalm 19:8	*rejoicing* the heart
Proverbs 17:22	a *merry* heart doeth good like a medicine
2 Corinthians 9:7	for God loveth a *cheerful* giver
Mosiah 4:3	having *peace of conscience*
Alma 42:18	brought *remorse of conscience* unto men
John 14:27	my *peace* I give unto you

Galatians 5:22	fruit of the spirit is *love, joy, peace*
Enos 1:27	then shall I see his face with *pleasure*
Luke 3:14	and be *content* with your wages
2 Nephi 4:32	my heart is broken and my spirit is *contrite*
Deuteronomy 20:1	be not *afraid*
Alma 15:4	his heart began to take *courage*
Jacob 2:7	whose feelings are exceedingly tender and chaste and delicate before God, which thing is pleasing unto God
1 Corinthians 12:31	covet *earnestly* the best gifts
1 Nephi 3:25	did *lust* after it
Deuteronomy 11:18	lay up these words *in your heart* and *in your soul*
Luke 24:32	did not our heart *burn* within us.
Alma 5:14	mighty change in your *hearts*
Alma 32:28	*swell within your breasts;* and when you feel these *swelling motions . . . enlarge* my soul . . . *delicious* to me
1 Nephi 8:28	they were *ashamed,* because of those that were scoffing
D&C 6:33	*fear not* to do good
1 Corinthians 13:4	charity *suffereth* long
Alma 14:11	the Spirit *constraineth* me
1 Nephi 16:2	the guilty taketh the truth to be hard, for it *cutteth* them to the very center
Proverbs 10:1	a wise son maketh a *glad* father
Ecclesiastes 11:9	Let thy heart *cheer* thee in the days of thy youth
Alma 3:26	to reap eternal *happiness* or eternal *misery*
D&C 59:18	all things . . . to *gladden the heart*
D&C 59:23	*peace* in this world
Psalm 97:10	ye that *love* the Lord, *hate* evil
2 Corinthians 11:2	I am *jealous* over you with godly jealousy
2 Nephi 2:25	men are, that they might have *joy*
John 3:16	for God so *loved* the world
Leviticus 19:18	nor bear any *grudge*

Thus you can appreciate that this is another area in which you should be in the world but not of the world. You ought to be much more open to your emotions than the worldly modern culture teaches. You ought to be much more willing to recognize emotions, talk about them, share them, and enjoy them, than perhaps you have been. With your husband or wife, and your children, you should use the emotions to provide a richness, a depth, and a fullness to your life that does not exist in the contemporary industrialized world.

Skills You Can Use in Managing Your Emotions

There are a number of skills that can help you manage the emotional part of your marital stewardship. Seven of them are discussed in the remaining pages of this chapter. They are:

I. Skills for expressing (sharing) feelings.
    1. Recognize emotions in yourself and others.
    2. Label your emotions when you recognize them.
    3. Express your feelings and share them with others.
    4. Express negative emotions in helpful ways.
II. Skills that help you understand feelings.
    5. Listen with your heart as well as your head.
    6. Accept rather than reject expressions of others.
    7. Recognize nonverbal and verbal messages.

EXPRESSING SKILLS

Communication is the process of sending and receiving messages in a way that creates understanding. Half of this process is being able to *express* yourself so the messages you want to send are the ones that are received. The following four skills can help you in this role.

Skill no. 1. How many young boys are told, "You should not feel that way"; "You're a big boy now, and big boys don't cry"; or "Just forget about it [the feeling]. It's not important." Unfortunately, this society systematically teaches individuals to be dishonest with their emotions. Many learn these lessons so well that they become insensitive to their emotions and don't know what they are really feeling. F. Alexander Magoun feels this is a part of honesty, and he suggests that most people would be better off if they had more *emotional honesty*. (*Love and Marriage* [New York: Harper, 1948].)

How can you become more aware of your emotions? First, you can look at your behavior to find clues about your emotions. If you are skipping along, whistling or humming, and have an extra spring in your step, this can say something about how you are feeling. If you find yourself a little more critical, negative, or disagreeable than usual, this too can provide some clues as to how you are feeling. Some people would do well to become more sensitive to these behaviors. They go through life acting pleasant in one situation and disagreeable in another, while being quite unaware of how they are acting and what these actions can tell them about their feelings.

One Bottled-Up Year

Don and I were married just one week after I had completed my education and only six months after his return from a mission. We had been high school sweethearts and had continued to date prior to his mission, and so everything seemed to fit into place. Our first two years of marriage were spent with Don in school and me teaching . . . with each of us leaning totally on our two sets of parents instead of on each other. And then it happened.

We moved away so that Don could attend medical school. By then we had our first daughter, and so without spending so much as a day with each other to make the transition, Don began his schooling and I once again began teaching to support our little family.

At first I didn't mind getting up a few hours earlier. Our daughter needed to be dressed and packed for her day with the sitter, and evening meals had to be planned as well as lunches made for us both. After about mid-year, however, I could feel myself becoming more and more resentful of the heavy burden that seemed to be placed squarely upon my shoulders. I was afraid to tell Don how I felt because I realized the great strain he was under. But, as in all situations that are not dealt with, by the end of the school year I was one giant exhausted crank. I'm sure now that this exhaustion was as much from mental frustration as from my actual load.

One Sunday morning on the way to church, tempers seemed to just explode. It had been a particularly hurried morning and Don had been frustrated with some exams he had taken that week. He was feeling down and mentioned how difficult the year had been for him. Not to be outdone, I snapped back, exclaiming that the year had "been no picnic for me, either!" From that moment all the frustrations we had both been keeping bottled up seemed to roll out with no control.

That afternoon we were able to sit down and for the first time really talk to each other. I was able to see that I had relied too much on my family for a sounding board and for mental recreation. Don, on the other hand, felt that I was more independent than I really was or wanted to be. We were able to calmly decide that we really needed each other more than either one had realized. We needed to talk more and to try to understand what the other was feeling and thinking. He needed to be more involved in my profession, and I needed to be made to feel important to his profession. I am not going to say that from this point on everything was perfect, but we both learned that we could give more than we had in the past, and that we could really sit down without blowing our tops and express our feelings to each other.

From that moment on we began to plan dates when we could talk and share what we were feeling. Now, with several daughters in our home, we still find that our most special dates are the quiet, personal ones where we can share and linger while we communicate in a loving environment.

A second thing you can do is pause and think about what is happening to you emotionally. This is the process of listening to yourself, listening to what is going on inside. The purpose of life is to have joy (2 Nephi 2:25), and you need to take the time to "tune in" to the experience of joy. You need to be alert to the response of joy inside you. Again, some people go through life not experiencing joy because they don't take the time to feel, to experience, to truly love. The Savior talked of people having "ears to hear" and "eyes to see" spiritual truths. He knew that some people would tune into spiritual experiences and some people would not. It is the same with one's feelings. Some have the ears to hear what is going on inside, and some do not. Some have the eyes to see their feelings, and some need glasses.

How can you learn to hear and see?

By practicing! If you want to learn how to recognize your emotions, you need to spend a few minutes listening and watching. You should pause to look inside and see what you can. At first you may only rarely get a glimpse of an emotion, and you may recognize a feeling only when it is extremely intense. Later, as you try to tune your antenna inward, you will find that your eyes become sharper and your ears can hear more and more. You will first recognize one or two emotions and then another and another, gradually awakening yourself to an important part of your experience.

Skill no. 2: Labeling your emotions. When you first get a glimpse of an emotion, it has no name. You are vaguely aware of a sensation, an experience, a feeling that you are living. Then, gradually, much like a sunrise that becomes more clear and bright, you see things more clearly. Usually you can then tell what the emotion is and find words which describe it. This is the process of *labeling* your feelings.

Some feelings, such as anger and happiness, are easy to label. Others are much more complex and subtle, and it is more difficult to label them. Sometimes you may find yourself saying things like, "I'm not sure how to describe what I'm feeling," or "I just can't find words that express it," or "words just aren't adequate."

The process of labeling emotions is important, because having names for feelings can help you communicate about your emotions. Davitz identified a list of hundreds of different emotions. (Joel R. Davitz, *The Language of Emotion* [New York: Academic Press, 1969].) A modified version of his list is reproduced below. Perhaps you and your spouse could walk through this list, verbalizing emotions you may be experiencing. Hopefully, this review will increase your vocabulary of emotions.

Labels for Emotions

1.	accepted	34.	connected
2.	accepting	35.	contemptuous
3.	active	36.	contented
4.	admiring	37.	cowardly
5.	feeling affection	38.	creative
6.	afraid	39.	cruel
7.	alarmed	40.	curious
8.	alienated	41.	cut off from others
9.	amused	42.	defeated
10.	angry	43.	dejected
11.	anxious	44.	delighted
12.	apathetic	45.	dependent
13.	appreciated	46.	depressed
14.	attractive	47.	deprived
15.	awe-inspired	48.	deserving punishment
16.	awkward	49.	desperate
17.	beaten	50.	determined
18.	beautiful	51.	disappointed in myself
19.	bewildered	52.	disappointed with others
20.	bored	53.	discomforted
21.	brave	54.	dislikeable
22.	calm	55.	dominated
23.	cheated	56.	domineering
24.	cheerful	57.	eager to impress others
25.	close	58.	eager to please others
26.	closed	59.	easily manipulated
27.	comfortable	60.	easy-going
28.	committed	61.	elated
29.	compassionate	62.	embarrassed
30.	competent	63.	enjoyable
31.	concerned for others	64.	envious
32.	confident	65.	evasive
33.	confused	66.	evil

67.	excited	105.	inconsistent
68.	exhilarated	106.	in control
69.	failing	107.	indecisive
70.	fatalistic	108.	independent
71.	fearful	109.	inferior
72.	feminine	110.	inhibited
73.	flirtatious	111.	insecure
74.	friendless	112.	insincere
75.	friendly	113.	inspired
76.	frigid	114.	involved
77.	frustrated	115.	irritated
78.	gay	116.	isolated
79.	generous	117.	jealous
80.	genuine	118.	judgmental
81.	giddy	119.	lonely
82.	grateful	120.	losing
83.	gratified	121.	lovable
84.	grief-stricken	122.	loved
85.	grudge-bearing	123.	loving
86.	guilty	124.	loyal
87.	gutless	125.	manipulated
88.	happy	126.	manipulative
89.	hateable	127.	masculine
90.	hateful	128.	masked
91.	harmonious	129.	melancholy
92.	hopeful	130.	misunderstood
93.	hopeless	131.	moody
94.	hostile	132.	needy
95.	humorous	133.	nervous
96.	hurt	134.	old beyond years
97.	hurt by criticism	135.	optimistic
98.	hyperactive	136.	out of contact
99.	hypocritical	137.	out of control
100.	ignored	138.	overcontrolled
101.	immobilized	139.	overlooked
102.	impatient	140.	odd
103.	inadequate	141.	panicked
104.	incompetent	142.	paranoid

143. passionate
144. peaceful
145. persecuted
146. pessimistic
147. phony
148. piteous
149. pitiful
150. played-out
151. pleased
152. possessive
153. pouting
154. prejudiced
155. preoccupied
156. pressured
157. protective
158. proud
159. quiet
160. rejected
161. relaxed
162. relieved
163. religious
164. remorseful
165. repelled
166. repulsive
167. resentful
168. restrained
169. reverent
170. rewarded
171. sad
172. satisfied
173. scared
174. secure
175. self-complacent
176. self-reliant
177. serene
178. shallow
179. shamed
180. shameful
181. shy
182. silly
183. sincere
184. sinful
185. sluggish
186. soft
187. solemn
188. sorry for self
189. strong
190. stubborn
191. stupid
192. sunshiny
193. super
194. superior
195. supported
196. supportive
197. surprised
198. suspicious
199. sympathetic
200. tender
201. terrified
202. threatened
203. tired
204. tolerant
205. torn
206. touchy
207. triumphant
208. two-faced
209. ugly
210. unable to communicate
211. unappreciated
212. uncertain
213. ungifted
214. unresponsive
215. unrestrained
216. up-tight
217. used
218. useless

219.	victimized	223.	weary
220.	vindictive	224.	weedy
221.	violent	225.	wishy-washy
222.	warm	226.	youthful

This list has been especially helpful to spouses who choose to write to each other about their feelings. As they write and are trying to identify how they are feeling at that moment, they can glance at the list and find an emotion that describes that feeling.

Skill no. 3: Sharing your feelings. Once you have learned to recognize emotions and label them, it is then possible to disclose these feelings to others. Becvar has identified several different ways in which you can express feelings. (R. J. Becvar, *Skills for Effective Communication: A Guide to Building Relationships* [New York: Wiley, 1974].) First, you can express them indirectly or *nonverbally* through your actions. If you are excited you tend to do such things as jump up and down, squeal, laugh, and gesture with your hands. Each of these behaviors sends nonverbal messages to those who are watching. When you are sad or depressed, you tend to move slowly, talk little, sigh, cup your forehead in your palm, move away from others, and look down; and thus different nonverbal messages are sent.

A Bucket of Tears

As I look back and realize how thick-headed I was, to this day I have a hard time believing it. But, as with most of us fellers, I married way over my head, and my dear wife finally brought me to my senses.

It all started (for me, that is) one evening when I was able to leave the office early. As I passed the grocery store I had a brilliant idea. I would buy up some morsels and cook my wife the most exquisite meal she had ever tasted. After all, she had been a slave to the kitchen for years, never complaining, and always feeding me with flair.

I arrived home with groceries in my arms, announced my intentions, sent my wife off to enjoy an hour of solitude without children, and rolled up my sleeves and went to work.

I must say that was one gourmet meal. Everything somehow turned out superb. As we ate I waited for her to begin praise of my gourmet touch, and yet as we scraped our plates clean, I hadn't received a word of compliment. Finally I could take the silence no longer. Clearing my throat I timidly asked, "What's the matter, dear? Is something wrong with my cooking?"

It was then that I should have had a bucket ready, for she let out with more tears than I'd have thought possible. After the flood subsided, and after shooing the children into the family room for TV, I anxiously approached her once again.

This time, collapsing into my arms, she revealed her long bottled-up feelings. It seems that old Social Retard here had been eating her well-prepared meals for years, and had never once told her how much I appreciated the meals or how grateful I was for the hours of toil and labor she had invested into them. And then with one wisp of an apron I come home, cook one meal, and demand praise!

I will tell you this. That evening shook me to my boots, and now, realizing that my wife needs and deserves praise and thanks, I have made a new resolve to vocalize the appreciation I have always felt. It's still amazing to us how this one bucket of tears washed away so many of the cobwebs surrounding our communication process—and how much better we feel toward each other now that we express the feelings we are having, rather than let them remain inside with an assumed understanding on the part of our partner.

You can also use verbal messages to share your feelings; there are two types of these. You can use *direct* statements such as:
"I'm angry."
"I think I feel lonely tonight."
"I feel so excited that . . ."
"It is depressing to . . ."
"I feel sad about . . ."
"Deep inside there is a feeling of . . ."

Or, you can use metaphors. They are analogies or figures of speech that describe a feeling. Some examples are:

"I feel like something that the dog dragged in."

"I feel like I'm floating on a cloud."

"I feel like I'm carrying the whole world."

"I'm tingling all over."

"I feel like I'm ten feet tall."

You can, of course, use combinations of these various methods of sharing your feelings. In fact, you always send non-verbal messages whenever you express a feeling verbally. You say it in a certain way, and an alert observer can usually get a lot more information from the nonverbal messages than from the verbal statements.

The important thing in this skill is being able to find some way to express your emotions so that your partner can understand what you are experiencing. One effective way to do it is to use "I" statements. These are declarative sentences in which the word "I" is the subject. (Thomas Gorden, *Parent Effectiveness Training* [New York: Wyden, 1970].) They are very different from "You" statements and "I-You" statements. They are especially useful when you are expressing negative feelings and someone else is involved with the feeling. Some examples of "I" statements contrasted with "You" statements and "I-You" statements are:

I statement:	I'm furious.
I-You statement:	I'm furious and it's your fault.
You statement:	You've made me furious.
I statement:	I'm so mad I could tear this place apart.
I-You statement:	I'm so mad at what you've done I could tear this place apart.
You statement:	You've ruined the whole evening with this mess.
I statement:	I feel like I'm useless and unimportant.
I-You statement:	It hurts me when you don't come home on time or call.
You statement:	You don't even care about me or how I feel.

It is obvious that the "I" statement has some advantages over the others. It clearly identifies your feelings, and it creates ownership.

Skill no. 4: Express negative emotions in a healthy way. A word of caution needs to be added at this point about expressing your intense feelings to each other. It is not the intent of this chapter to advocate the unrestrained expression of any feeling to anybody at any time. To express negative feelings just to "get them off our chests" *can be very harmful.*

Door Slamming

Brian and I have very different personalities, so we react to things very differently. Early in our marriage, if we had a disagreement, he would leave, sometimes for several hours. I felt abandoned. I wanted him to stay and work things out, preferably with his arms around me. I needed closeness in times of stress between us. He needed space and time to think.

Eventually I realized that he could not read my mind any more than I could his. If something bothered me as much as that way of his reacting did, I owed it to our marriage to find a solution. So one evening when all was quiet and calm, I brought the subject up.

Brian was very surprised at my interpretation of his action. He had never intended to hurt me by leaving. Quite the opposite. He was trying to protect me from his frustration and sometimes anger. By leaving he avoided saying things we both might later regret. Upon returning, he would be calm, have things sorted out in his mind, and be ready to discuss things quietly.

He had felt that my need for closeness was a "feminine ploy" used to manipulate him. He also felt crowded and even cornered. He simply needed to get away to think and to calm down.

Once we understood each other's motives, we were able to work things out. When he needs to leave, he tells me. I do not feel abandoned anymore, because I know what he's

*doing. If he finds he's going to be gone for a longer time than
fifteen to twenty minutes, he calls to reassure me and tell me
when he will be home. The phone call lets me know he still
cares very deeply about my feelings and needs.*

*When he returns we can sit down calmly and discuss the
problem and arrive at a solution. Understanding each other's
feelings under stress has helped us to communicate about all
areas of our relationship. We realize that while we deal with
our emotions in a different way, our goals are the same —
to have a happy and fulfilling marriage.*

There is an art to disclosing negative emotions and not hurting your partner, and it is seldom learned very well in today's
society. The natural thing to do when you have negative emotions is to release your emotion in an unrestrained way. It is easy
to lash out at others, get even, tell others off, blow off steam,
yell, or hit things. The unnatural way is to accept your emotion
for what it is and then be careful and loving in the way you
communicate your feelings to your partner.

It takes time and effort to express negative feelings in helpful
ways. It demands self-control and compassion and a loving concern for the other person. But in the long run it is well worth it
because it helps you work through your emotions while preserv-
ing respect and love in the relationship. If you share your feelings
in the more natural ways you will very quickly destroy the
precious and delicate parts of your relationship — such as feelings
of trust, openness, concern, and helpfulness. These fragile and
lovely things will be replaced with suspicion, defensiveness, and
resentment, and they will eventually retreat from the relationship.

How can you express your negative feelings helpfully? How
should you act? The following guidelines can be very helpful.
The authors and many of their students have found them so.
They can help you pause and realize what you can do. Again,
you may not be at a level of progress where you can do all of
the things in the following list. If this is so, you ought to try to
do a few of them, and when you have developed that ability,
you can try to do the others. Also, you may not be able to

follow these guidelines all of the time. Again, following them some of the time will help you develop this ability, and if you practice, practice, and practice, you will get better at it. Those of you with trouble in this area may find it useful to make several copies of this list and tape them on places such as the refrigerator door, medicine cabinet mirror, and dashboard.

The guidelines are these:

First: *Is the "total environment" right?* Check out the time of day, distractions, noise, privacy, outside pressures in the home, etc.

Second: *Am I in control of myself?* Intense feelings will inter- fere—in ways we may not even recognize. Therefore, we need to find out where we are. Perhaps we need to go and vent our intense feelings first, alone, if they are strong enough to get in the way.

Next: *Is the other person receptive?* We need to ask ourselves whether the other partner is defensive, preoccupied, tired, or overworked. We can ask by saying such things as: "Where are you now?" "Can I share another feeling?"

Then: *Be careful and slow.* Use tact, love, consideration, and don't dump too much at once. If the receptiveness leaves, wait until it can be recreated.

Always: *Be sure to include yourself in the problem.* Almost all problems which cause intense negative feelings between people are the result of interaction between them rather than just the fault of one of the partners. To include yourself, you can use "I" statements when discussing the problem. The information previously given about separating the issue from the personality is also helpful in expressing negative feelings effectively.

Afterwards: *Show an increase in love.*

RECEIVER ROLES

Communication between a husband and wife is a two-part process. A person plays the expresser role when he is the one who is experiencing feelings and expressing them to his spouse. A person plays the role of the receiver when he listens to the feel- ings from his spouse. The preceding pages have dealt with some skills that can help you be a good expresser. Would you now please turn your attention to the receiver role in marriage.

Skill no. 5: Listen with your head and your heart. Some important skills in being able to perform his receiver role were emphasized by King Benjamin in the Book of Mormon. As he gathered his people around him to instruct them and to bare his feelings to them, he prefaced his remarks with the following:

> My brethren, all ye that have assembled yourselves together, you that can hear my words which I shall speak unto you this day; for I have not commanded you to come up hither to trifle with the words which I shall speak, but that you should hearken unto me, and open your ears that ye may hear, and your hearts that ye may understand, and your minds that the mysteries of God may be unfolded to your view. (Mosiah 2:9.)

In this passage of scripture, there are found two of the skills necessary to understand expressions of emotions: (1) an attitude of attention and interest, an "I care about what you are about to say" attitude; (2) a desire to listen with the *ears,* the *mind,* and the *heart* so as to be able to comprehend the messages sent.

Skill no. 6: Accept rather than reject. When someone else is expressing a feeling, it is so easy to look at things only from one's own point of view. We may say things like: "You couldn't possibly feel that way," "That's a terrible way to feel," "That's not how you really feel," or, "Ha . . . !" Again, the easy thing to do, the natural thing, is far from the wise thing to do. The natural man is again an enemy to God and that which is good (Mosiah 3:19).

The key to being an accepting person is to recognize that whatever is happening emotionally is real, and you cannot change or alter or deny that moment. It has happened. If the emotion is a pleasant one, you can savor and enjoy it. If it is a negative feeling, you need to admit it and accept it as a fact, just as you would some physical object. You will immediately recognize what it would mean if someone looked at a tree or car or physical object and tried to convince himself that it was not there. It would be a distortion of reality that would have implications for his mental stability. The same is true for denying the existence of emotions. It has implications for your emotional and mental stability.

Once you accept the existence of an emotion, you can do many things about it. If you don't like it, you can do things to help the feeling go away. If the feeling is immoral or bad, such as a feeling of jealousy, of coveting, of lust, or of unjustified anger, you can also try to repent of the feeling. You can change your situation so that the feeling will leave. You can hope and pray and try to prevent the feeling from recurring, and you can avoid similar situations in the future. What you don't want to do is deny it. That merely puts it out of your awareness, where you aren't in control of it or its effects.

There are at least three specific behaviors that you can avoid by trying to be accepting. One of these is *denial.* This occurs when you reject your mate's revelation of feelings by discounting or refusing to accept that he or she feels that way. You pass judgment on feelings as inappropriate or unrealistic, and you refuse to accept the possibility that such feelings are real. When you do this, you are telling the sender that you know more about his feelings than he does, and that he should listen to you instead of to his stomach. The following examples of a husband-wife conversation are illustrative.

W: I just feel devastated by what's happening lately.
H: Come on, dear, you couldn't possibly feel that way.

H: When dinner is late every night, I turn into a raving monster.
W: A little thing like that shouldn't upset you so.

A second behavior to avoid when we are trying to be accepting is to *defend* ourselves. Examples of this follow.
W: I feel terrible when you're rude to my mother like that.
H: I'm only trying to help you cut the apron strings and grow up.

H: I'm terribly embarrassed when we're always walking into church late. Can we do something about it?
W: Well, if I were bald like you it wouldn't take very long for me to get ready either.

A third behavior to avoid is to *ignore* expressions of feelings.

Some people fall into this pattern by lack of attention and by being so preoccupied with seemingly more important interests that they just don't pay attention to the messages that are being sent by their mates.

W: George, I'm so upset with you. I've decided to go to my mother's.

H: Hmmm! (Continues to read the paper.)

W: Furthermore, I'm going to set the house on fire as I leave, to show you how mad I am.

H: Hmmm!

Skill no. 7: Recognize nonverbal and verbal messages. One important source of nonverbal messages is watching the *way* a person says something. Is he talking casually or is he intensely emotional as he says things? Does he have to pause and get control of himself as he talks? Some of the nonverbal messages sent are so obvious that anybody can pick them up. For example, when a person is crying or speaking in a loud voice it is easy to get information from these nonverbal messages. But other messages are subtle and difficult to detect, and they take more skill. For example, small things like a curled lip, a glance out of the corner of an eye, tightly closed hands, and a slightly longer than usual breath can send messages if a person is alert enough to hear them.

Two parts of the body provide a lot of clues about what is happening emotionally—the eyes and the upper lip. The eyes can be clear or red, fixed or moving, downcast or looking at the ceiling, dry or watery, looking at someone else's eyes too little or too much, wide open or partly closed; and each of these changes can give clues to what is happening. The eyes, however, can be voluntarily controlled to a great extent, and so it is possible to receive incorrect messages when trying to interpret the nonverbal clues. The upper lip has fewer nerve endings and it is more difficult to control voluntarily. Therefore, it frequently is a better indicator of what is really going on inside a person. If the lip is quivering, this is a pretty good indicator that the person is upset. If it is straight and slightly tight, this indicates tension and stress. If it is relaxed and moves easily, this indicates that emotions are less intense.

Nonverbal messages are sometimes unique to the person. For example, Bill may sigh at a certain time, and those who know him know that it means a certain thing. Another person may talk fast or slow or not talk at all, and those who have been around him know what these nonverbal messages mean. Sometimes a person misinterprets the nonverbal messages, they don't know what the messages mean. When this happens to you, you can turn the nonverbal into verbal. Talk about it. Get it into the open. Discuss it.

Summary

The purpose of this chapter has been to expose you to ways in which your emotions influence your communication within your marriage relationship. You have learned the difference between your *emotions* and your *thoughts,* and have then gained insight into the five different aspects of emotions. These aspects are as follows:

> The *source* of your emotions
> The *intensity* of your emotions
> The *consciousness* of your emotions
> The *effects* of your emotions
> The *decreasing intensity* of your emotions

You then learned that it is important for both you and your partner to properly manage the emotional part of your relationship. Several ways of managing your emotions were then presented to you.

You are now ready for the next discussion, that being on the crucial nature of communicating consistently. Press on!

5

I suppose it was something you
*   said*
That caused me to tighten
and pull away.
And when you asked, "What is it?"
I, of course, said, "Nothing."

Whenever I say, "Nothing,"
You may be very certain there is
*   something.*
(Author unknown.)

Communicating Consistently

One of the rules of good communication is to have all of the messages you send say the same thing. If you're angry you ought to admit it, because your nonverbal messages will communicate how you feel while your verbal messages deny it—and people around will either be confused or know that part of you is lying while another part is telling the truth.

Look if you will at four different couples and see how consistent they are in their communication; then discuss the effects it has in their relationship.

The Joneses

Shiela says, in an emphatic way, "You hold the priesthood, so lead. You should be the leader in family home evening."

The Smiths

The home teachers leave a message about priesthood leadership and the wife comments about how important it is to let the head of the family preside. Then, as the home teachers are about to leave, they turn the time back to the father for a closing prayer. The father stands up as he folds his arms and says, "All right, children, let's gather around so we can have a prayer." As he and the children begin to move into a circle, the mother slips off her chair onto her knees and bows her head, ready to pray.

The Barkers

Sue is excited as she tells her husband about a new development at her job. Harry doesn't seem too interested, so she says, "Are you sure you want to hear more?" He responds, "Of course, I'm listening," as his eyes continue to scan the sports page of the evening paper.

The Berretts

As Bill slips into the car seat beside Ethel, she reaches for his hand and gives it a squeeze. She then looks over at him and says, "I've really wanted to go to this play, and I appreciate your postponing your business appointment. You're a jewel."

In the Jones family there is an important inconsistency. The wife is actually assuming the leadership in the relationship as she verbally tells her husband to assume the leading role, and she does it in a demanding way. She is taking command, and when this is done the husband can't really be the leader, whatever he does. If he doesn't take charge of family home evenings, he won't be the leader, and if he does, he is doing it under her instructions. Either way he is still a follower. This inconsistency could be eliminated in several ways:

One way:

The wife could move out of the leadership role but still bring up the problem. She could say things like, "I have a problem, and I'd like to talk about it." Then, after they agree that it is an appropriate time to talk, she could say things like, "It seems to me that I'm the one who always gets family home evening organized and started, and I don't feel good about it." Or, more to the point, "I'm uncomfortable about our family home evenings. When I go ahead and organize them, I feel like I'm doing something that should be a part of the priesthood." This way the wife is bringing up her problem by describing her feelings and opinions. She is not giving him instructions. She is taking initiative, but she is not usurping the presider's position.

Another way:

The wife could exert more leadership in this situation but do it by consensus and under the direction of the presiding authority in the home. She could say things like, "It seems like I'm the one to get family home evening going all the time. Is that the way you (or we) want it, Fred?" In doing this, she is raising an issue for them to deal with together. She recognizes her role as a partner and also recognizes that the priesthood role in the family is one of management or directing the process rather than one in which the husband should have all of the power, initiatives, and tasks.

In the Smith family, the husband gave several verbal and nonverbal messages to the family. He verbally asked them to join in a prayer. Then, by standing up and folding his arms he also sent the following nonverbal messages: "This time let's all stand up to pray, and we ought to get ready now. Stand up around me so that we form a circle." The wife then sent very different nonverbal messages to everyone in the room. Nonverbally, she said, "This time let's all kneel down to pray." More importantly, however, her message occurred after her husband was standing, and she therefore also communicated, "I'm the leader here. Let me, rather than my husband, indicate what ought to be done. It doesn't matter that he indicated we should stand up. Kneel down." This mixing of messages from the parents was difficult for the children to deal with and also was difficult for the parents, because the conflict all occurred on a nonverbal level. And it may have all happened unconsciously.

The Smiths could have established consistency in a number of different ways. The wife could have waited until the next visit to kneel. Another way would be for her to use a verbal request such as "I feel like kneeling down this time. Would that be okay?" At a deeper level, she is probably unhappy with the way he leads. If she is, it would be much better for her to initiate a conversation about her feelings at another time rather than non-verbally disagreeing with him in front of the children and the home teachers. She needs to follow the skills in chapter 4 of recognizing, labeling, and expressing her true feelings.

The problem in the Barkers' communication is more obvious. He is verbally telling her that he is interested in what she has to say, but then he doesn't pay any attention. This kind of inconsistency is easier to cope with because it is more in the open, and we have some conventions for dealing with it. If Mrs. Barker just wanted to deal with that particular inconsistency, she could say things like, "When you're through with the paper, I have something exciting to tell you," or "I get the feeling that I'm not being listened to," or "Hey, choose between what I have to say and the paper." This could be a unique situation, or he could have a habit of giving mixed messages. If it is a rare occurrence, it can be handled with these simple comments, or just ignored. If it is a habit, she could bring it up another time as a "problem" in their relationship, and they could try to correct it.

The Berretts are an example of the way we ought to communicate. Ethel is verbally expressing appreciation, and the nonverbal messages she is sending are all consistent with her verbal message. Reaching for his hand and giving it a squeeze reinforces the verbal messages rather than canceling them or giving a different message.

To summarize, consistency in communication means that all of the messages you send, both verbally and nonverbally, fit together. You say things that are compatible. Inconsistency means that some of the messages you send say one thing and others say others. When you are consistent, your communication flows smoothly and is efficient and pleasant. When you have inconsistencies, especially with nonverbal messages, you are uncomfortable. You misunderstand, and unnecessary problems appear in the relationship.

> *At the end of a long day, in came Brian carrying a bouquet of beautiful long-stemmed roses. Attached to the flowers was a quaint little card which read, "For no reason, except to say I love you."*
>
> *The flowers have long since died, but I keep the tiny little card on my bulletin board just to remind me that Brian really cares.*

Different Types of Consistency and Inconsistency

There are three different types of consistency, and they have different effects on the quality of communication. They are verbal/verbal, verbal/nonverbal, and nonverbal/nonverbal.

VERBAL/VERBAL CONSISTENCY AND INCONSISTENCY

Verbal/verbal consistency deals with whether all of our sentences agree. Note, for example, the following situation: The school-age child does not want to go to sacrament meeting and says, "Do I have to go?" The mother responds, "No, you don't have to go. Now, put on your coat and let's get in the car."

The mother's two verbal messages are inconsistent. One sentence indicated the child didn't have to go, and the other said he did have to go. To be more consistent, the mother would have had to say something like, "Yes, you do have to go. Now put on your coat and get into the car." Or if the mother did not think the child had to go, she would need to say something like, "No, you don't *have* to go, but you should go, and I want you to go. Please decide, so those who are going can get into the car." If she were a patient mother who felt in a helpful mood, she could have said, "I realize that you want to stay home, and you may not fully understand why you need to go. Nevertheless, put your coat on and get into the car. If you want to talk about why you need to go, we can after the meeting."

Verbal/verbal inconsistencies are usually so obvious that most people recognize them, and when they point them out, everybody involved can see them. People learn to recognize and deal with them while they are children, and virtually everyone has these skills. They usually do one of these things: they (a) resolve the inconsistency by correcting one of the statements; (b) write the comments off as irrelevant, unimportant, or unintended; or (c) enjoy the humor in them. These inconsistencies are like detours when driving a car. They are short inconveniences that can be dealt with in a minute or two. It is very rare that these inconsistencies seriously disrupt the overall quality of communication, probably because it is so easy to detect them and correct them.

VERBAL/NONVERBAL CONSISTENCY AND INCONSISTENCY

Most nonverbal messages are consistent with verbal messages. A person may wink or smile as they say hello to an old friend. They turn and face someone when they say, "What was it you said?" and their turning says nonverbally, "I'm interested," "I want to hear you," "You have my attention." When people are around someone they respect, they nonverbally act and verbally speak in a respectful manner.

If all married partners were always this consistent it would be lovely. Unfortunately, they are not. Remember the Joneses and the Smiths and the Barkers at the beginning of this chapter? They are not examples that rarely happen. Situations like theirs happen all too frequently in husband-wife and parent-child relationships. Some people are involved in inconsistent communication situations only occasionally. Others have a habit of being inconsistent much of the time.

Words and Meanings

Now I had really done it! I had been doing just great after having our fourth baby—great, that is, until I passed the mirror and had time to really study my poor figure.

"Oh, honey, I look terrible! Just look at me. I look like the Goodyear Blimp, like a beached whale, like Miss Piggy.

I look like someone's mother!"

And then, hearing me, my husband responded, "Well, you are someone's mother. You look . . . fine."

I could tell that he had really been hunting for a word to describe me. "Fine!" I breathed. Yep, that's what he said, only somehow that word sounded like "better get those pounds off, babe!" I just wonder if he will ever just say what he means instead of leaving the subtle interpretations to me and my imagination.

What happens when this type of inconsistency occurs?

This type of inconsistency is quite different from verbal/verbal inconsistencies. This problem is (1) harder to detect; (2) harder to talk about when you do find it; (3) easier to deny and avoid when you are confronted about it; and (4) harder to solve when you want to correct it. In other words, *this type of inconsistency tends to seriously disrupt things in marriage.*

John: Darling, you're so fond of good meat, you really should try the rib-eye steak.

Mary: Thank you, darling, but I'd much prefer the filet mignon. It's a little more expensive than rib-eye, but I do think it has a better taste.

John: (Sensing that Mary has not accepted his superior knowledge of meat) But people order filet mignon because of snob appeal—missing an opportunity if you don't order it. Many restaurants don't even carry it.

Mary: I really appreciate your advice, John, but I do feel like having a filet mignon tonight.

John: I'm not giving you advice. I'm just telling you the facts.

Mary: You are giving me advice, and I don't need it. If it's all right with you I'd like filet mignon—or do I have to order fish?

John: Order what you _____ well please! (William J. Lederer and Don D. Jackson, *The Mirages of Marriage* [New York: Norton, 1968], page 165.)

In this kind of interchange, those involved usually do not understand what is *really* going on. They think that the other person is just being inconsiderate, too rigid, impolite, ornery, ignorant, or insensitive. Few persons realize that two of the things that are occurring in such sessions are (1) a difference of opinion about the nature of the relationship, and (2) the fact that both parties are using nonverbal messages to try to create the type of relationship they want.

There are several skills that can help you recognize and eliminate these inconsistencies, but the third type of discrepancy should be identified before the skills are discussed.

NONVERBAL / NONVERBAL DISCREPANCIES

Nonverbal / nonverbal discrepancies are the most difficult and disruptive messages of all, because all of the messages are nonverbal. Some examples of them may help you realize that they do occur and that they interfere with effective communication:

Courteous Only at Home

Whenever Bill and Sue are in public, Bill is a warm and attentive person. He goes out of his way to be courteous to her, and most of their friends think he is a model husband. When they are alone, however, other things seem to get in the way. He is too busy to be affectionate, and he seldom does the nice little things he does when others are around.

Wife Turns to Children

Since George got out of medical school, things seem to have changed. George's schedule is very demanding and erratic, and he is always on call. This means he is gone a lot. Mary has found an increasing fulfillment in her relationships with the children, especially with the oldest boy, George, Jr. She turns to him for advice about many things, and enjoys long chats in the evenings when George is at the hospital. The resulting pattern is that Mary's nonverbal messages about a companionship type of intimacy are sent more to her older son than her husband, yet she still tries to think of George as her marital partner.

Nonverbal / nonverbal inconsistencies seem to be more rare than the other two types. This may be because they occur less frequently, or it may be because they are so difficult to identify. And when they *do* occur, they are extremely difficult to solve. They are harder to deal with because they are less obvious, and it is easy to deny them. They are also frequently contrary to one's intentions, and people don't like to admit that they would be that inconsistent.

The Consistency Principle in the Gospel and in Science

Before we discuss the skills you can utilize with the consistency principle, you need to realize that this principle is an important part of the gospel *and* of modern social science.

Its role in the gospel can be seen in the emphasis that the Savior gave it in the Sermon on the Mount. He taught: "Not every one that saith unto me, Lord, Lord, shall enter into the kingdom of heaven; but he that doeth the will of my Father which is in heaven." (Matthew 7:21.)

In this verse he is dealing with verbal claims and nonverbal behavior, and he is teaching that verbal/nonverbal inconsistencies are unacceptable to him. His admonitions about prayer also teach that people should be consistent. He taught that we should not pray as the "hypocrites" do (3 Nephi 13:5), who pretend to be humble but pray without humility. His analogy of "false prophets, who come . . . in sheep's clothing, but inwardly they are ravening wolves" (3 Nephi 14:15) is an example of nonverbal/nonverbal communication.

Paul also commented on this principle. He asked "For if the trumpet give an uncertain sound, who shall prepare himself to the battle?" (1 Corinthians 14:8). An uncertain sound occurs when part of the message gives one signal and part of it gives a different one. Paul's insight into the effects of this confusion helps because he observes that it will lead to confusion, ambivalence, and inappropriate behavior, and that is exactly what it does in marital relationships.

The Consistency Principle is also an important discovery in modern science. It was initially discovered by psychiatrists who were trying to understand several different types of mental illness. They observed that the families of schizophrenic children tended to have more inconsistencies in their communication than most other families. (G. Bateson et al., "Toward a Theory of Schizophrenia," *Behavioral Science* vol. 1, 1956, pages 251-64.)

It has been difficult to empirically test this principle (Jay Haley, *Strategies of Psychotherapy* [New York: Grune and Stratton, 1963]) because it is so difficult to measure the variables with present techniques, but psychiatrists and counselors who work with troubled families have found that the principle is a very valuable insight for them.

The most recent review of the research and theory about this principle is Broderick and Pulliam-Krager's review of its role in family relationships. (Carlfred B. Broderick and Harvey Pulliam-Krager, "Family Process and Child Outcomes," in W. R. Burr et al. [editors], *Contemporary Theories About the Family*, vol. 1 [New York: Free Press, 1979].) They suggest that a continuing pattern of inconsistencies can create several unfortunate results in families. It can lead to mental illness such as schizophrenia, and deviant behavior such as juvenile delinquency. Of course it does not always lead to these effects, because individuals can sometimes find ways to correct the problem or circumvent its effects, but it tends to create serious problems in a large number of families.

What Can You Do to Create Consistency?

There are a number of ways you can learn to be consistent. Four of them are: (1) learn to recognize when you are consistent and inconsistent; (2) be sensitive or alert to inconsistencies; (3) recognize that nonverbal messages are usually the most accurate; and (4) learn to metacommunicate. Perhaps it would be helpful to closely examine each of these:

SKILL NO. 1: ABILITY TO RECOGNIZE CONSISTENCY AND INCONSISTENCIES

Most communication with others is consistent, and it proceeds in a normal, uninterrupted, and comfortable manner. It is therefore easy to recognize consistency, just as it is easy to tell when a car is running well or the weather is pleasant. Recognizing inconsistencies is a different matter. It is harder and takes more skill. First, you need to recognize that something is wrong, and then you need to realize that the problem is an inconsistency.

One thing you can do to help recognize inconsistencies is to remember, whenever you are trying to evaluate your communication, that they *do* happen. Anyone can get into situations in which communication isn't going well, and then there is a checklist of problems to think about, such as:

Are we too upset?

Are we too tired?

Is there something else bothering us?

Are we being too vague in the way we are saying things?

Is there a hidden meaning?

Is it the wrong time of the month?

We need to add at least one more question to this mental checklist:

Are you being inconsistent in the way you are saying things?

There is also a unique kind of clue that can help you recognize inconsistencies. It is that they usually lead to a general, vague feeling that something is wrong. You feel uncomfortable, puzzled, or ill at ease, but it is hard to put your finger on what is causing the feeling. Other communication problems, such as not speaking loudly enough, are easily recognized because they have a specific effect in your marital system. For example:

If we speak too softly, others can't hear.

When we are highly emotional, we say things we don't mean.

When there is too much noise around us, it interferes with hearing.

If we lie, others will stop believing us.

If we don't listen, we will misunderstand.

Now there can be another one added to this list:

If we have inconsistencies, we get a vague, general feeling that something is wrong, but it is hard to put our finger on it. If you are sensitive to your emotions and are alert to the possibility that inconsistencies may be causing the feelings, it will help you to be skillful in recognizing them.

SKILL NO. 2: SENSITIVITY TO INCONSISTENCIES

Everyone pays attention to the things that they think are important. Physicians several hundred years ago didn't pay attention to cleanliness because they didn't think it was important. Physicians today are very sensitive about cleanliness because they know it makes a difference. Some people are like the ancient physicians; they haven't realized the importance of inconsistencies in communication. Others are like the physicians of today; they are concerned about consistency because they know it is important.

This doesn't mean that you need to pause every few minutes and sniff the air for inconsistencies. What it means is that whenever you feel uncomfortable about what is happening in a relationship, you ought to have high on your mental checklist the possibility of inconsistencies. You ought to have an appropriate sensitivity, not too much or too little.

SKILL NO. 3: ABILITY TO RECOGNIZE THAT NONVERBAL MESSAGES ARE USUALLY THE MOST ACCURATE

All people sometimes say things that conceal how they really feel. Someone asks how you are, and you respond with a "fine" even when you aren't really fine. At other times you may choose to be tactful or evasive because you don't have the time to go into detail or the situation isn't right to reveal your feelings.

It is much more difficult to conceal one's true feelings in nonverbal messages than in verbal ones. This means that whenever verbal messages are inconsistent with nonverbal messages, the chances are pretty good that the nonverbal messages are closer to the truth. This, of course, isn't always true, but it occurs often enough that the following is often applicable: "How can I hear what you are saying, when what you are doing rings so loudly in my ears?"

You should also realize that sometimes the nonverbal message that is received is less accurate than the verbal message. For example, you may misunderstand the nonverbal signal, or it may be sent for a different reason than you think. This means that you need to be tentative and cautious in making conclusions, and that it is frequently useful to check out your interpretation of nonverbal messages.

SKILL NO. 4: METACOMMUNICATION

The three skills that were just discussed will help you recognize inconsistencies, but they do little to help you correct them. There is, however, a skill that is very useful in turning inconsistent communication into consistent communication. It is called metacommunication.* It is the process of talking about your communication. It occurs when you talk verbally about the verbal and nonverbal communication in a relationship. It is useful in resolving all kinds of inconsistencies, but it is especially useful in dealing with problems in nonverbal communication — because it turns the nonverbal messages into verbal messages.

The following example illustrates metacommunication. It builds on the Mary and John case history mentioned earlier.

Statement

John: I was awfully uncomfortable at dinner tonight.
Mary: Yes, I was too. What happened?
John: I'm not sure, but we really got into it.
Mary: We seem to be having kind of . . . uh . . . fight quite a bit lately.
John: Yeah . . . I wonder why. We used not to . . .
Mary: You know . . . one thing that might help us find out what's going on would be to think back about what we said to each other.
John: You mean earlier tonight?
Mary: Um hmmmmm.
John: You mean, talk about what we said?
Mary: Yes, but even more than that I get the feeling that . . . uh . . . some things were going on that weren't even said, and if we said them to each other we might be able to get a better picture of what happened.
John: Yeah, okay . . .

---

* The term *metacommunication* has two different meanings in the communication literature. The meaning that is used here comes from Paul Watzlawick *et al.*, *Pragmatics of Human Communication*, New York: Norton, 1967. Some scholars also use this term to refer to the nonverbal messages that accompany all of our verbal messages. Examples of those who use it in that way are J. W. Keltner, *Elements of Interpersonal Communication*, Belmont: California, Wadsworth, 1973; and Harold L. Rausch et al., *Communication Conflict and Marriage*, San Francisco: Jossey-Bass Publishers, 1966.

Mary: It seemed to start when we were talking about what to order.

John: I remember talking about the different things on the menu . . . and you seemed to get all upset.

Mary: Um hmmm . . . Before that I don't think I was upset.

John: Well, let's see what happened . . . I thought you'd enjoy that rib-eye steak.

Mary: And I probably would have.

John: I guess maybe I came on a little bit strong, for some reason.

Mary: Yes, and I resented it. It made me feel like you were trying to dominate me, tell me what to do.

John: You know, I'll bet that the reason I did was . . .

This conversation illustrates metacommunication about the conversation the couple had earlier. Metacommunication can also involve a discussion about the trends in a couple's communication that tend to occur in conversation after conversation. All relationships develop their own set of norms or rules about communication, and most people never stop to identify or analyze their norms or rules. They are aware of many social norms that are characteristic of their larger culture or society. For example, they are aware that they ought to say "please" and "thank you" at certain times in their communication, and that it is more appropriate to use "proper" language in some situations than in other situations. Many persons tend to be unaware, however, of many of the norms or rules that gradually develop in their marital and family relationships. Examples of such norms: "Don't talk about those subjects"; "The wife is the one who will always win in the end anyway"; "She can criticize him, but he can't criticize her"; "He has to think it's his suggestion or he won't go along with it"; "Children can't talk back to parents"; "She shouldn't get so sentimental"; and "Never make people feel guilty about something they've done." We may want to keep some of the rules in our relationships, but there are others that we would probably want to eliminate if we knew they were there.

A. Lynn Scoresby suggests that one or all of four basic things can be discussed when a couple metacommunicates. (*The Marriage Dialogue* [Reading, Massachusetts: Addison Wesley, 1977].) They are these:

1. We can clarify the literal meaning of words spoken so that correct understanding occurs. (Example: "I didn't understand what you just said.")
2. We can discuss how the nonverbal behavior and context of a message is related to what is actually being talked about. (Example: "When you told me you were happy to see me, why were you frowning?")
3. We can go back to the beginning of the misunderstanding and try to clear up the difficulty first realized, which could prevent the problem from leading to a deeper misunderstanding later. (Example: "I didn't understand what you said at first, and you didn't understand the response that I gave to you.")
4. We can discuss each person's feelings so that each can disclose what is felt and why.

Metacommunicating is not a cure-all for all communication problems. But it is a technique that can get certain types of problems in the open where they can be faced and eliminated. Few people would want to spend a great deal of time metacommunicating, but most people would probably benefit from some metacommunication. The following exercise provides an experience to help you increase your ability to metacommunicate.

Metacommunication

Goal: To increase the ability to metacommunicate by practicing it.

1. Set aside fifteen to thirty minutes for this activity.
2. Discuss how effectively you usually communicate in this relationship when you encounter a problem, a difficulty, or an issue on which you need to make a decision. Some of the things you may want to discuss are listed below. *First, try to identify some good things you do.* Then, if you want to, you can talk about some things that can be improved.

a. Does one person do certain things when communicating that the other person especially appreciates, such as being open-minded, considerate, or empathetic, or taking the time to listen rather than to think of what to say next?

b. Does one person do certain things when communicating that the other person doesn't like, such as clamming up, not listening, dominating the conversation, or ignoring the other person?

c. Sometimes norms or rules develop about how to communicate in a relationship, and couples are not even aware of them. You may want to think about whether you employ any of these norms and then evaluate whether you like or dislike them. Examples of these norms are these:

1) One person can criticize, but the other can't — or at least always seems to pay a psychological or emotional price for doing so.

2) Certain topics can never be discussed.

3) If the two people disagree, one of the two should have more say than the other one in deciding what to do.

4) It is acceptable for one individual, but not the other, to use covert techniques for controlling the situation (crying, getting a headache, withdrawing affection, whining, sweet-talking, etc.).

Summary

The purpose of this chapter has been to explore the effects of inconsistencies in communication. Three different types of consistency-inconsistency were identified: verbal/verbal; verbal/ /nonverbal; and nonverbal/nonverbal. You learned that verbal/ verbal inconsistencies are usually easy to recognize and correct; hence they seldom have a detrimental effect on your communication. Verbal/nonverbal inconsistencies are a different matter. They are harder to detect and harder to eliminate when you do recognize them. You also tend to deny them when someone suggests that they are present. Therefore, these inconsistencies tend to disrupt the communication in one's marital system. The nonverbal/nonverbal inconsistencies are the most difficult to deal with because all of the messages are in the elusive nonverbal part of communication. Many inconsistent messages are unintended, so a person giving them won't even know they are there.

The last part of the chapter discussed four skills that you can use to help yourself be a wise steward in managing this part of your material system. The skills are: (1) being able to recognize inconsistencies; (2) being appropriately sensitive to them (not too concerned about them); (3) recognizing that when inconsistencies occur, the nonverbal messages are usually the most accurate; and (4) being able to metacommunicate. Metacommunication is the process of communicating verbally about the way you are communicating, and this means that you verbalize the nonverbal messages that you think are causing problems.

It is now time to move into the next chapter, where you will climb even deeper into this thing called "marriage" and discover ways you and your partner can solve the problems you encounter.

6

Neither will ye suffer
that they transgress the laws of
God, and fight and quarrel one
with another.
(Mosiah 4:14.)

Though Problems May Arise

In weak or tired moments in your marriage, it would be only natural for you to think that your life would be better if you could do away with problems and crises. While it is true that life would be more simple and less painful if you encountered no problems, this is actually a very short-sighted view of things. By removing yourself from the immediate crisis and taking a long thoughtful look, you will realize that problems are actually *desirable*.

Our first parents, Adam and Eve, learned this in the Garden of Eden. Lehi taught his children that if it were not for the first transgression and fall (which of course brought problems on our now-telestial earth) "they would have had no children; wherefore they would have remained in a state of innocence, having no joy, for they knew no misery; doing no good, for they knew no sin. . . . Adam fell that men might be; and men are, that they might have joy." (2 Nephi 2:23, 25.)

This joy apparently is not possible without our first experiencing the "opposition in all things" spoken of in the scriptures (2 Nephi 2:11). Your own special package of problems is designed to give you this experience and teach you to become like our heavenly parents. Without this opposition there would be no test —and without the test there could be no meaningful future for you.

Problems, obstacles, and challenges, then, are the key to your reaching your potential. Without them you would become like trash fish such as carp, who float and drift with the prevailing currents. Fish like trout and salmon, however, swim upstream and are driven with an insatiable desire to overcome all obstacles to reach their goals. Obstacles are one of the reasons why there is a difference between carp and salmon.

The Prophet Joseph Smith provides a tremendous example of a life filled with challenges and problems that needed to be overcome. He was not perfect in mortality and even complained on occasion. The Lord hearing his prayers in Liberty Jail did not send a legion of angels to avenge the wrongs committed against him and his people. Instead he said:

> And if thou shouldst be cast into the pit, or into the hands of murderers, and the sentence of death passed upon thee; if thou be cast into the deep; if the billowing surge conspire against thee; if fierce winds become thine enemy; if the heavens gather blackness, and all the elements combine to hedge up the way; and above all, if the very jaws of hell shall gape open the mouth wide after thee, know thou, my son, that all these things shall give thee experience, and shall be for thy good. (D&C 122:7.)

As Joseph learned, one reason why difficulties are desirable is that it is only as a person experiences pain, frustration, disappointment, tragedy, and other adversities that he is able to experience the deepest and most satisfying joy, happiness, and peace. Consider, for example, the situation of Adam and Eve in the Garden of Eden. They did not have problems, frustrations, difficulties, sin, opposition, or adversity. They were in the condition that some Latter-day Saints think would be ideal—free from problems. Unfortunately, their sterile and uneventful life was also without happiness or growth. As the scriptures teach, they were "in a state of innocence, having no joy, for they knew no misery; doing no good, for they knew no sin" (2 Nephi 2:23). The paradox is that opposition is necessary. Problems and happiness, difficulties and satisfaction, misery and joy, go together. You cannot have one of these opposites without the other.

Therapeutic Tennies

I have played racquetball for over twenty years, ofttimes with business associates who have advanced skills and techniques. Now, before going further, let me say that my wife came from a very active, athletic family, and is not afraid to put on her tennies and work out. Anyway, about three years ago my wife and my married daughter took racquetball lessons, and they have subsequently become excellent players. Now I find we have a great time playing as a family. In fact, many of the games are equally as competitive, and they become somewhat therapeutic, for we actually solve and unravel family problems and sometimes make family decisions while we are on the racquetball court. For us, sharpening our racquetball skills has served to help us sharpen our problem-solving skills.

A second reason why problems are desirable is that without them you would be incompetent. You wouldn't grow and progress. When you face problems, you can learn to deal with them in creative, imaginative ways, and they can help you develop resourcefulness and a capacity to get things done. If you did not face obstacles you would remain forever in a state of ignorance and inability as well as innocence. This would frustrate you even in this life if you truly want to grow and progress. Also, when you think about your eternal goal—to become as God is—you realize that it will be important to learn how to cope with problems and difficulties. You will need to learn these things if you are to be an effective leader. And you can only learn the skills you will need by having problems and then learning how to stand on your own two feet as well as your companion's two feet in dealing with them.

In addition to the ideas mentioned above, there are several other reasons why it is wise to improve your problem-solving skills in this life. They are:

Problem solving as a couple is different than as an individual. Most people learn early in life to make decisions and deal with their problems as individuals. They learn to make many decisions about their lives, such as what type of clothing to wear, which classes to take at school, whom to have as friends, etc. This type of problem solving is very different from the kind we will be doing in our adult life and in our post-mortal life. It is different because we have been making these decisions as individuals. After we marry, we make decisions as a pair, and the process of making pair decisions is often different from that of making individual decisions. At whatever point we are in our marriage, most of us have considerable room for improvement, and we would be wise to improve our *couple* problem-solving ability.

Many of you have been too sheltered from problems. As you grew up in families, your parents made most of the important decisions about your life. You may not have had the opportunity to make your own decisions, and as a result you may not have developed much skill in problem solving. It is only when you need to make decisions and you have the responsibility for your own lives and the freedom to do your problem solving in your way that you really learn how to do it. In this process you stub your toes a few times. You make some bad choices, and you then have to live with their consequences. This process helps you learn how to make good decisions.

A final reason it is important to improve your problem-solving skills is that there is a principle to be learned that will pay off in your marriage. The principle is this:

The better you can solve problems, the better your marriage.

One aspect of this principle is that problem-solving ability isn't like height or weight, where one single factor goes up or down. Problem solving is a part of an emotional and interpersonal system, and it is an immensely complex process. Like all complex systems, 99 percent of it can be in tip-top shape, but if one crucial part operates poorly, the whole system suffers. It is a little bit like a chain; a chain is only as strong as its weakest link. Your problem-solving ability isn't as weak as its weakest part because, unlike chains, you can get by with a weak link or two. A few weaknesses, however, add up quickly, and they disrupt the whole process. For example, crucial things like listening carefully to each other's opinions, being decisive when it is necessary, and following through on decisions are crucial skills in problem solving. You can be highly proficient in many of the other parts of the process, but if you do several of these crucial things poorly, your overall problem-solving ability suffers. Thus one's problem-solving ability is not the sum of all of its parts. It is a complex process in a system, and gradations between poor and good problem solving can be determined by a few parts of the process.

CLOUD NINE

Why is it
whenever I reach for the sky
to climb aboard cloud nine,
it evaporates and rains
upon my dreams?
Is it a matter of science,
or simply a matter of fact,
that not even a cloud
with a silver lining
can hold the weight of our dreams
without some precipitation?
I think I've found the answer
to this dilemma —
keep on reaching for the sky,
but don't forget your umbrella.
                        (Susan Stephenson.)

All marriages have problems, and the successful marriages are the ones in which couples learn how to deal with them successfully, turning them into assets rather than liabilities. President

Spencer W. Kimball has discussed this principle many times in pointing out that effective problem solving can eliminate the need for divorce. He has counseled as follows:

> There is a never-failing formula that will guarantee to every couple a happy and eternal marriage; but like all formulas, the principal ingredients must not be left out, reduced, nor limited. The selection before courting and then the continued courting after the marriage process are equally important, but not more important than the marriage itself, the success of which depends upon the two individuals — not upon one, but upon two.
>
> When a couple have commenced a marriage based upon reasonable standards, no combination of power can destroy that marriage except the power within either or both of the spouses themselves; and they must assume the responsibility generally. Other people and agencies may influence for good or bad; financial, social, political, and other situations may seem to have a bearing. But the marriage depends first and always on the two spouses, who can always make their marriage successful and happy if they are determined, unselfish, and righteous.

Later in this address, President Kimball said:

> It has come to be a common thing to talk about divorce. The minute there is a little crisis or a little argument in the family, we talk about divorce, and we rush to see an attorney. This is not the way of the Lord. We should go back and adjust our problems and make our marriage compatible and sweet and blessed. (*Marriage and Divorce*, pages 16-17, 30.)

Using Spiritual Resources to Improve Your Problem Solving

Knowledge is very limited in this mortal life. You came to the earth as an infant and then gradually learned as you grew up. But even as an adult, there are many truths that are hidden from you by the veil that separates you from the spiritual realm. Your limited knowledge can be increased dramatically, however, if you can get in touch with the spiritual part of life and then use it. Using your spiritual resources will be an invaluable aid in dealing with your problems in marriage and family living.

We Achieved

Ron always found it difficult to verbalize those feelings that were closest to him. I don't know if this is a trait of all men, but in our marriage it was very difficult for me to patiently expect feedback. In an effort on my part to openly share my feelings, even when I knew he wouldn't reciprocate (without my getting upset because he wouldn't), I gradually saw a change as he learned to share some of his feelings with me and the children. For a person who was always so caring and tender it was difficult for me to understand why this was so difficult for him to do, especially since, in comparison, I was a babbling brook and thought anyone should be able to say what he thought.

And then lightning struck in our family. Ron found he had cancer which had spread throughout his body, and as the last year of his life passed, he lost 130 pounds. With the loss of each pound I could see his struggle for composure, to say what was important to him that he was feeling way deep inside.

Finally, one day approximately two months before he died, we shared our last open verbal exchange of feelings to each other. The pain of feeling his pain was almost more than I could bear.

Through those last days, as we had for several years before, we held hands and prayed together. We could share our feelings, openly shed tears, and discuss our concerns with our Heavenly Father, even though we could not do this face to face. It is my hope and prayer that other couples will not have to wait for a disaster in order to begin communicating and sharing feelings with each other. By then it is too late.

HOW DO YOU RECEIVE SPIRITUAL ASSISTANCE?

The scriptures teach that scriptural truths are learned in a very different way than natural truths. We learn natural truths by focusing the mind, thinking about natural things, and reasoning to make sure they are consistent with our previous experience. We use our natural senses of hearing, seeing, touching, smelling, and tasting, and we couple these with our mental process of reasoning. The result is knowledge of the natural world around us.

The things of God are learned in a very different manner. They are sensed with senses that are different from the five senses we use in learning natural things. Spiritual truths are learned through becoming in tune with the Spirit of God, and the senses we then use are the senses that can recognize spiritual truths. Each of us knows the delicate feeling inside that whispers to us as we go out of our way to do something good for someone else. We get a feeling of peace, of quiet, pleasant joy. This is a spiritual experience. It is the sensing of the Spirit of Christ that is inside all of us to help us know when something we are doing is right. A different spiritual sense operates when we do something that we know is wrong. We get an uncomfortable feeling, a dullness, a twinge, a hurt. These two feelings, a feeling of rightness and one of wrongness, are two spiritual senses. They do not occur first in the head or mind. They do not occur first in the eyes or ears or mouth or nose or fingers as they would if one of our five senses were the source of the information. They occur in what is referred to as the "heart" — not the organ that circulates the blood, but that part of the body or soul that receives spiritual messages.

We can learn a little more about how to receive spiritual messages by reading several scriptural passages closely. By comparing an idea or message to a seed, Alma explained how to "listen" for spiritual information.

> Now, we will compare the word unto a seed. Now, if ye give place, that a seed may be planted in your heart, behold, if it be a true seed, or a good seed, if ye do not cast it out by your unbelief, that ye will resist the Spirit of the Lord, behold, it will begin to swell within your breasts; and when you feel these swelling motions, ye will begin to say within yourselves — It must needs be that this is a good seed, or that the word is good, for it beginneth to enlarge my soul; yea, it beginneth to enlighten my understanding, yea, it beginneth to be delicious to me.
>
> Now behold, would not this increase your faith? I say unto you, Yea; nevertheless it hath not grown up to a perfect knowledge.

But behold, as the seed swelleth, and sprouteth, and beginneth to grow, then you must needs say that the seed is good; for behold it swelleth, and sprouteth, and beginneth to grow. . . .

And now, behold, are ye sure that this is a good seed? I say unto you, Yea; for every seed bringeth forth unto its own likeness.

Therefore, if a seed groweth it is good, but if it groweth not, behold it is not good, therefore it is cast away. (Alma 32:28-32.)

The key phrases of Alma's message are these: "behold, it will begin to swell within your breasts," "feel these swelling motions," "enlarge my soul," "enlighten my understanding," "delicious to me," and "sprouteth." These are the sensory experiences that occur when we are receiving spiritual messages that something is good and true.

The Lord describes this process by saying "by my Spirit will I enlighten them, and by my power will I make known unto them the secrets of my will" (D&C 76:10). Joseph Smith also has described the process of receiving spiritual insights:

A person may profit by noticing the first intimation of the spirit of revelation; for instance, when you feel pure intelligence flowing into you, it may give you sudden strokes of ideas, so that by noticing it, you may find it fulfilled the same day or soon; i.e., those things that were presented unto your minds by the Spirit of God, will come to pass; and thus by learning the Spirit of God and understanding it, you may grow into the principle of revelation, until you become perfect in Christ Jesus. (*History of the Church,* vol. 3, page 381.)

Even though you may never have given yourself credit for being in tune with the Spirit, it is possible to change so that you are highly receptive to spiritual messages. President Marion G. Romney gives a four-fold formula for increasing one's spiritual sensitivity:

If you want to obtain and keep the guidance of the Spirit, you can do so by following this simple four-point program.

One, pray. Pray diligently. Pray with each other. Pray in public in the proper places, but never forget the counsel of the Savior:

"When thou prayest, enter into thy closet, and when thou hast shut thy door, pray to thy Father which is in secret; and thy Father which seeth in secret shall reward thee openly" (Matthew 6:6).

Learn to talk to the Lord; call upon his name in great faith and confidence.

Second, study and learn the gospel.

Third, live righteously; repent of your sins by confessing them and forsaking them. Then conform to the teachings of the gospel.

Fourth, give service to the Church.

If you will do these things, you will get the guidance of the Holy Spirit and you will go through this world successfully, regardless of what the people of the world say or do. ("The Guidance of the Holy Spirit," *Ensign*, January 1980, page 5.)

A second thing you can do to increase or decrease your ability to hear spiritual messages is to listen and respond or to ignore and not respond when the messages come. The more you listen for the messages and respond appropriately to them, the more you are able to hear them. This, in turn, allows your spiritual senses to become more keen. And the opposite is also true. The more you ignore the messages, the less able you are to hear them. Alma explained this process very well by showing how it will ultimately lead to the extremes of knowing vast amounts or losing all of one's ability to hear spiritual messages:

And now Alma began to expound these things unto him, saying: It is given unto many to know the mysteries of God; nevertheless they are laid under a strict command that they shall not impart only according to the portion of his word which he doth grant unto the children of men, according to the heed and diligence which they give unto him.

And therefore, he that will harden his heart, the same receiveth the lesser portion of the word; and he that will not harden his heart, to him is given the greater portion of the word, until it is given unto him to know the mysteries of God until he know them in full.

And they that will harden their hearts, to them is given the lesser portion of the word until they know nothing concerning his mysteries; and then they are taken captive by the devil, and led by his will down to destruction. Now this is what is meant by the chains of hell. (Alma 12:9-11.)

The Savior had a slightly different way of explaining this same process. He was aware that we have natural ears to hear natural sounds, *and* also spiritual ears to hear spiritual messages. This is why he commented, "He that hath ears to hear, let him

hear" (Matthew 11:15; 13:9). Moses was another who talked
about spiritual communication, as he observed that he could not
see God with his natural eyes:

> But now mine own eyes have beheld God; but not my natural,
> but my spiritual eyes, for my natural eyes could not have beheld;
> for I should have withered and died in his presence; but his glory
> was upon me; and I beheld his face, for I was transfigured before
> him. (Moses 1:11.)

In summary, the things of God are known by the Spirit of
God. Therefore, if you want spiritual help in solving your problems, you must be spiritually in tune. You become in tune by
living the commandments as well as you can, repenting when
you make mistakes, and increasing your ability to receive
spiritual messages.

WHAT SHOULD YOU DO WHEN YOU WANT SPIRITUAL HELP?

The Lord gave some very specific instructions to Oliver
Cowdery as to how he was to ask and not ask for divine assistance in translating from the plates of the Book of Mormon. The
instructions are also useful in assisting you as you solve your
marital problems. Oliver Cowdery was told:

> Behold, you have not understood; you have supposed that I
> would give it unto you, when you took no thought save it was to
> ask me.
> But, behold, I say unto you, that you must study it out in your
> mind; then you must ask me if it be right, and if it is right I will
> cause that your bosom shall burn within you; therefore, you shall
> feel that it is right.
> But if it be not right you shall have no such feelings, but you
> shall have a stupor of thought that shall cause you to forget the
> thing which is wrong; therefore, you cannot write that which is
> sacred save it be given you from me. (D&C 9:7-9.)

The Spirit of the Lord can help in other ways. For example,
James taught:

> If any of you lack wisdom, let him ask of God, that giveth to
> all men liberally, and upbraideth not; and it shall be given him.
> But let him ask in faith, nothing wavering. For he that wavereth
> is like a wave of the sea driven with the wind and tossed. (James
> 1:5-6.)

Sometimes you may have problems for which you feel you need wisdom before you can study them out in your mind and get confirmation about your decision. When this occurs, it is appropriate to pray for wisdom concerning what you should do. In his unique situation, this was what Joseph Smith did in the Sacred Grove in Palmyra, New York. No doubt he had previously studied the matter out in his mind to the extent that was possible, but there just was not enough information available for him to come up with a tentative conclusion that he could take to the Lord. So he went in supplication, asking the Lord what he should do. Anytime you likewise are perplexed about a problem you can do the same, and if you are in tune the Lord will help you in the way he deems best.

WHEN SHOULD YOU SEEK SPIRITUAL HELP?

Amulek gave one of the great sermons in the Book of Mormon; in it he touched on this issue. He gave this counsel:

> Yea, humble yourselves, and continue in prayer unto him.
> Cry unto him when ye are in your fields, yea, over all your flocks.
> Cry unto him in your houses, yea, over all your household, both morning, mid-day, and evening.
> Yea, cry unto him against the power of your enemies.
> Yea, cry unto him against the devil, who is an enemy to all righteousness.
> Cry unto him over the crops of your fields, that ye may prosper in them.
> Cry over the flocks of your fields, that they may increase.
> But this is not all; ye must pour out your souls in your closets, and your secret places, and in your wilderness.
> Yea, and when you do not cry unto the Lord, let your hearts be full, drawn out in prayer unto him continually for your welfare, and also for the welfare of those who are around you. (Alma 34: 19-27.)

USING THE PATRIARCHAL ORDER

The way to get spiritual assistance with problems is to use the proper priesthood system. This system, known as the patriarchal order, provides an efficient, harmonious method of solving problems as well as directing other processes in your marriage relationship. The patriarchal order is explained in more detail in chapter 14 of this volume, and that discussion is very relevant to the issues discussed here. You should realize that the information covered there will be very helpful in getting valuable spiritual assistance in dealing with your problems.

Using the Social Sciences to Improve Our Problem Solving

The social sciences have discovered a number of techniques that can also help us solve problems. One of these is that it is useful to divide the problem-solving process into several stages. Five stages in problem solving are these:
1. Identify the problem.
2. Agree to work (or not work) on the problem.
3. Identify and evaluate alternative solutions.
4. Make a decision by selecting one of the alternatives.
5. Implement the decision.

One of the important skills in problem solving is being able to tell which of these stages you are in. This is important because when the wife is in stage four and she's ready to make a decision, and the husband is way back in stage one (he doesn't even know what the problem is), perhaps the method of problem solving being used is itself one of the problems. There are also a number of other skills that can help you in each of the five stages. They are discussed in the following paragraphs.

SKILLS FOR IDENTIFYING PROBLEMS

Skill no. 1: To be able to tell when you are in this stage. How can you tell when you have a problem? Usually one spouse becomes aware of a problem or need and communicates his or her concern to the other. In a family, one member senses the problem and then others are told about it. The following statements are typical of this problem-defining stage:
"We need to talk about . . ."
"What is really bothering you, dear?"
"I feel we ought to make some changes around here."
"As I see it, the problem is that . . ."

"I have a problem, and I'd like us to do something about it."

Many times, previous events in your relationship permit you to move very quickly over this stage. Sometimes such indicators as the way a person acts, a gesture, or just a certain type of silence can communicate that a problem needs attention. But other times you can assume too much when you rely on gestures or other nonverbal methods of identifying problems, and you later find out you did not really have consensus about whether a problem or issue existed or what it was. The best way to identify a problem is to use words, to describe it in sentences, trying not to threaten the other person's self-esteem.

Skill no. 2: Using "I" statements. Whenever you try to identify problems, it is useful to make "I" statements rather than "You" statements. This is done by identifying how you respond personally to the problem, or by identifying the effect that something has on yourself, rather than describing what someone else has done. Statements such as "I feel uneasy" or "I am very uncomfortable about . . ." are examples of "I" statements. One advantage of "I" statements is that they are not judgmental of the other person. "You" statements are judgmental of the other person, and they make that person uncomfortable. "You" statements like "You yell too much" or "Your yelling makes me uncomfortable" tend to put the other person on the defensive. Also, "I" statements don't imply that you alone know what should be done, an impression that is sometimes communicated when you make "You" statements. An example of a "You" statement is trying to identify a problem by saying, "If you would only quit yelling, everything would be better." You could say that same thing in an "I" statement: "I'm uncomfortable when I hear that. Can we talk about how I'm feeling?" When you use "I" statements, you "own" your feelings rather than blame others, and it usually helps this stage of problem solving go more smoothly.

Skill no. 3: Using "summary" statements. One effective way of making sure that there is consensus about the definition of a problem is for one person to make a summary statement. This can be a very brief statement about what the problem or issue is, and the other person can then either agree or disagree. When the feelings, reactions, or behavior of one member of the couple is the problem, one way to summarize is to reverse roles and see if that member can describe the problem. One advantage of summary statements is that they tend to move couples into the next stage of decision making after they agree on what the problem is. Sometimes, of course, they can mutually recognize a problem nonverbally, and when this happens, summary statements are unnatural and useless. But at other times these summaries are very helpful.

Skill no. 4: Turning an "individual" problem into a "couple" problem. When you are solving problems alone, you can go on to the second stage as soon as you are aware of a problem. But when you are a couple, it is very different. If one member of the couple recognizes a problem, it is at that moment the individual's problem, not the couple's problem. Only when one person communicates to another that there is a problem and the other person recognizes the problem does it become a couple problem. And as many married couples know, the process of convincing a spouse that there really is a problem is sometimes a very difficult task. In fact, it is occasionally impossible, and the individual who has recognized the problem has to treat it as his or her own problem rather than as a couple problem.

There are several techniques that can help you turn individual problems into couple problems. For example, if you have strong feelings about something, you can share these feelings, and this may help your spouse realize that there really is a problem. You can also compare problems by saying things like, "Look, this is as big a problem to me as when we . . ."; or, "I'm more upset about this than . . ." You can also avoid making a mountain out of every molehill that comes along. If you think that everything is a serious problem, it would be like the "wolf, wolf" story. Your spouse will justifiably learn to ignore your attempts to convince her or him that you indeed have a problem.

Skill no. 5: Being sensitive to the emotions that accompany this stage. Little problems like "Who's going to pick Jane up at the bus station?" or "Should we go to the movie or concert?" create few emotions. Many problems are more complex, and when you bring them up there are intense feelings. In marriage, many problems are closely tied to feelings of masculinity or femininity, feelings of adequacy or inadequacy as a person, and delicate feelings of love, acceptance, tenderness, and caring; and any attempt to bring up problems in these areas creates strong feelings. Many times in marriage, the emotions that accompany a problem are much more important than the problem itself. It is therefore useful to go slow when you are trying to identify a problem, and also to pay close attention to the overall situation. Ask yourself these questions: "Is it a good time? Are there other feelings that will get in the way? Do we have enough privacy? Will the other person be threatened? How do I feel about the situation? And, would we have enough time now to deal with the problem?" If you haven't been able to find a time, you may want to only mention that you have a problem that you need to talk about as soon as it can be arranged. Above all, you ought to be as supportive as possible of each other when problems are identified that create negative emotion; and beautiful processes like tact, patience, caring, consideration, and gentleness are tremendously important. *As valuable as these loving behaviors are when things are going well, they are much more valuable when problems are being discovered.*

SKILLS IN IDENTIFYING AND EVALUATING ALTERNATIVES

In some ways the process of identifying solutions is similar to identifying a problem. Both situations evoke emotions, and you need to be sensitive to the feelings that are created. Also, both demand attention, listening skills, and the ability to express yourself in nonthreatening ways. In other ways, the process of thinking of solutions is different, and it demands unique skills. Following are several of the skills that are unique to this stage.

Skill no. 1: Being able to recognize when you are in this stage. You can move into this stage when there is consensus about what the problem is. Sometimes this is simple and automatic, and both spouses recognize it at the same time. At other times, you may need to check out whether you are ready to move to this stage or whether you are already in it. You may say things like, "Are we ready to try to figure out what to do?" or, "Okay, we agree on what the problem is. What can we do about it?"

While you are identifying alternative solutions, statements like the following are called for:

"One thing I've thought of is . . ."

"You know what _____ did about that?"

"Have you any ideas about what we can do?"

"As I see it, we've got two choices . . ."

"I'm wondering what you'd like to see done about it."

Skill no. 2: Being creative. Research shows that creativity is very valuable when you are identifying alternatives. This means that you ought to think blindly as you are trying to find ways to solve problems. Let your mind go. Think up alternatives that are unusual, different, and even bizarre. Since you will be evaluating the alternatives later and can reject the inappropriate ones, there is no harm in getting some "creative" solutions on your list.

Shirts

The task that I least enjoy among my homemaking duties is to iron. Because of the nature of my Cliff's job, he wears dress shirts every day of the week, and with Sunday's shirt added, that brings the total to six shirts a week that I must keep ironed. Many times I put off the ironing until he is out of shirts in his closet and then it takes me half a day to get caught up again. Cliff knows how much I hate to iron, and how frustrated I become as I attempt to get his collars and cuffs wrinkle free.

The other day, as I begrudgingly set up the ironing board for another marathon of wrinkle smoothing, I waded through the morning mess to get his shirts, only to find them all gone. Immediately I felt guilty as I suspected he had taken them to the cleaners, and that he had done it while he was righteously hot-under-the-collar because of my slothfulness. I just knew that Cliff was trying to make me feel guilty so that I would change my ways.

That evening however as he came home and I had the chance to question him about the shirts, he simply said that he understood how difficult it was for me to get such a dis-

tasteful job completed, and so he had merely taken them to the cleaners to give me a break.

As I melted appreciatively into his arms, I once again knew that I was the luckiest wife in the world, as I had a husband who not only was sensitive to my frustrations, but did what was necessary to remove them from my already-too-muddled life.

Skill no. 3: Avoiding the evaluation of alternatives when you are trying to be creative. One characteristic of humans is that certain mental activities encourage similar activities and discourage different activities. For example, when you are in a reverent or sacred mood there are a number of behaviors that are encouraged and a number that are discouraged. Reverence tends to create quiet and respectful behaviors such as speaking softly and moving slowly, and loud or boistrous activities are then inappropriate. If you are cheering at an athletic contest the opposite behaviors are called forth.

Some scholars have suggested that this is important in problem solving because being creative in thinking up new alternatives and evaluating the alternatives call for opposite mental processes. When you are doing one it will tend to discourage the other. This means that when you want to be creative in thinking of new alternatives, you may want to refrain from evaluating the alternatives. You can write the new ideas down on a piece of paper and add to the list. Then, after you are through brainstorming, you can shift into the evaluative processes, where you are a more cautious and more hesitant to think up new ideas in a carefree manner.

One thing you can do to foster a creative frame of mind is agree beforehand that the next few minutes will be to think up as many ideas as possible. You can call it a "brainstorming time." You can then be as creative as possible and not make any negative comments or evaluative comments during that time. Then, after the brainstorming is over, the ideas can be sorted, evaluated, and modified.

Skill no. 4: Getting several alternatives. Some couples usually make up their minds about what to do as soon as they think of the first good solution. They take the first workable idea that pops into their heads. This is illustrated in the following situation:

First Option Taken

Phil and Jennifer, an engaged couple on a tight budget, were deciding where to look for housing. "Basement apartments are usually most inexpensive," said Jennifer. Phil agreed, and they looked in the newspaper listing, jotting down the addresses of basement apartments. They found one they liked pretty well, and decided to take it although they didn't like the neighborhood.

It may be this couple have found an apartment that fills their needs well, but the small number of options they considered may have excluded other possibilities that would have been wiser choices. For example, they might have found a mobile home, an upstairs apartment, or a duplex that would have given them a better combination of their desires in housing; but these possibilities were excluded by their narrow range of alternatives. Research in this area shows that the quality of decisions is usually lower when very few alternatives are identified, and it tends to improve when more alternatives are identified.

Apparently, however, after an optimum number of alternatives has been identified, attempts to find additional alternatives tend to interfere with decision making. This may be because couples get bogged down in considering too many alternatives.

Skill no. 5: Recognizing how many alternatives you usually have. Another important skill in this stage of decision making is recognizing how many alternatives you usually identify in decision-making situations. Some couples ordinarily seek only one. Others think of a few, still others of a large number. You need to have an accurate understanding of how many you tend to seek.

Skill no. 6: Changing your usual patterns. Another skill that is useful is to be able to increase or decrease the number of alternatives you usually consider in decision making—depending on whether you usually have too few or too many to be optimally efficient.

Skill no. 7: Changing and reorganizing the alternatives. Sometimes there is little you can do with the alternatives. For example, if you are deciding whether to go to a ball game or a movie, you may wind up with a simple choice of one or the other. Many times, however, you can be creative in shaping up one or two alternatives so that they are more attractive.

As an example, the problem is that the wife wants the husband to pick up his clothes and put them in the hamper rather than leave them lying around, for he has a rather deeply ingrained habit of leaving them all over the place. They have talked about it many times, but the wife hasn't changed her expectation and he hasn't changed his behavior. The only alternatives they have identified are that she quit being so fussy or that he pick up his clothes. Had they been a bit more creative, they could have also thought of the additional alternatives of his at least throwing them all in the same corner and her picking them up, of getting three more hampers so it would be easier for him to pick them up, and of getting a valet (chair with a rack on the back) so he would have a place he could hang things easily.

After getting these five alternatives they could combine or modify them in creative ways. For example, they could agree that the clothes he may use again soon could be put in a certain place such as over a chair or valet, and all of the dirty clothes could be placed in a new hamper that could be placed in the bedroom.

SKILLS IN SELECTING AN ALTERNATIVE (DECIDING)

Skill no. 1: Recognizing when you are in this stage. Some couples are very skillful at the decision-making practice. They have a knack for knowing when the alternatives have been rearranged or modified enough and they are ready to make a decision. They can also tell when they have made the decision and are ready to move on to implementing it. Others aren't so blessed. They can't make up their minds or aren't sure what the decision is when they're finished. They find themselves saying things like, "Oh, I thought we decided to . . ."; or "But we were going to . . ."

Here are some of the comments typical of this stage:

"OK, Rod, which do you think is best?"

"It looks to me like the best way to handle this is for us to have separate closets. What do you say about that?"

"Then let's do a little of both, but . . ."

"It sounds as though we agree best on that last idea. What do you say we go ahead on it?"

Skill no. 2: Being decisive. One essential ingredient in decision making is to come to a conclusion about what to do or not do. Some couples raise issues and problems and talk about the relative advantages and costs of various alternatives, but they find it difficult to come to a conclusion about which course to take. This is illustrated by the following situation:

Fran and Roger were upset about some of the behavior of their three-year-old son. They had discussed the matter and had recognized that a large part of the problem was that each of them responded to him differently—they sensed that they were defeating each other's goals. They made a few suggestions but agreed upon no plan. Time went on, and their son's troublesome behavior continued.

It is easy to see that Fran and Roger did not really come to a decision; it is this decisiveness that is important.

As with so many other skills, the first step for you is an introspective analysis to determine where you are as a couple or a family. Are you or your spouse too indecisive? Or does one of you move to the deciding stage too quickly? Or is this an area that is not a problem in your relationship?

Skill no. 3: Taking appropriate risks. Researchers have suggested that the willingness of couples or families to take risks is also related to the quality of their decision making. As they point out, too little or too much risking hinders the quality of decisions. There is therefore a certain optimal level of risk taking. It is important to identify in general how much risk taking is desirable, because you can legitimately take more risks in some situations than in others.

Each couple, of course, needs to decide just how risk-taking they should be. Some couples may be more daring than is wise, while others may be so afraid of breaking traditional patterns that they make much less wise decisions than they could.

Skill no. 4: Getting consensus about decisions. Consensus refers to the degree two or more people agree that the alternative chosen is the best one. The goal, of course, is for a couple to achieve a high degree of consensus in their decision making.

Not all decisions can be highly consensual, even in "ideal" relationships. Couples can, however, get consensus often if they work at it, and this will promote high morale, satisfaction, and harmony.

Sometimes it takes more time and effort to keep working at consensus than it does to settle for an accommodating or coercive decision, but the resulting increase in satisfaction is usually worth it. At other times couples may find that achieving consensus is too costly and that they would be better off with lower satisfaction and an accommodating or coercive decision. Each situation has to be assessed on its individual merits, but knowing that getting consensus usually creates greater satisfaction makes it worth more than a little effort.

Some of the Lord's instructions to the General Authorities help explain another aspect of consensus in decision making. He indicated that decisions made by presiding quorums in the Church receive more blessings if they are unanimous decisions. When they have to resort to majority votes rather than have consensus "their decisions are not entitled to the same blessings which the decisions of a quorum of three presidents were anciently" (D&C 107:27-29). This same consideration probably also applies to the "presiding quorum" in the home. If a husband and wife can work at their decision making until they come to a consensus, they will probably receive more blessings than if they have to resort to less desirable methods, such as the husband getting the last say or either one forcing his or her will on the other. And it is also probably true for family decisions. The members of the family will probably be blessed more if they can find a consensus than if the parents have to force their will on the children or if the children manipulate the parents into doing what they want.

Skill no. 5: Being able to work out quid pro quo's. A *quid pro quo* is "something for something," something given or received for something else. One way to use the principle is for one person's behavior to stimulate the other person to behave in a certain way. Many quid pro quo's are unconscious and automatic. For example, we all know that a smile is contagious. If we smile at someone, he will tend to smile in return. In a marital relationship we soon become conditioned to the quid pro quo pattern even though we don't realize it. Each of us informs the other of his response pattern with little clues, and we each learn how to recognize the responding clues of the partner.

The value of quid pro quo's in this stage of decision making is that we can consciously work out some reciprocal arrangements as strategies for solving problems. If the husband wants the wife to behave in a certain way and she doesn't, it may be possible to solve his problem and, at the same time, solve one of hers if a quid pro quo can be worked out. He can agree to do something that he hasn't previously done if she will also make the change he desires. An example is a situation in which the wife wants the husband to express his affection with words by saying things like "I love you" more often, and the husband wants the wife to respond to his sexual advances more frequently. They may find that a quid pro quo in which he agrees to be more verbally affectionate and she agrees to be more physically affectionate will solve both problems and add considerable pleasure for both of them.

SKILLS IN IMPLEMENTING DECISIONS

Making a decision does not solve a problem unless the decision is actually carried out. Sometimes this involves some detailed planning about what the couple or family is going to acquire or how things will have to be changed. Several scholars who have analyzed decision making suggest that this stage should also include some way of evaluating the plan of action later to make sure that the solution is really solving the problem.

Here are some comments that are typical of this stage of decision making:

"Now that we've decided what to do, how are we going to do it?"

"Where are we going to get the money for . . . ?"

"For the next two weeks I'll . . ."

"Could you help me . . . ?"

"There isn't any way we can . . ."

This stage of problem solving calls for many of the same skills that are needed in other stages, but it also demands some unique skills. Some of these are discussed below.

Skill no. 1: Sticking with it until a method of implementing the decision is found. Some couples think a problem is solved when they agree on decisions or solutions. And sometimes they are. When problems are mere choices between several desirable things, they are solved when a decision is made, providing the person concerned follows through. However, most of the problems that occur in marriage are more complex, and couples need to stay in a problem-solving mode after they have selected a solution. Usually the most difficult process is over. They're over the crisis, or over the hump, but there is one final thing that must be done if they are to be effective in problem solving:

> *They need to take the time to figure out how to implement the decision and then implement it.*

This demands a "stick-to-itiveness" that is difficult for many couples.

Skill no. 2: Showing an increase of love. Another thing that can help after problems are solved is to take the time to provide reassurance, support, or love to make sure that everyone feels good about the situation. You ought to go out of your way to be supportive if any feelings were hurt or if some things you said were unkind or hard to swallow. Research has shown that supportiveness is an important ingredient in problem solving, and you ought to be sure to include it at the end. It will help put the problem behind you and help you to be less reluctant to deal with other problems in the future.

The Bread Box

*Wanting to personalize my Christmas gift to my sweet
wife, I decided to make her something with my "own hands."
After giving the house a careful perusal, I came up with the
idea of constructing a wooden bread box for the kitchen. She
had been using a large "ugly" plastic bread container that did
not fit with the wooden kitchen cabinets.*

*I roughed out a few bread box designs in my spare mo-
ments at the office, which included fitting the common bread
loaf sizes used by our family. I experimented with painted,
glass fronts, flower designs, and tole painting decorations.
All the while I became more enthusiastic about the project
and had visions of how excited my wife would be over my
creation, and how delighted and proud I would be over my
handiwork.*

*Finally, after deciding on the pattern, I went to the BYU
hobby shop to start the initial construction of my Christmas
project. Using the power woodcutting tools at the hobby
shop required my studying the safety manual and taking the
appropriate test for each power tool I would use. At last,
after successfully passing the safety tests, I selected some relatively knot-free pieces of kiln-dried fir and began my project.
My plans worked out well, and I was able to cut out all the
pieces without any particular hangups. I used a power router
to put a nice edge on the top, bottom, and main door to my
creation.*

*With all the pieces cut, I brought my project home to
sand and assemble in my garage on the work bench. I hid my
prize in an orange box and told all family members to keep
out. I made it a point to stress that I had a special Christmas
project going on in the garage. The family got caught up in
the spirit of things, wondering what Dad was making in the
garage when he was out there sanding and nailing away. It
was a fun "ego" trip for Dad in several ways. I was making
something creative that gave me a lot of personal satisfaction
as a product of my own doing. I also "knew" my wife would
appreciate something that had required more effort than*

merely going to the store and purchasing a ready-made item. I had given of my time and effort to please my mate. A lot of basic "needs" were being fulfilled.

Then it happened. The bread box was constructed. All it needed was some final sanding, then a stain and varnish job. By now the suspense was very high. Each member of the family had, over the past few days of construction, made guesses as to what Dad was making. Fortunately, none had come up with the idea of a bread box. One evening on our way home from a Christmas program, the guessing started again. As fate would have it, one of the children finally guessed a wooden bread box. I faked it and asked for the next guess. But Mom casually picked up on the bread box guess and proceeded to describe how she loathed wooden bread boxes, never dreaming in a million years that was the correct answer. As a child her mother had an old wooden bread box that was always smelly, and as she remembered, it even had bugs in it.

Wow! All my efforts and good intentions shattered in one innocent, casual off-hand remark. All kinds of feelings flooded over me. I was hurt to think that I had given of myself, and now my "baby" was perceived as an "old smelly wooden bread box." In the next breath, I was angry. How could she be so cruel! My feelings were written on my face. I could not fake it any longer. The children in their open, sensitive way, knew the truth had been discovered. They also sensed the awkward dynamics that now were present. What does Dad do next? Will he be "big" enough to see the moment in its total perspective? Or will he let his emotions rule his rational person?

I let anger and hurt sweep over me. Quickly reacting, I struck back at the person who had attacked my "pet project." "Fine, I'll give the bread box to my mother! She will like it, I'm sure!" I said in a cutting voice.

The hurt, pained look that came over my sweet wife's face was not what I had bargained for. My "winning" was very hollow. When we arrived home, my wife went tearfully into the house and to our bedroom. I stayed in the garage to nurse my hurt pride. The children, caught in the crossfire, could see the comic tragedy of it all. They loved us equally and understood how we both had quickly and innocently backed ourselves into an emotional impasse.

Today, Dad's bread box sits in the kitchen in full view of the family at meal time. There are no bugs in the box. It doesn't smell. In fact, it fits in quite nicely with the other kitchen woodwork, thanks to the stain that was mutually decided on by my dear wife and myself, as well as the neat, brass hinges that match the cupboard handles. Sometimes, as I look at my "pet project," I wonder how I would react were I to have the experience all over again. Would I be more open and perceptive, as my children had anticipated their Dad would be?

Summary

This chapter has identified a number of things couples can do to solve the problems that occur in marriage and family living. First, you need to realize that problems are not just bearable and unavoidable. They are, paradoxically, desirable. You wouldn't want to be without them. As you try to solve problems, you ought to seek spiritual assistance, and the chapter discussed several ideas on how to do this. It discussed some methods of getting in tune so you can "hear" spiritual messages, some ways to seek help, and times when you ought to seek help.

The chapter then suggested that you also need to recognize the different stages of problem solving so that you know what you are trying to do—what the issue is. Five stages were identified, and the next part of the chapter discussed several skills that can help you in these stages.

While this chapter explored only some of the keys to successful problem solving, the authors hope it has stimulated you toward a more effective management of your problems.

7

*Unity does everything when it is
perfect. It satisfies desires,
simplifies needs, foresees the
wishes, and becomes a constant
fortune.
(Senancour.)*

Creating Unity

Lloyd and Virginia have finally come into some unexpected money and have decided to spend it on some things they have been needing for some time. Lloyd says this is a good time to buy the new tires for the car, since they are on sale. Virginia insists that the children really can't go on any longer without new clothes.

An impasse has been reached, and the initial excitement that came with the discovery of the money has turned to frustration. The problem is an age-old one that few married couples have been able to escape — how to balance their limited resources with their seemingly unlimited needs and wants, particularly when the marriage partners have differing perceptions of what is a *need* and what is a *want*.

Alvin and Christine do not have this particular problem at the present time, but Alvin is waiting in the car honking the horn while Christine continues to get ready for church. Alvin looks at his watch, grits his teeth, and starts to tap his fingers on the steering wheel.

This couple is experiencing an obstacle that few marriage partners have been able to avoid—differing expectations of the way partners should behave in marriage.

Differences Are Inevitable

Most concerns that arise in marriage seem to fall under these two categories, and it is doubtful whether any married couple has successfully been able to avoid these types of strains for very long. These difficulties can work like other adversities, and the effort that it takes to overcome them can strengthen a marital relationship just as hard work strengthens our physical muscles. And yet, if these obstacles are not successfully scaled, they can act like a divisive wedge, driving a couple further and further apart.

Many couples enter marriage believing that such difficulties and disunities will never happen to them. They feel their marriage will be different because their great love for each other will prevent them from having the problems that "normal" couples have and they will always act as one. It is good to enter marriage optimistically, even though not long into marriage the idealistic visions of an eternally blissful marriage soon fade as the two partners discover the differences in each other which they hadn't noticed before.

For most there is a numbing effect during courtship and early marriage. Differences go unnoticed, and tolerance for each other's weaknesses and mistakes is very high—and this is probably good, because it motivates most people to marry. If it were not for this early love and its blindness and forgivingness, many persons may never have married, but would even now be looking for some mythical Mister or Miss Perfect!

Football Frosting

When we married, my husband found quickly just how utterly "bored" I was with his interests in sports. But . . . being the dutiful wife, I grudgingly agreed to attend the season basketball and football games with him.

The first couple of football games were an opportunity for us to be together, and I was flattered that he included me, but I was totally unenthused watching a game that I knew nothing about. I had heard husbands tell their wives to be quiet (only not that politely) when they would ask for an explanation of what was happening on the field, so I hesitated to say anything. I just didn't want to sound dumb or be told to be quiet. After some time, however, I decided if I was going to go to the games, I wanted to know what was happening, and so in addition to watching carefully to pick things up, I also started asking questions. I found that I had a husband who seemed genuinely pleased that I wanted to learn, and he kindly answered my questions and tried to explain so I would understand (I just had to learn to ask when we weren't in the middle of a critical play!).

Over the years of our sports marriage my husband has included me in his many interests (as I have him in mine), and we've grown closer as a result. The frosting on the cake was when one time I said to him, "Would you like me to stay home from the game so you can ask one of your friends to go with you?" His reply was that he was already taking his best friend! Needless to say, this put a warm feeling in me, and because of statements like this and helping each other to learn, we are able to eliminate some of the potential areas of contention some couples are burdened with.

It is unrealistic to believe that you and your spouse should not have differences in marriage. Your backgrounds, your experiences, your interests, and the examples for being married that you observed while growing up are usually quite different from your mate's. It is inevitable (and *not* sinful) that these differences will sooner or later create situations in which differences of opinion will need to be resolved. To be otherwise would deny you both an important opportunity to learn to work in cooperation with each other—to be unselfish, to be empathetic, and to place the interests of your companion above your own. Unfortunately this is an age in which it is taught that personal development, self-assertion, making a name for oneself, finding oneself, rugged individualism, independence, and other forms of "me-ism" are seen as more important than sacrificing one's personal desires for the good of relationships. Selfishness and putting one's own interests first are becoming a more acceptable and "realistic" way to deal with others. The result of this form of hedonism is that there are few marriages in the world today that are experiencing the immense joy that is possible in a relationship where mutual self-sacrifice and the resulting harmony and love make it possible to resolve differences and to become truly one.

Not Fishy at All

I grew up as the daughter of a coach, and so I have always loved a variety of physical activities. One sport I had never particularly wanted to engage in was fishing, because to me it was a total bore. And another that I couldn't imagine doing or even going along for was deer hunting. It wasn't long after our marriage that I found out that fishing and hunting were his greatest second loves! In fact, he'd built a very strong bond with his father partly through their hunting experiences each fall.

At first I thought that I would just ignore his interest in these activities, and when he asked me to go with him I would decline and say things like, "I don't see what you like about fishing," or I would snidely comment, "To me, hunting is just a waste of time." But after a couple of years I realized I wasn't going to change him and I was also being left home, and so I decided to start accepting his invitations so that I could be with him. And do you know that even though there are other activities I would rather do than fish,

I am starting to enjoy it (when the fish are biting). Last fall I even went on the deer hunt with my husband and his parents, and we had a fantastic time building stronger ties of love for each other.

There are a couple of activities that I love, such as the ballet, that he has no interest in. But who knows? If I could learn to like to fish . . . then maybe he could . . .

This type of unity, however, like a testimony, often must pass through a trial of faith or a refiner's fire before it can mature and possess the enduring strength that is characteristic of a truly eternal, celestial marriage. For this reason you should thank the Lord for your differences, as they, like adversity, give you the opportunity to grow and prove that you are both capable of overcoming all things and are worthy of greater challenges and responsibilities in the celestial kingdom.

Your natural differences can be worked through and unity achieved by adherence to correct principles and skills for marital interaction. For most couples, there are few things in premarried life that teach how to live with someone of the other sex in peace and harmony, and yet there are many examples presented daily on the TV, in movies, newspapers, commercials, and elsewhere that exemplify horrible ways to treat each other. Good models, unfortunately, are rare and hard to find in today's world.

As a result, couples are at various levels of development in their ability to work through the differences that naturally arise in marriage. Four of these levels are presented next, with suggestions as to what it would take for you to be able to function at each level.

PROBLEM SOLVING: LEVEL ONE

The Level One attempt to resolve differences is often characterized by physical fighting, swearing, and throwing things. This level consists of excessive selfishness and an undeviating stubbornness, communicating that "my way is the only way, as I am obviously much wiser and greater than my partner can ever become. To make sure that my partner gets this point and believes it, I create and deliberately (although maybe subconsciously) choose an emotional outburst that is designed to put my partner down where he or she belongs—beneath me and my wants."

Those functioning at this level bring out the worst in each other. They often will do things which they know will start the spouse off on one of these emotional tirades aimed in their direction, just to reinforce their belief that the mate is an ogre. What is most surprising about this repeating cycle of hurting and retaliation is how long such couples can remain together. Often when they separate they find themselves lonely and unable to blame anyone for their faults and will rejoin each other in order to have a scapegoat to attack and sacrifice so they can build their own self-esteem at the partner's expense.

To function at this level is easy. It takes little practice and comes very naturally to many people. Many of these people functioned at this level as children, and all they need to do to continue as adults is not to grow up emotionally. The majority of people interacting on TV and in the movies solve their differences in this manner. All one really needs in learning to act this way is to not think, be undisciplined, not read the scriptures, ignore the teachings of the Savior, and do what one sees most of the world doing.

PROBLEM SOLVING: LEVEL TWO

The Level Two method of resolving differences consists of pretending the differences don't exist and then trying to bury the emotions that come from feeling hurt. The only problem with this method is that a person buries his feelings alive in the bottom of his stomach. These feelings most often refuse to die and keep surfacing to disrupt the couple's lives and the lives of all those who are close to them. Some people have managed to successfully bury issues that have remained alive in their stomachs, eating away at them for years and years. These unresolved feelings of resentment, anger, disappointment, frustration, hurt, etc., are capable of destroying a person's physical health, ruining his marriage and family unity, and even sending him to an early grave.

Those using this technique seldom reveal just what is bothering them. They are not, however, able to hide from their spouses that they are upset. Early in the marriage of one of the authors, his wife would occasionally interact at this level. On one such occasion where their limited resources could not keep pace with their unlimited wants, he tried to convince his wife how badly he needed a larger motorcycle to get to work. He had a perfectly logical presentation of why this was where their resources should be invested at that time, and he presented his case to her with an air of "I've been inspired in this decision, and if you are in tune with the Spirit, you too will see that it is best." His wife swallowed her feelings and went along with the "inspiration."

The day came when he brought the motorcycle home. He was excited and happy, but his wife's greeting kiss at the door was about forty degrees cooler than normal. He ignored this nonverbal innuendo, not wanting to believe it meant what he thought it meant. The next event was supper, during the course of which his wife spilled the soup in his lap and made the comment, "Oh, I'm sorry, but, you know, these pots and pans did come across the plains with the pioneers, and the handles are a bit loose." He then knew what she was saying—she wanted (and needed) a new stainless steel cookware set and was upset about the motorcycle that had been purchased in its place. Following a discussion, he returned the motorcycle and bought for his wife the stainless steel cookware. How much easier things would have gone had he been more sensitive to his wife's needs, and had she not tried to bury her feelings about the issue!

To function at this level is a small step of progress, even though it requires that a couple practice some self-control. Those practicing this technique usually learned it from such sayings as, "If you don't have anything good to say, then don't say anything." There are occasions when this is sound advice, and when a person carries this philosophy into his marriage by repressing important feelings, there may be fewer people physically hurt and less furniture damaged than if he used Level One. But at this level the marriage will never produce the great joy that is possible. The partner who feels hurt will continue to feel hurt, and the silent mate will always be wondering what the problem is and will feel continually frustrated.

Level Two is more common than the fiery first level. Even

though there appears to be more peace in the home, such marriages may well be even less stable than Level One marriages. This level is not recommended for those trying to create an eternal marriage.

PROBLEM SOLVING: LEVEL THREE

Level Three is advocated by specialists in communication to help people resolve differences. It is particularly useful in helping to solve problems that grow out of limited family resources. It is a process similar to that used by nations to negotiate peaceful settlements of their differences.

Couples functioning at this level usually go through a sequence of steps in settling their differences. First, they recognize that a conflict exists and communicate to each other that they would like an appointment to negotiate a settlement. During the negotiation period each partner recognizes that the other also has rights and makes an effort to be sensitive to the other's needs.

At the appointment bargaining session, each partner states what he or she would like and then demonstrates a willingness to make compromises and trade-offs in the negotiation process. For example, if the wife and husband had been functioning at this level when the motorcycle/cookware issue arose, it might have been settled by their agreeing that one of the purchases could be made now and the other later, and then by flipping a coin to see which came first. Or he could have agreed to do the dishes for a year if he got the motorcycle first, or he would have offered some other type of compensation to make the settlement fair and equitable.

This level of problem solving is popular among many couples in the world today and is a definite improvement upon levels one and two. It takes work, self-control, at least a small amount of empathy, and a desire to place the relationship on at least an equal level of importance with one's own personal needs and wants.

PROBLEM SOLVING: LEVEL FOUR

The skills associated with Level Four are based on gospel principles that deal with a couple's treatment of each other. The following discussion contains some practical suggestions about how a couple can put these gospel teachings into practice in everyday living.

Be charitable. This aspect of problem solving means that a person has as much *love* and *concern* for his mate as he has for himself. It also implies *empathy*, in that an individual tries to understand as completely as possible his mate's feelings and needs, and he values their relationship *more* than his own wants and needs.

Music to My Ears

Throughout our married life, Ray taught me to be an individual. He appreciated and encouraged my interests in music and with people. He encouraged my work with the aged and handicapped because he knew the satisfaction I received from giving what I could to these special people. In every way he would watch the children and help about the house so that my personal development was not stifled. In return, I tried to follow his business in science (which is not my bag as an artist) and to keep up with his interest in sports.

As I reflect on our life together, I think the most valuable lesson we learned is that he made the effort to appreciate music of all kinds (he even went to the operas with me) and I learned to appreciate athletics. Even though he has now passed away, I relive daily the many, many sharing moments that we gave to each other. For us, marriage was truly a heaven on earth.

When Paul and Mormon defined charity (1 Corinthians 13, Moroni 7), they used such words as, "suffereth long, is kind, envieth not, vaunteth not itself, is not puffed up, seeketh not her own, is not easily provoked, thinketh no evil, rejoiceth not in iniquity, beareth all things, believeth all things, hopeth all things, endureth all things, never faileth, is the pure love of Christ, endureth forever."

Using some synonyms for these phrases of Paul and Mormon, one can easily see how applicable their counsel is to the problem-solving process. When resolving differences, a couple should use patience, gentleness, appreciation, humility, consistency, dependability, and unselfishness, and should think loving thoughts toward each other. They should also live righteously, trust each other completely, be optimistic about their marriage and their ability to resolve differences, use more patience and more consistency, and each show daily a genuine and sincere love and concern for his mate that will turn their mortal relationship into an eternal companionship.

Unless you as a couple learn these important charity skills first, the rest of the suggested skills in Level Four will be of little worth and can, if misused, even make you more skillful in manipulating your loved ones. To be charitable as defined by Paul and Mormon is to have achieved 95 percent of the skills necessary to function well at Level Four. It means you treat your mate at all times like the king or queen he or she is becoming. It means that the level and tone of voice you use in problem solving is the same as it would be if you were talking to the Savior, the prophet, or any other important person.

Listed next are several suggestions which can help you to use charity in solving your marital problems.

Be sensitive to timing and deal with feelings first. This skill consists of being able to recognize when it *is* or *is not* a good time to share your feelings about your concerns and then having enough control to wait until the best time arrives. Choosing the right time of day when neither marriage partner is too tired or pressured or harassed to discuss important feelings can go a long way to successfully resolving any differences.

Also associated with this skill is that of being aware of what feelings you are experiencing at the time you are going to express your concern. This is important because intense feelings affect your rational control, which in turn influences your ability to be charitable and communicate clearly. Therefore it is highly advisable to deal with these feelings and reduce their intensity before you try to talk to your mate about the issue. This "cooling off" period can be accomplished in a variety of ways. The best way is to discipline yourself not to get upset in the first place. This is a difficult thing for most, but it can be done if you understand the nature of your emotional responses.

Many of your initial feelings of anger, hurt, revenge, frustration, defensiveness, etc., cannot be avoided. If you continue to feel this way, however, it is because you have chosen to do so; you have learned that it is an effective way to make others look bad and wrong while allowing you to look innocent and right. Imagine, for example, a person functioning at Level One, shouting and screaming about how terrible things are — and then receiving a phone call. The transformation that takes place seems miraculous as he greets the caller in a pleasant or at least a neutral voice. The reason these transformations are possible is that this person is in control of these secondary emotions and uses them to his advantage.

The first step in reducing the intensity of your secondary emotions is to stop wanting to make others look bad or to find someone else to place the blame on. The first thing to look for is the beam that is in your own eye, rather than to try to make a scapegoat out of others. If you are in the habit of using your emotions for this purpose, change will be a difficult process, but it will be feasible if you are determined enough. One of the best ways to do this is to first study the teachings in the scriptures about how you should see and treat others. The Savior's teachings are replete with such examples. In the Sermon on the Mount he taught, "Blessed are the pure in heart: for they shall see God." (Matthew 5:8.)

To be pure in heart is to be completely honest — with others, the Lord, and yourself. To be emotionally dishonest by being overly sensitive and defensive to save face when you have erred is the opposite of being pure in heart. Likewise, it is dishonest and impure to try to hurt or offend others by extending and inflating your initial emotions. The Savior taught, "But I say unto you, that whosoever is angry with his brother, shall be in danger of his judgment; and whosoever shall say to his brother, Raca, or Rabcha, shall be in danger of the council; and whosoever shall say to his brother, Thou fool, shall be in danger of hell fire."

(Joseph Smith Translation, Matthew 5:24.) The terms *Raca,* or *Rabcha,* were terms in Jesus' time which indicated unholy and contemptuous feelings.

It appears that the intent of the Lord's teachings here is to condemn any language which expresses harsh or contemptuous feelings about another. It is also interesting to note that the King James version of Matthew 5:22 states, "That whosoever is angry with his brother *without a cause* shall be in danger of the judgment . . ." (italics added). Both the Joseph Smith translation and the Book of Mormon account omit the phrase "without a cause," perhaps suggesting that by higher gospel standards unrighteous anger is impure whether one has been provoked or not. This is consistent with the Savior's teachings later in the same sermon, as he instructed his followers to turn the other cheek and to forgive each other rather than engage in the "eye for an eye and tooth for a tooth and I'll get even" practices that were common then—and are now.

To put these teachings into practice, some find it helpful to do such things as count to ten, read poetry, play the piano, or even to cry as a means of reducing the intense emotions, before the two married partners discuss the bothersome issue. However you choose to do it is generally not important; the important thing is that you gain control of the initial feelings you experience before you engage in a serious problem-solving discussion. In addition, you should not use your emotions in ways that are dishonest, impure, or lacking in charity.

Home at Last

We decided to build a new home because there were several advantages to the new location. At that time we were excited at the challenge, and so I invested a great deal of time, imagination, and planning in the project, and Warren invested a great deal of money. In fact, all of our money.

As the project was nearing completion, we still had not been able to sell our present home, and so one day Warren announced he was going to sell the new house (we had received an offer on it out of the clear blue sky). The house was sold, and when I expressed my disapproval Warren be-came very, very angry and accused me of being extravagant by wanting him to work night and day to pay for the house. I continued to resent Warren and felt that he was selfish. Anything he wanted we could afford and he was willing to pay for, but anything I wanted we couldn't afford. The prob-lem was compounded when Warren decided to buy some in-vestment property with the money from the house. He re-sented that I could not see that we were headed for financial disaster if we didn't sell one of our homes, and we had a buyer for the new one. He also felt that I didn't appreciate how he provided for us. He thought I didn't like the house he had provided, and so consequently he felt threatened.

I resented that he would sell so easily and so unfeelingly all that I had worked so hard to create, and so I thought he didn't value me or my efforts. Neither of us realized how the other felt. It was some time later that we finally sat down and talked about our feelings. When we had shared these feelings with one another, we could both see how and why we had acted as we did. Also, we both were very sorry that we had let the problem go so far before talking about it and dealing with our feelings.

Another way to use charity in bringing your concern to the attention of your spouse is to begin your disclosure of feelings with a *sincere*, positive statement that is related to the issue. When you are angry, this is a difficult thing to do, and you can't do it sincerely until you are in control of your secondary feel-ings. An example of this would be if you were concerned about continually being late for church with your family and wanted to bring it to the attention of your spouse. You might do the following: First, make sure that you are in control of your feelings and that your spouse is also in a receptive mood. This can be done by simply saying: "Dear, I have a concern I'd like to talk to you about. Is now a good time to do it?" If your spouse says yes, then you might say something like this: "Dear, I ap-preciate how good you and the children look when we go to church. It makes me feel proud to be seen with you each week."

In this way, you are communicating to your spouse that this is not an attack and that he / she does not need to become defensive and counterattack.

Your next task is to honestly and in kindness state your feelings that are associated with this concern. "I've been a little embarrassed and anxious the last few weeks when we've walked into church late." In this way you let your spouse know exactly what you've been feeling and help him or her to be able to empathize with you and understand your feelings better.

You should next state what the concern is and do it in a tentative manner rather than use absolutes. By doing this you are acknowledging that what you are saying is only the way *you* see it and that your partner's views are just as important as your own.

Continuing this example in a tentative way, you would say something like this: "It appears to me that we're either taking too much time to get ready or that we're not starting to get ready soon enough." Other tentative phrases include: "As I see it . . ." "I may be wrong, but . . ." "It seems to me . . ." "In my opinion. . . ."

Next you need to be descriptive in your explanation of the problem rather than saying it in such a way that you are passing judgment upon your companion and thus causing him or her to react to you defensively. The object is to describe what you believe the facts to be in the way you would in giving testimony in a court of law, rather than making judgments such as, "You don't even care if we are late or not." An example of this would be: "As I remember it, the last three weeks when I arrived home from leadership meeting, three of the children were still in bed. That gives them only an hour to wash, eat, get ready, and travel to church. That doesn't appear to me to be enough time. . ."

After you are sure your partner understands both your feelings and your perception of facts about the problem, and after you have given him a chance to state his feelings and perceptions of the facts as he sees them, then it is time to move on to the resolution step. Unfortunately, too many people try to skip all of the above steps and just blurt out such things as, "Why do you always make us late for church?" This type of attack is dishonest and nearly always makes the situation worse.

To resolve the issue, then, you need to do three things:

1. State what you would like to do about it. "I would like the children to get up and start getting ready by eight, and for all of us to be in the car ready to go by nine forty-five."

2. State what you are willing to do to help make it possible for your suggestions to be accomplished. This shows that you are not just a "complaint filer" but are also willing to put forth the effort to see the changes made. An example would be, "To help make this possible, I'm willing to stop chatting with my friends so long after meeting. I'll come home earlier and help get the younger children ready. Is there anything else you can think of that I can do to help?"

3. Be willing to compromise. If your suggestions are not acceptable, be flexible and accommodate your mate's perceptions of how the problem can best be resolved.

For some, the steps to problem solving suggested in Level Four are natural and easy. Others may have a need for some serious soul-searching, repenting. It is obvious that no man has ever reached perfection in a moment, and that perfection is a step-by-step process. The important thing is that you be on a charted course, continually improving, accepting your failures as new starting points, and not giving up.

For those willing to pay this price, unity in marriage is eventually possible, and that which couples are given the potential to become, through their temple ordinances, can be achieved by self-mastery and adherence to gospel principles.

The Secret

I have frequently read that financial woes are one of the leading causes of divorce. Because my parents frequently quarreled over money and how it was spent, I especially wanted to avoid this type of problem in my own marriage. I can remember carefully planning out a budget with my sweetheart in the days preceding our wedding. We would be living on a shoestring, but were sure that whatever we lacked in money, could be made up for by living on love. I had been working at a good paying job for two years, I had money saved, I had purchased a nice wardrobe of clothes, and I felt no great financial pressure. My husband-to-be would receive the GI bill to finance his education, and I planned on being content with having babies and being the "heart" of our little home. I was eager to make the necessary sacrifices to accomplish these goals.

Our schooling years were some of the happiest of our lives. However, after earning two degrees, we left the comfortable protection of our student housing project and were cast into the very real world of increased financial responsibility. We had four children, and our dream of steady employment was finally a reality. The "harsh" reality, though, was that the paycheck barely stretched to meet our new, increased financial needs. We had been living on love for so many years, with the dream of the "pot of gold at the end of the degree," that it was disappointing to realize we still had to go without. By this time, my wardrobe was terribly outdated and I felt very frumpy after four pregnancies. (And it wasn't only my wardrobe that was out of style. My sweetheart had been wearing the same, one-and-only sportscoat for six years.) It was at this particular time in our marriage that I learned one of the great lessons of my life.

I have always had a flair for fashion, and one day I found myself in one of the beautiful shopping malls in our city. I noticed a gorgeous white turtleneck sweater in one of the stores. It was just what I felt I needed for the coming winter months. I quickly paid for it and headed for home, ignoring all feelings of "I can't afford it." I arrived home before my husband and suddenly felt guilty that I had spent the money. Consequently, I hid the sweater in the back of my closet.

For the next few weeks, I kept my secret, and one snowy morning, when I could resist no longer wearing it, I put the sweater on. My husband immediately noticed it and commented on how pretty it was and how nice I looked in it. He asked me where I got it, and I burst into tears, confessing how I had hidden it from him. (It was the only thing I had ever kept from him. I was miserable and felt like a "real sneak.")

I will never *forget the look on his face. He gently communicated to me that it really hurt him that I was "afraid" to purchase something that I felt I needed. He told me how much he loved me and that he would give me the world if he could, but since that wasn't possible, he trusted my judgment in keeping my purchases within our budget. I cried, not only because I had been found out, but because I had hurt the person most near and dear to me. And yet, I felt a great relief to be rid of my carefully hidden secret.*

Though this was just one small isolated incident in a marriage of six years, I will never forget it, as it taught me the sweetness of total honesty between spouses. It also was important to me to know that my husband trusted *me, that I could make a decision about something I needed and it would be perfectly acceptable to him. Also important to me was the fact that he had faith in me that the decisions I would make in the future would be responsible ones. That precious trust has deterred me many times in the past eighteen years from indulging my sometimes impulsive, extravagant "flairs" for this or that, and yet has allowed me the freedom to express my personality and choose for myself as an equal partner in our financial world.*

Summary

This chapter first served to legitimize for you the fact that even Latter-day-Saint couples have differences.

The discussion then focused on the four levels of resolving conflict used by persons in their marriage relationship. You then learned how to operate at Level Four. The bottom line in this discussion is to provide a "Christlike" way of solving problems. Hopefully, this approach has given you new determination to resolve your differences.

Continue your journey now, if you will, into the comfort zone of roles.

Love is not love
which alters when it alteration finds.
(Shakespeare.)

8

A Comfort Zone
of Roles

Every married couple has experienced unexpected changes, yes, even ups and downs, throughout their married lives. For many persons, dealing with the "down times" has not been easy, and frequent mistakes have been made in how they treat their partners. This is to say that they are simply human. It has no bearing on their love for each other, and yet they must eventually understand that inappropriately responding to each other during these "down moments" can eventually disrupt the bonds of love they share.

A Pound of Minced Meat

In the early years of our marriage, when Milt was in medical school and I was working, we had some problems defining roles. We didn't really discuss roles, but we each just assumed the role we felt most comfortable with. I would cook the meals, clean the house, take care of the baby, get up with him in the night when necessary, do the shopping, and work full-time at the hospital. Milt would go to school all day, read the paper at night, and spend four or five hours every night and all day Saturday studying.

Our problem arose on Sundays. Milt was in the bishopric and as such went to meetings and sat on the stand during meetings. I would take care of our son during meetings. He did not like to sit quietly, and when meetings were over, I felt like a pound of minced meat. When we went home I was exhausted and resentful that I had to slave over making dinner while Milt read the paper and relaxed. I would be steaming by the time we had eaten and I had done the dishes all alone.

I felt that I was tired and deserved a little help. After all, my dad always pitched in and helped my mom with Sunday dinner. In contrast, Milt felt that he worked hard and deserved to have one day of rest.

Finally, after keeping these feelings pent up inside for over a year, I dropped the bomb on Milt. For several hours we worked through the garbage that had been building up, and from then on we have been able to express our feelings when we have been uncomfortable in our roles. We have both learned that it just doesn't pay to harbor feelings and build a case against each other just because we don't want to deal with our feelings, but rather our marriage has deepened tremendously just through sharing and trusting.

President Spencer W. Kimball has vividly described what often occurs in a marriage as traits of humanness (or personal weaknesses) surface:

> One comes to realize very soon after marriage that the spouse has weaknesses not previously revealed or discovered. The virtues that were constantly magnified during courtship now grow relatively smaller, and the weaknesses that seemed so small and insignificant during courtship now grow to sizeable proportions. The hour has come for understanding hearts, for self-appraisal, and for

good common sense, reasoning, and planning. The habits of years now show themselves; the spouse may be stingy or prodigal, lazy or industrious, devout or irreligious, kind and cooperative, or petulant and cross, demanding or giving, egotistical or self-effacing. The in-law problem comes closer into focus and the relationship of the spouses to them is again magnified. (*Marriage and Divorce,* page 13.)

Some undesirable behaviors occur because all people are in a mortal condition in which no one is perfect. The scriptures describe this kind of state by saying, "all have sinned, and come short of the glory of God" (Romans 3:23). A person may become impatient when tired, when dealing with small children for the eighteenth hour in a day, or when paying the monthly bills. Many feel resentful and want to get even when someone takes advantage of them, and some stretch the truth when they are in a tight spot.

Even though individuals compromise in various situations, not all undesirable behavior is so wrong that it can be called sin. Sometimes it is a result of differences in one's background, as with the neighbors of one of the authors:

Peter grew up in a family where the mother handled the family money and paid all of the bills. Sue was raised in a family where the father took care of the finances. When they were married, they both assumed that the other one would be the one to handle the money. For the first few months of their marriage, the bills stacked up. In fact, the light bill and the telephone bill were so much overdue that the power and telephone were turned off twice. Both partners felt more than a little frustrated because the other one wouldn't assume his or her "rightful" obligation in this part of their marriage.

Is this a case of "undesirable behavior?" Definitely! When Peter did not pay the bills, it was undesirable to Sue, and vice versa. Situations like this are all too common, yet they are quite different from sinful behavior such as physical abuse, dishonesty, adultery, exploitation, or cruelty.

Since everyone is imperfect, and since all husbands and wives grow up in different kinds of homes, individuals must learn to recognize and then cope with both types of behavior problems in marriage. They need to learn to manage their marriage in such a way that they turn these situations into productive rather than destructive experiences. This chapter develops several strategies that can help you deal with these situations.

The BB Principle

One of the first areas you can examine in your marriage is your BBs. Simply, these are your *beliefs* and your *behaviors.* The first B is your beliefs about how you feel you ought to act, and the second B is your behavior, or how you actually do act. The key to a successful marriage is to keep your BBs the same; that is, have your behavior consistent with your expectations about how you should behave. When your BBs are out of whack, it fouls up a marriage. Yet all is not lost when your BBs are out of harmony, for you can change either one — the beliefs or the behavior — to get things back on an even keel. This principle especially holds true for beliefs or expectations that at least one partner deems important. (Note: We speak here of beliefs and behaviors in the marriage relationship, and not of, for instance, gospel principles, wherein there is a right and a wrong.)

How do you apply the BB principle?

When you keep your BBs the same, you are actually experiencing a *congruence* between your beliefs or expectations and your behavior. So that you can understand what your options are in your marriage relationship, consider using this word *congruence* rather than simply the BB principle.

The first thing we must do in applying the congruence principle is to think *congruence and incongruence* rather than *right and wrong.* In other words, when the wife thinks the husband is spending too much time with his friends and too little time with her, she may not be correct in taking the "simple" way out and merely telling him that he's wrong and he ought to stay at home. It may not be that simple. While obviously he is wrong if he neglects her, she needs to realize that there are no absolute laws about how much time a husband spends at home. It may be a situation wherein her expectations and his behavior are incongruent.

Going even deeper, this wife has expectations, her husband has expectations, and he also has certain behaviors. His expectations and behaviors may be just as correct and wise as hers, if she were to completely understand his view of things. By looking at it through the eyes of "congruence," each may see that the situation is not one wherein one is right and the other wrong. Both have beliefs and both have behaviors, and their relationship would be better if some things were changed.

This sounds simple, but most individuals are not very good at changing. They assume that their opinion about what should be done is the Truth (with a capital *T*). For example:

—If the wife doesn't want to do the housework, and her husband thinks she should, he thinks he is right, right, right, and she should shape up.

—If he thinks that kids should not be spanked, and she disagrees, she assumes he ought to change—pronto!

—If she visits her parents at least once a week and he thinks that visiting monthly is enough, he thinks she should be more reasonable and independent and that she ought to be the one to change.

—If the husband can't keep on the budget because he's an impulsive buyer, she thinks he ought to change his behavior and be more responsible.

Notice that people tend to think in terms of absolute rights and wrongs. And each usually assumes that he is the one who is Right (with a capital *R*). *Married partners would be so much better off if they would approach all of these situations in terms of expectations and behavior*—and search as a couple for a point at which to change one or the other, or both.

IS THE BASIC PROBLEM DISUNITY OR INCONGRUENCE?

The thing you can do in your marriage in coping with what seems to be undesirable behavior is to approach a given situation as a problem, a problem which needs to be solved.

The Possibly Perfect Partner
or
What is the Eggbeater Doing in the Silver Chest?

You've fallen in love, you two who were friends. You look at each other and the world around you with an eye single to your own needs. Out of all the faces in all the world, this one face is your kind of face, this one smile, the warming one.

You build your dreams, set the date, and go through the motions of becoming betrothed. And while that enchanting spell spreads over you, you marry. Then, holding hands, you walk off into the sunset to live happily ever after.

New in your discovery of each other's ways in the daily tasks of life, you are full of wonder — you wonder how you could not have known that this marvelous skier decorates the bedroom with socks, ties, and used lift passes. And when he dries the dishes, he absent-mindedly puts the eggbeater in the silver chest.

He wonders how you, his beautiful and sensible wife, could possibly emerge as a toothpaste tube mutilator, a cap leaver-offer, and a financial hazard with the checkbook. What's more, you starched his no-iron shirts.

You each wonder if two people so different, cloaked with love and some frustration, can ever become one.

It is at such moments that you are glad that you are friends as well as husband and wife. You are thankful for an understanding of the plan of life and the potentiality of the human spirit. In all your differences there is one important quality you share — imperfection and the right to grow.

So you pick up the socks; he replaces the toothpaste cap; you retrieve the eggbeater; he copes with the overdraft one more time. Then you kiss each other.

Maybe not the perfect partner yet, but you keep trying because you promised you would.

Two imperfect children of God who look at each other and the world around them with an eye single to another's needs — friends still and forever. (Author unknown.)

The first stage in problem solving is to determine what the problem is. You may say to yourself, "That's easy! The problem is that someone is misbehaving. Someone is not doing what he ought to do. The problem is the behavior, so let's change the behavior." If you say this, you may be falling into a trap, and you'll probably create more problems than you'll solve. You need to realize that most of the time when there appears to be a behavioral problem, the root or basis is not behavioral. It is not that someone is misbehaving. Sometimes it is, but not often. Most of the time the root problem is *disunity*.

What is the difference?

Examine the following three couples. Some of their problems are only behavior problems (in which behavior is incongruent with expectations), but some of them involve disunity.

The Smiths

Incongruence only: She thinks he should pick up his soiled clothes rather than leave them where he takes them off. He agrees, but he gets so busy that he forgets every other night.

Expectations: Both agree. There is unity.
Behavior: His behavior is incongruent with both of their expectations.

Incongruence and disunity: She thinks he should pick up his clothes rather than leave them where he takes them off. He disagrees. He thinks that part of her tidying a bedroom in the morning ought to include gathering the soiled clothes from the chairs. It is easier to do it in the morning than to go to the bother at the end of the day when people are tired. So he leaves them on the chair.

Expectations: They disagree. There is disunity.
Behavior: Congruent with his expectations but incongruent with hers.

The Johnsons

Incongruence only: He thinks they should visit their folks at least monthly, and so does she. He's "so busy" that he doesn't go very often. She takes the kids and visits the folks monthly.

Expectations: Both agree. There is unity.
Behavior: His behavior is incongruent with both expectations.

Incongruence and disunity: He thinks they should visit the folks weekly. She thinks that is too often. She thinks once a month is plenty, and once every other month would be best. They visit them weekly.

Expectations: Disunity. They disagree.
Behavior: Congruent with his wishes but incongruent with hers.

The Tuckers

Incongruence only: He thinks the house should be much straighter than it usually is, in case someone drops in. He also thinks it is the wife's job to keep it clean. She agrees that it is her job and that it should be straighter, but with five small children it is not straight very often.

Expectations: Unity. They think the same.
Behavior: She is not behaving the way they both think she should.

Incongruence and disunity: Same situation as above, except that she thinks that while the children are small it is all right for the house to be less tidy. She thinks that it is straight enough.

Expectations: Disunity. He wants it neater than she does.
Behavior: Her behavior is consistent with her expectations, but not with his.

There are two reasons why it is important to know whether a problem is merely an incongruence or whether there is also disunity. First, whenever you have disunity it is a more basic or fundamental problem that the behavioral problem. Beliefs precede behavior. This means that you have to deal with the disunity problem before you can solve the behavioral problem. If you try to solve the behavioral problem when you have disunity, it is like trying to fix a flat tire by putting air into it before you fix the hole. And as long as the disunity is there, it will somewhere cause incongruence between beliefs and behavior. Oh, you can solve the behavioral problem. For example, if you want more affection shown than your spouse does and you have had little affection shown (which is what your spouse wants), you can become more affectionate. Unfortunately, this merely makes the behavior incongruent with your spouse's views rather than with yours. It gives your partner the problem rather than you. You still have a problem as a couple.

The second reason why it is important to know whether there is disunity whenever there is undesirable behavior is that you solve the two problems very differently. When you have disunity problems, you solve them by talking about your beliefs. You try to change your opinions, your wishes, your desires, and your expectations to bring them into line with each other's. While there may sometimes be emotional or psychological overtones, this is dealt with as a mental issue, since it concerns differences of opinion. But when the problem is incongruence of expectations and behavior, you have more options. You can change your expectations *or* your behavior, or both, *and you use very different techniques to change your behavior.* Trying to solve disunity problems by changing behaviors is like putting a cast on your arm because you have a sore throat, or getting the car tuned up because the TV won't work, or vacuuming the rug because the dishes are dirty. These analogies may seem ridiculous, but many persons actually make similar mistakes in their marriages. For instance, a husband tries to get his wife to change something she is doing *because he thinks it should be changed,* when the problem the couple need to solve is not the behavior at all. *It is the difference of opinion.*

REMEMBER — DEAL WITH FEELINGS FIRST

After you have learned that you have a problem, what do you do next? Do you jump right into the process of solving it? Only if you like to fight and destroy precious things like love and peace. The answer? *Wise couples deal with their feelings first.* Before entering into a discussion you should ask yourself, "Is the total environment right? Is the time of day right? Will there be distractions, noise, outside pressures interfering? Am I in control of myself? Is my partner receptive? Is he or she defensive, preoccupied, tired, overworked?" You should check out these questions with your partner by asking him or her if the time is right before you sit down for the discussion. If everything seems to be in order, you are ready to move ahead.

The next step is to gain an understanding of how each of you *actually feels* about the discrepancy. In this stage each of you will concentrate on trying to gain an understanding of how the other feels. As you do this, you are building the foundation for other processes to occur *after* each of you has as complete an understanding as possible of the other's feelings about the discrepancies. To do this, you each should take turns first playing the expresser role and then the listener role. The expresser shares his/her feelings about the discrepancies in a helpful manner without attacking the self-esteem of the other partner. In order to accomplish this, it is often helpful to restrict the expression to (1) what was done and (2) how it made you feel. The expresser can do this by either verbally expressing his feelings or by writing his feelings first and then sharing this with the partner before trying to verbally explain how he feels. During this stage, you may say things like:

"If you leave me here and go overseas to improve your training for six months, I'm afraid that I won't have enough money to pay the bills and keep food on the table for the kids. I'm also afraid that I won't be able to handle all the problems that will come up with the kids. The older ones challenge me on everything that I ask them to do right now. Without you around, I'm afraid I'll lose control of them. I'd also be very lonely."

In this situation the wife states her views on how she sees the discrepancy. She sees that the husband is suggesting going away for a period of time and leaving her without the support she feels she should receive from him. She has stated what he has done or is planning to do. She then explains her feelings about what he is about to do. She would be less wise if she attacks or blames:

"You're just irresponsible! You jumped at this opportunity to get away from me and the kids. You don't love me anymore, and you can't stand the kids. You don't even care if we eat or not.

I'm going right over to the bishop and tell him all about your plans to abandon us!"

It is doubtful that this approach will do a great deal of good in resolving the discrepancy between how the wife feels her husband should act and how he proposes to act. She has attacked the *person* instead of the *issue* and has assigned motives to his intentions rather than describing how she feels about what it is he is proposing to do.

Perhaps she could more constructively identify her feelings and express them, rather than throwing verbal darts at her husband. She could do this by saying,

"I'm feeling abandoned and empty. I'm questioning your love for me as well as the children, and I just don't know how to respond. Why are you leaving?"

As you can see, identifying feelings instead of merely projecting the blame on the spouse provides a constructive balance and will allow the partners to respond without being defensively harsh with each other.

WHAT ARE YOUR ALTERNATIVES?

After you understand the feelings on both sides, you can then turn your attention to resolving the discrepancies. What is the next step? As with any other problem, step number two is to *identify and discuss your alternatives.* What are the alternatives? With undesirable behavior, there are four main ones: (1) change the expectations, (2) change the behavior, (3) change the importance of the expectations, or (4) learn how to live with what is seen as less than ideal behavior. The following situation can help us understand these alternatives:

Glenda's side:

Harry and Glenda have been married for six months, and their marriage isn't what she thought it would be. She thinks Harry spends too much time with his buddies. Since he is working and still finishing school, he doesn't have much free time, and what he has seems to go to his friends. There isn't much time left for her. This leaves her with a lot of time on her hands. At first she didn't mind, but she resents it more all the time.

Harry's side:

Harry has some close friends, and he doesn't want his marriage to mean that he has to give them up. It takes time to keep friendships. He does spend a lot of time with the friends, but he also spends a lot of time with Glenda. His marriage is first, but it is not the only thing.

Assume that this is a behavioral problem, not a disunity problem. They have agreed that they should spend a lot of time together. Assuming this, consider their alternatives:

1. *Change expectations:* It may be that their expectations are unrealistic. Both want to spend time together, but they have so many other things they also want that there aren't enough hours in the day, especially for Harry. Therefore, they may help solve the problem by adjusting their expectations. They could change them in several different ways. For example, they could decide to spend less time with friends, even though that might be painful. Or they could agree to get by with less interaction with each other than they would like — temporarily, until they get out of school. Or Harry could take an extra year to finish school.

2. *Change behavior:* It may be that Harry has not yet fully realized some of the changes that occur with marriage. He has assumed that his spouse would be his best friend, but he hasn't realized this means that some of his other friends must become less important. In trying to keep everybody happy, he has unwittingly neglected Glenda. If this is so, the problem could be solved by his adjusting his behavior so that he spends more time with her and less with his friends. He and Glenda could also make sure that the time they do spend together is "quality" time.

3. *Change the importance:* It may be that they can't find a way to change their expectations or behavior enough. He just can't give up his buddies even though he realizes he should. The best solution they may be able to come up with is to live with their problem, letting Harry spend a lot of time with his buddies. Glenda may be able to change her opinion about how important it is by saying to herself, "This certainly isn't the most important thing in our marriage. It would be nice to have it better, but it is not necessary. He recognizes that he has a fault in this area and

will try to improve, but it is not as important as some other things, and we are going to work on them first."

4. *Learn to live with it without any changes:* (This is what people do when they can't find a better solution.) Harry continues to see his friends a lot and Glenda can't tell herself it isn't important because it *is* important to her, and it is important to him. What can they do about it? They realize that they have a lot of other great things going for them in their marriage, and aren't going to let this one problem ruin their life. They try to avoid the issue and just accept it as a "less than ideal situation." They tell themselves, "After all, all couples have a few areas in which things aren't perfect. Besides, Harry is a good husband in many other ways."

There are a number of strategies that can help us with each of these alternatives. The following pages discuss some of them.

Strategies for Coping with Undesirable Behavior

METHODS OF CHANGING EXPECTATIONS

Talk about why. Set aside some time to talk about the reasons for your expectations. In the case of Harry and Glenda, they could talk about why she wants him to be with her more and why he wants to be with his friends a lot. When a couple spend a few evenings talking about their feelings and all of the subtle variations and possibilities, they frequently find a way to rearrange their views so that these are compatible, or change them so that they are more workable or realistic.

Another advantage of this strategy is that it helps you better understand each other. Also, just spending the time together creates a feeling that the other one cares enough to do what he can in working things out. It can help you feel that your partner is trying to understand your point of view. That type of emotional support is very helpful.

Talk with other couples. It can be very helpful to talk with others about their expectations in marriage. You can make statements such as these:

—We have some differences of opinion about _____
and we're interested in getting some other opinions.
—How do you work out a budget?
—What do you do when one person does . . . ?

You need to be careful in using this strategy to make sure that you do not discuss parts of your marriage that would be better kept to yourself. For example, it would be unwise for couples to discuss the intimacies of each other's sexual interaction or to use these conversations to embarrass or coerce either person. There are, however, hundreds of areas in marriage about which it is useful to get opinions from others. For example, it can be very useful to discuss ways of relating to in-laws, budgeting, disciplining children, what to do about insurance, finding time to get everything done that you'd like to, etc.

Recognize that most expectations should be flexible. There are a few role expectations that are tied to important moral and ethical ideals. For instance, you should not physically abuse a spouse, you should never be cruel to each other, you should not commit adultery, and you should not bear false witness about each other. But these rigid and inflexible expectations are surprisingly few in marriage. Most of your expectations are cultural beliefs that you glean from your parents or some other part of your culture, and they can be altered and changed according to your personal needs and wishes. Notice how flexible all of the following issues are:

—Who should handle the money?
—Who should do the cooking, cleaning, and ironing?
—Should the main meal be in the middle of the day or in the evening?
—How often should we visit in-laws?
—How should we discipline the children?
—How much influence should in-laws have with us?
—How often should we express affection?
—How frequently should we go out?

Most individuals grow up assuming that their way of doing things is the right way. They need to learn that their way is only *one* way. There are other ways that can be equally good and wise. Thus you can have a tremendous amount of flexibility in how you arrange or rearrange your interactions in marriage.

Avoid unrealistic expectations. Sometimes couples set their goals so high that they assure failure. You need to realize that you both need a little time to attain perfection — and you may need more than a *little* time. You climb mountains one step at a time, and you need to progress and grow the same way. This means that you can have long-term, ultimate goals of being at the top of some high mountains, but your immediate goals and desires should be some short-range goals that are within your immediate reach.

There is a common pattern in the LDS culture of setting unrealistic goals and then feeling guilty and defeated when they are not reached. This is delightfully illustrated with the following tongue-in-cheek description of Sister Patti Perfect.

Patti Perfect

Many LDS women unconsciously compete with an idealized image of the already-perfect wife and mother who successfully incorporates all the demands of family, church, and society into her life. Although we have never met such a woman, we persist in believing she's out there somewhere. We can just imagine what she must accomplish in a day . . .

Patti gets up very early and says her personal prayers. She zips her slim, vigorous body into her warm-up suit and tiptoes outside to run her usual five miles (on Saturday she does ten). Returning home all aglow, she showers and then dresses for the day in a tailored skirt and freshly starched and ironed blouse. She settles down for quiet meditation and scripture reading before preparing the family breakfast. The morning's menu calls for whole wheat pancakes, homemade syrup, freshly squeezed orange juice, and powdered milk (the whole family loves it).

With classical music wafting through the air, Patti awakens her husband and ten children. She spends a quiet moment with each and helps them plan a happy day. The children quickly dress in clothes that were laid out the night before. They cheerfully make their beds, clean their rooms, and do the individual chores assigned to them on the Family Work Wheel Chart. They assemble for breakfast the minute mother calls.

After family prayer and scripture study, the children all practice their different musical instruments. Father leaves for work on a happy note. All too soon it is time for the children to leave for school. Having brushed (and flossed) their teeth, the children pick up coats, book bags, and lunches they have prepared the night before and arrive at school five minutes early.

With things more quiet, Patti has storytime with her pre-schoolers and teaches them a cognitive reading skill. She feeds, bathes, and rocks the baby before putting him down for his morning nap. With baby sleeping peacefully and the three-year-old twins absorbed in creative play, Patti tackles the laundry and housework. In less than an hour, everything is in order. Thanks to wise scheduling and children who are trained to work, her house never really gets dirty.

Proceeding to the kitchen, Patti sets out tonight's dinner: frozen veal parmigiana that she made in quantity from her home-grown tomatoes and peppers. She then mixes and kneads twelve loaves of bread. While the bread rises, Patti dips a batch of candles to supplement her food storage. As the bread bakes, she writes in her personal journal and dashes off a few quick letters — one to her congressman and a couple of genealogy inquiries to distant cousins. Patti then prepares her mini-class lesson on organic gardening. She also inserts two pictures and a certificate in little Paul's scrapbook, noting with satisfaction that all family albums are attractive and up to date. Checking the mail, Patti sees that their income tax refund has arrived — a result of having filed in January. It is ear-marked for mission and college savings accounts. Although Patti's hardworking husband earns only a modest salary, her careful budgeting has kept the family debt free.

After lunch, Patti drops the children off at Grandma's for their weekly visit. Grandma enjoys babysitting and appreciates the warm loaf of bread. Making an extra call, Patti takes a second loaf to one of the sisters she is assigned to visit teach. A third loaf goes to the nonmember neighbor on the corner.

Patti arrives at the elementary school where she directs a special education program. A clinical psychologist, Patti finds this an excellent way to stay abreast of her field while raising her family. Before picking up her little ones, Patti finishes collecting for the charity fund drive.

Home again, Patti settles the children down for their afternoon naps. She spends some quiet time catching up on her reading and filing. As she mists her luxuriant house plants, the school children come through the door. Patti listens attentively to each one as they tell her about their day. The children start right in on their home-work, with mother supervising and encouraging them. When all schoolwork is done, Patti and the children enjoy working on one of their projects. Today they work on the quilt stretched on frames in a corner of the family room.

Dinnertime and father arrive, and it is a special hour for the whole family. They enjoy Patti's well-balanced, tasty meal, along with stimulating conversation. After dinner, father and the children pitch in to clean up so that mom can relax. She enjoys listening to the sounds of laughter and affection that come from the kitchen.

With the teenage children in charge at home, mother and father attend an evening session at the temple. During the return trip, they sit close together as in courting days. "Well, dear," says Paul Perfect, "did you have a good day?" Pat reflectively answers, "Yes, I really did. But I feel I need more challenge in my life. I think I'll contact our family organization and volunteer to head up a reunion for August." (Margaret B. Black, Midge W. Nielson.)

The unreality of this story is not to say that you should go to the other extreme and abandon all your high standards and goals. You need to find a middle ground. You ought to keep your lofty long-term goals and realize they are just that—long-term. You ought also to have many intermediate goals and short-term goals so that you are "anxiously engaged" in improving yourself. And this can include some "godly sorrow" about the imperfections that are yours; but it ought also to include confidence and pride in what you are able to do. You should have enough goals and areas you are working on to make you stretch and lengthen your stride, but you ought not to try to run faster than you can lest you stumble on your own intentions.

METHODS OF CHANGING BEHAVIOR

Sometimes it is easy to change behavior. Here are some examples:

—Sam never calls Sue when he's going to work late, and she would like him to. Sue tells him how important it is to her, and from then on he does it.

—Jack hasn't been praying as regularly as he should. He has good intentions. He just forgets. He and Jill decide that they will have their prayers at the same time, as that will help him remember. After that, he prays each morning and evening.

—Bernard thinks Barbara toasts the bread too dark. He recognizes that she grew up that way because her whole family likes it dark, but he prefers it just barely a light brown. She thanks him for letting her know how he wants it and toasts his lighter.

At other times it is hard to change behavior. Some habits are formed over many years and are difficult to change. It takes a lot of discipline and work to change them even a little.

What can you do to change these behaviors?

There are many things you can do to change behavior. Four of them are these: (1) change habits a little at a time, (2) use conditioning, (3) use Deutsch's principle, and (4) discuss the consequences.

Changing habits a little at a time. You haven't built your habits overnight; you have built them slowly and gradually. You break them the same way. Those of you who think you can break a deeply ingrained habit quickly are apt to discover later that you haven't really changed it.

Habits are like threads in a rope. If you try to break one thread or a small piece of string, you can do so easily. If you put two pieces of thread together, it is a little harder, but you can still break them. When you put three or four together, it is difficult; but if you wrap the threads around your finger and pull hard, they pop. Breaking this many at once hurts the hand a little. When you add a few more and try to break them, it hurts you to try, and you can't break them. If you were to continue to add threads one by one, you would gradually create a piece of twine and then a small rope. Then you'd have a large rope, and then a massive rope that could tow the largest of ships and hold up thousands of tons. Gradually it would become so strong that there is no way it could be broken by pulling on it.

But even the strongest rope can be broken by reversing the process. You can take one thread away from the large rope and break it; then another, and then another, and so on. As you do this, gradually even the largest and strongest rope will get smaller and weaker. Eventually you will only have one or two strands left, and you can easily break them. In this manner the strongest ropes on earth can be broken by the weakest of people.

What does this teach you?

Habits are like ropes. They are made up of small, thin little acts that are easy to change when you change them one at a time. When you act the same way hundreds and thousands of times, you have a habit; and, like the rope, it is so strong that it is impossible to break immediately. You can try as hard as you can, and all it will do is hurt you to try. You cannot break the habit. You cannot change your behavior all at once. You can, however, change the way you act in any small moment. That time won't break the habit, and it takes concentration to go against it; but, just as with the threads on the rope, even the weakest person can take one thread and break it. Then, after you have changed one act many times, you will observe that your old habit is becoming weaker. It then gets easier and easier to take a thread away and break it (change the way you act). Gradually you can break the most troublesome and difficult habit.

This has many implications for how you ought to act in marriage. For example, it means that you need to be patient and long-suffering with yourself and with your partner when you are trying to break bad habits. It means that some of them take months and years, even a lifetime, to break. And since you may have several different bad habits (large ropes), you cannot work on all of them at the same time with the same energy and dedication. This means that you may have to live with some of them for a while, while you work on others. It means that you ought to be accepting and tolerant of your limitations and imperfections and be willing to forgive and forgive and forgive while you are in the slow process of perfecting yourself.

Use conditioning. You have undoubtedly heard about the Russian scientist Pavlov and his dogs. As all dogs will in such circumstances, his dogs would salivate when they saw him bringing their food. Pavlov started to ring a bell when he brought them the food, and he kept doing this till eventually the dogs would salivate when he rang the bell and didn't bring food. They had been *conditioned.* They had learned to associate the bell and the food so closely that they responded to the bell the same way they did to the food. This discovery about a century ago led scientists to more and more discoveries about how humans learn to do some things and avoid others. You can use these discoveries to help you change your behavior in your marriage.

One of the best ways to use conditioning employs a principle called the Success Principle. It is a simple idea:

The more often a person's behavior is rewarded, the more likely he is to perform the activity.

The opposite is also true: the more a person is punished, the less likely he is to repeat an activity. How can you use this principle to help change your behavior? You can use it by going through several simple steps. These are:

1. First, use this principle in connection with specific actions that you can easily observe and count. You can use it to help do specific things like doing three kind acts a day or giving one compliment a day to someone else or "giving in" every other time when you have a disagreement.

2. Before you try to change, spend a period of time monitoring how you really do act. It is usually best if this is done on paper. You ought to chart, count, tally, or check your behaviors for several days. This gives you a clear indication as to what you are doing, and sometimes you are surprised.

3. Next, think of some way to reward yourself for doing something right or punish yourself for doing something wrong. Even little ways can do it, like putting pennies in a jar every time you act the way you should. You can also tell yourself that you will get a certain reward, such as a movie, new dress, ball game, dinner out, when you have performed at a certain level.

4. While you are trying to change, you need to again keep track of how you are actually behaving. This means you need to go through the tedious process of counting, monitoring, tallying, etc.

In today's society, people value economic and materialistic things, and so these things can be very effective reinforcers. You can use them to reward yourself, and deny them to yourself or take them away to punish. You need also to learn that there are social reinforcers. These are more subtle, but they can be extremely powerful. Things such as recognition, attention, praise, encouragement, thanks, affection, closeness, etc., can have extremely powerful effects. In fact, modern scientists believe that many undesirable behaviors were learned through reinforcement patterns having social rewards. For example, when you were a child you may have unconsciously learned that the only way you could get your parents' undivided attention was to misbehave. When you did things right you were ignored; you just blended into the woodwork. But when you got into trouble, your parents were right there, and they were concerned about you, really concerned. Gradually you learned to misbehave, and thus you created some undesirable habits.

There are two other aspects of this process that you ought to remember if you are going to use it in your marriage. These are so important that if you ignore them, you may be like your parents and experience unintended consequences that you do not want; *you may actually do more damage than good in your marriage.* What are these cautions?

First, rewards make much more difference than punishments. As the old saying has it, "It is easier to catch flies with honey than vinegar." If you use punishments to change your own behavior or the behavior of others, it creates resentments, animosity, and anger. Therefore you would be well advised to use rewards liberally and punishments very rarely and cautiously.

Second, most adults resent it when they are manipulated by others. They like to be in control of their own lives. They like to do things the way they want to do them. They appreciate their free agency, and they don't like to have it threatened or taken away from them.

A Man Convinced . . .

For many years we have had a conflict in our marriage which centers around the supper hour. Regardless of careful planning or coordinating, Michael is always late for supper. He has always had a good excuse, as he is in business for himself, which entails many unexpected things happening each day, but I found it hard to believe that this was the case every night of the week, especially when he could be on time for a golf date or fishing trip.

I wondered many times if it was just not rewarding enough for Michael to come home to the disaster our supper table was, with five young children, so I tried to make the food especially attractive and the children amiable . . . but to no avail.

I tried fixing supper later and later until we were eating at 7:30 in the evening. This was undesirable simply because by that time the children were so hungry and tired and cross that no one could live with them.

Then there were some evenings when Michael could extricate himself from the office early, but then he couldn't stand to waste the nice weather by being indoors and would go golfing until after dark. I felt totally frustrated because I could not get the family all together for supper, and if I fed the children early and left a plate for Michael I felt guilty that I was neglecting my wifely duties.

After fourteen years of married life and unhappy supper hours, I have come to the conclusion that food and supper have little value on my husband's list of priorities. Unlike my father, who lived his whole life so that he could sit down to eat supper with his wife and family, Michael is quite happy to eat a warmed-up supper at his convenience, all alone if necessary, and come home to a smiling, happy wife. I feel badly it took me so long to realize that what was important to my dad is of little importance to my husband. I also found the old adage true that "a man convinced against his will is of the same opinion still." Perhaps with this new understanding we will live happily ever after, after all.

What does this have to do with conditioning?

If you use conditioning on someone against his will or in a way he wouldn't like, you are taking away part of his agency. You are *manipulating* him, and this is unkind, unethical, and usually unwanted. It can cause very undesirable side effects in a marriage. So what do you do? Whenever you want to use conditioning to change someone else's behavior, you need to be sure that he would agree with the goals you are trying to reach. If you are trying to change some undesirable behavior, it ought to be a *mutual* decision. You need to make sure that you are unified in what you are trying to do. The person who is being conditioned has the right to decide that this is what he or she wants.

This means that the well-intentioned wife who wants her husband to be more active in the Church should not punish him for his behavior. She should also not try rewarding him with such things as affection or attention when he does things her way. Such behaviors will build resentment and animosity toward the wife and the Church—and most of the time the husband and wife will not know what is happening.

Another thing this means is that the husband who wants his wife to stay more within the budget will just make matters worse by getting after her, scolding her, or berating her (punishing her to get her to change her ways). They need to first find out if they are unified about what ought to be done, and then, after they are unified, work out a plan together to change the behavior. When this is done the wife (or husband) agrees to the reward or punishment arrangement, and not only will it be more effective, it will create solidarity in the relationship rather than divisiveness.

Use Duetsch's principle. Duetsch's principle is so useful in changing behavior that it needs to be applied in this situation. The principle is this:

> *The more you act in a certain way, the more others around you tend to act in the same way.*

This idea can help you change behavior when you want to help your spouse change his (or her) behavior. If you want him to become more considerate or kind (and he agrees that he wants to change), you can become more considerate or kind yourself, and this will help him change. If you want him to become more generous or helpful, you can become more generous or helpful. If you want your spouse to give in more, you can give in more than you have been doing. If you want your spouse to be more attentive and listening, you can be more interested in and pay more attention to what your spouse is saying. If you want your partner to be more sensitive to your feelings and goals, you can be more sensitive to his feelings and goals.

This principle is beautiful to use because it is so subtle and soothing in relationships. It is giving some of yourself to and for the other person. It is going the second mile. It is like oil on troubled waters, soft music, or a gentle rain. It usually creates more of what you want than you think possible, and somehow it also makes other things better, as you feel good about the changes you are making and you feel closer to and more deeply in love with each other. Perhaps this is why the Savior relied so much on this principle in his teachings about going the second mile, judging not, returning good for evil, turning the cheek— the classic rule of doing unto others as you would have them do unto you, and the ultimate commandment of all—to love even as the Savior has loved you.

Evaluating Consequences. Social scientists, in evaluating different ways of trying to change behavior, find that one of the effective ways is to evaluate the effects of what you are doing. This is accomplished by asking yourself and each other questions such as:

"What will happen if I keep doing what I am doing?"

"Is that what I want to happen?"

"If I act in this way, what will be the consequences or results?"

"How will it affect me and those I love and care about?"

"Will it make things better or worse?"

Social scientists have discovered that this is a very effective strategy for guiding children. It helps them discover some of the reasons for acting in correct ways, and then they feel much better about doing the right thing. It is much more effective than telling a child to do something "because we said so." It is the same with yourself and your spouse. As you think and ponder about the effects of what you do, it helps you find the strength and determination to correct undesirable things, and it gives you reassurance and confidence in the things that you are doing right.

CHANGING THE IMPORTANCE OF YOUR EXPECTATIONS

When you can't change your *expectations* or your *behavior*, you can resort to the third method of coping with undesirable behavior. You can tell yourself that it is not important. This is easy for little things like those in the following situation:

William is never on time. He walks into church at the end of the opening song, and if he tells others he will pick them up at a certain time, they know he'll never be there when he says he will. He has good intentions. He's just never on time. He and his wife have talked about it, and he has tried to change, but he doesn't seem to be able to. They've given up trying to change him, and she's adjusted her life to it. After thirty-five years of marriage, she'd still rather have him change, but he probably won't. She tells herself that it doesn't make much difference in the eternal scheme anyway. After all, "time only is measured unto men" (Alma 40:8).

A Fish Story

Because my husband and I spent our first eight years of marriage sending him through school, we drew very close together during this time. We had no car and very little money, and consequently we became best friends, entertaining ourselves in any way that we could dream up. We had five children in seven years and kept pretty close to home for lack of a baby-sitter. By the time our marriage reached the twelve-year mark, however, we were financially more secure and the children were able to be left alone. We began getting out more and indulging in extra-curricular activities, but still always "together."

My father has been a great sportsman all his life, and one summer morning he invited my husband to go fishing with him. I felt a twinge of jealousy, almost resentment, that I was "stuck" home with the kids on a beautiful Saturday. These feelings, in turn, made me feel guilty and selfish. The fishermen were gone all day, and when my husband returned home with a limit of eight beautiful trout, he was ecstatic and was also smitten with the "fishing bug." I tried to be ecstatic too, but his clothes were filthy, the car was a royal mess, and I thought his fish were stinky. To put it plainly, I was jealous and yet frustrated, because I really didn't have the slightest desire to be invited to go alone.

As the summer progressed, the fishing trips increased. My resentment also grew by leaps and bounds. My sweetheart, the love of my life, my buddy, was waking me up at 5:00 A.M., keeping me up late at night, smelling up my kitchen and garbage, and in general having a wonderful time! It wasn't long before I made a scene. I simply could not stand to have him enjoying such a good time without me! He would somehow always select a time to head for the hills, just when I felt I needed his companionship. Things went from bad to worse, until I was really making both of us miserable. He still went fishing, but he felt guilty about it, and I felt guilty for making him feel guilty. Then, after two years, I took a good look at myself. I had to ask the question, "Is the resentment you feel really worth damaging the sweet relationship you have always had with your husband?" I had to honestly answer that no, it was not. I also began to have an understanding that though we had always been like two peas in a pod, everyone needs his "space" and time alone. I had become a clinging vine, without really intending to. I realized I was going to have to find some interests of my own to avoid the feeling of being "stuck" at home with the kids.

For two summers I struggled with it. I literally forced myself to smile and say "tight lines" as he walked out of the door. I even learned to enjoy eating trout. (And if you freeze the heads and tails until garbage pick-up day, they don't smell up the trash cans.) By the third summer, I was amazed to discover that I really didn't mind the fishing trips, and in turn my sweetheart was more considerate in sensing when it was appropriate to head for the hills and when it was appropriate for him to stay home and meet the needs of his family. Now I take our girls shopping, have my hair done, work on projects I am involved in, or take part in any one of a number of interests, while my husband is out enjoying a hobby that renews and refreshes him.

Clearly, then, some behavior problems can be solved by changing your opinions about their importance. Another example might be when a couple has problems over who is going to cut the meat at the dinner table. They can probably resolve them by sharing their feelings and then agreeing that it is not necessarily a sign of being a good husband to cut the meat, nor should it be interpreted as challenging the husband's authority if he is asked to do so. The couple can agree to deemphasize any underlying means that had been assigned to this matter and decide that whoever is least busy at meal time could be the one to cut the meat.

Your success in changing the importance of misbehavior will depend upon how closely it is tied to things you value. One wife, when faced with the continual frustration of having a husband who refused to become active in their church, decided that in order to relieve the weekly tension in the home she would decrease the amount of importance she placed on religion, so she too became inactive. In doing so, she did not take into account her own conscience and guilt feelings, and she was unable to continue being inactive. Behavior problems in an area of great concern usually cannot be resolved by simply convincing oneself that it is no longer important.

LEARN TO LIVE WITH IT WITHOUT ANY CHANGES

When you can't change your *expectations*, your *behavior*, or your beliefs about the *importance* of it, you're stuck! You don't like the behavior, and you can't get rid of it. Does this happen, really? Unfortunately, the answer is yes. In fact, it happens to all couples. It happens to saints and sinners, the good and the bad, the rich and the poor, the smart and the less gifted.

It would be pleasant never to have this happen in *your* marriage, and you may even be so idealistic that you tell yourself, "That won't happen to *us*." Unfortunately, life is sufficiently complicated, and humans are sufficiently human, that it usually happens in a number of areas in a marriage.

What do you do when this happens?

Again, there are several strategies that can help. One of them is to use the old saying "Keep your eyes wide open before marriage and half shut afterwards." Keeping your eyes half shut afterwards means that you need to ignore some things. It means that you keep those things in the attic of your mind. Of course, you can't do this with a large number of things, and you should not do it when the undesirable behavior is extremely serious, but can do it after. For example, if your spouse squeezes the toothpaste in the middle and it bothers you, you can buy two tubes at a time and never be reminded of your spouse's imperfection in this area.

A second strategy is to use a mechanism we have mentioned earlier, which psychologists call "compensation." Whenever you are bothered by undesirable behavior, you think about all the other positive things. If you are concerned about your own behavior, you can remind yourself that you have been doing pretty well in several other areas. If you are upset by the behavior of your spouse, you can think of all his other virtues. This at least helps put the imperfection in a larger perspective, and it will keep you from being too distressed by one particular fault.

A third strategy is to use what sociologists call *relative deprivation*. This means looking at your situation relative to others' situations. If you can observe that others also have problems, it can help you live with your situation. This process can work both ways. It can make your life either more or less difficult. If you are always comparing yourself (or your marriage) with the most outstanding trait in outstanding people, you are apt to have low esteem and feel miserable. Someone who evaluates his abilities in terms of Donny Osmond's singing, Elder Paul Dunn's ability to speak, President Spencer W. Kimball's humility, President Joseph Fielding Smith's gospel knowledge, the Prophet Joseph Smith's spirituality, and Robert Redford's charisma will have a difficult time living with his imperfections. Those who do this are picking out a person who is outstanding and then selecting his most outstanding trait as their standard. Relatively speaking, they're bound to be inadequate.

This is unwise for several reasons. These outstanding people are in the public eye because of their outstanding traits, but each of them also has his imperfections, and there is no way to become acquainted with his less admirable characteristics. This gives observers a limited view of them. Observers would be much wiser to compare themselves with those they know well enough to be aware of both their strong points and their limitations rather than just their strong points. Also, they would be wise to think as well about those who are less adequate and gifted than they. It will help them enjoy themselves and their marriage much more and help them find ways to live happily with those undesirable behaviors they are still trying to change.

A final strategy in helping you learn to live happily with your limitations and those of your spouse is to memorize the inspiring and helpful lines of the following well-known poem:

> God, grant me the serenity
> To accept the things I cannot change,
> The courage to change the things I can,
> And the wisdom to know the difference.

Give-n-Take

Although we come from similar backgrounds and have always had many common interests, many of our interests are different and seemingly incompatible. In school, Tom was always extremely poor in sports, while I was a P.E. major. On the other hand, Tom's vocation is that of a historian, while my worst subject was history. Both of us were anxious about our first date, since we knew our vocations were so different. Nevertheless, we found ourselves quite compatible, were engaged on the third date, and married six months later.

In the twenty-one years since our marriage, we have both taken an interest in each other's vocations. Tom has taken up racquetball and has learned to enjoy attending football and basketball games. He also has taken up skiing, which we do together. I now attend historical conventions with Tom, often critique his papers, and have taken an interest — quite absent before — in the past. Our interests have converged somewhat, and this convergence has helped in cementing our marriage.

Summary

This chapter has discussed ways of coping with undesirable behavior. Some undesirable behavior in marriage occurs simply because the man and the woman were reared in different families with different customs, traditions, and habits. Other undesirable behavior occurs because everyone is in a mortal and imperfect condition in this life. These two factors make it unlikely that most marriages will avoid all undesirable behavior. They will have some in their marriage (though these should tend to diminish with time), and they'd also have some if they didn't marry.

The chapter pointed out that the first thing to do in coping with behavioral problems is to determine whether there are also disunity problems. If the situation also involves disunity, a couple needs first to try to deal with it. After they have dealt with the unity issue, they have three main alternatives in coping with undesirable behavior. These are: (1) changing their expectations, (2) changing the behavior, (3) changing the beliefs about how important it is. (A fourth possible strategy, not mentioned in the chapter, is learning to live with the situation—happily or unhappily.) Several strategies for effecting each of these alternatives were then discussed.

You are now prepared to consider an area which is crucial in marriage, and which, if understood, can remove much of the destructive powers in most failing marriage relationships.

Money is a good servant
but a poor master.
(D. Bouhours.)

9

Loosening the Financial Yoke

While it may come as a surprise to you, the financial area of marriage causes more arguments than any other area, including in-law relations, religious differences, intimacy problems, and children. It is not the lack of money or the love of money that causes these problems, but simply the way a couple *manages* their money. The problems arise when they don't plan wisely, don't spend wisely, don't keep track of what they do; or when they differ on what they want and can't find ways to agree. Too many couples are like the following couples:

"The more we make the worse off we are. There just isn't enough to go around. And then George bought those golf clubs last week. I was so upset! I told him that if this is the way he was going to act, I was going to go out and buy me a new dress. I need it a lot more than he needs those old clubs."

"But the loan company said that we could combine all of our payments into one, and it would be less than we are paying now. If we do that we might be able to buy the TV now."

"We just don't have enough to pay tithing now. It all goes for rent and food and the car payment and other necessities. We're just barely getting by; we're not making enough. Maybe if I took that other job we'd be getting enough to pay tithing."

Even though at this point in your marriage you may either view yourselves as having your financial act together or as being a lost "$$" cause, drop back ten marital yards and consider the following discussion from fresh financial eyes.

The Management Cycle

There is a cycle in the way you ought to manage money, and every couple repeatedly moves through it, albeit haphazardly. They begin each week or month as they sit down with their bills and as they pay for their groceries. The cycle is the sequence of *planning, acting,* and *recording,* as shown below. The *way* they conduct this cycle (as you surely know!) makes a lot of difference in their lives. If they pass through the cycle wisely, they will be able to accomplish economic goals that poor managers never reach.

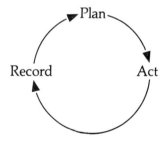

A Thrifty Beginning

After hearing a priesthood lesson, James came home and gave me a few dollars for myself. It was not to be spent on family needs, food, or clothing for the children, but was for

*me to spend on just myself. We were struggling students try-
ing to work our way through school, and there never seemed
to be enough money left over for the things I needed. Thus,
I very much appreciated his thoughtfulness.*

*All through school I did sewing for other people. The
money I earned in this manner, James always insisted I keep
and use for myself. With this money I would buy clothing,
needlework kits or knitting projects (to be given as gifts),
books to read, or music to play. Many times I saved those
few dollars to buy James a gift for Christmas or for his birthday. Perhaps the thing I remember most about those days is
that we never went into debt, but worked extra hard to meet
our needs, and then lived within these same needs. Because
we disciplined ourselves at that time in our marriage, doing
so now (with inflation as it is) is just second nature to us
both.*

One fortunate aspect of this cycle is that there is more than
one way to complete it. There is no standard "right" way to do it
effectively. Some people are detailed planners. They like to make
precise budgets and then stick to the budget by keeping accurate
books. Others are impulsive and like a freer style of life. They
enjoy doing things on the spur of the moment and having a lot
of flexibility in their plans. Still others like to plan but prefer to
keep their plans in their heads rather than on paper.

Is it possible for all of these couples to use the management
cycle wisely?

The answer is yes. It depends on *how they act* in the cycle.
The cycle allows for flexibility if they understand what they are
doing and do it well. This leads to the question of how to be
wise in each phase of the cycle.

PLANNING

The planning phase occurs as you decide where your money
should go. It is important, because if you don't decide beforehand where your money will go, you'll wonder later where it
went.

An example of a lack of planning was provided by a young married couple known to the authors. They had set a preliminary financial goal to save a certain amount of money before their marriage. This they did, then they got married. What they did not do, however, was to plan precisely what it was they were going to do with the money they had saved. They had a general plan of using portions of it each month to supplement their part-time employment while they went to school, but they made no specific plans. They also knew they enjoyed pizza, particularly at a certain restaurant.

Five months into the school year, they discovered that their entire summer's savings were gone. Trying to reconstruct the disaster, they traced backwards in their checkbook and discovered that 80 percent of their savings had been spent on pizza. They had discovered they were pizzaholics and were in need of better planning and restraint.

Who should do the planning? It depends on the couple. Some couples want the husband and wife to sit down together to develop and revise their budget. Others want to divide the planning. Still others will want one person to do most of the work but get the partner's approval before the plan is implemented. *Flexibility is the rule.* It doesn't matter who does it, as long as the couple (1) do a minimum amount of planning, and (2) work out a system that they both feel good about.

A Balanced Balance

I'm sure many divorces are a result of the inflationary times we live in when people feel they make pretty good money but at the end of the month they don't have enough cash to pay the bills. At this point of our lives (married over twenty-seven years) we're actually making considerably more money than ever before, and yet have less spendable cash because of our high tax bracket.

Several years ago my wife and I made a deal—I would make the money, and she would spend it! Really, we determined it was best for one of us to write the checks and man-

*age the family finances. This game plan has worked better
for us, since she is accurate and very conscientious about
paying the bills on time. She has done a much better job by
herself than we used to do* together. *We've found that our
marriage has a much more peaceful financial balance when
just one of us balances the bank account.*

If you have been experiencing financial pressures or difficulties, perhaps you could ask: "What type of budget should we
have? Should it be a weekly budget, a monthly or annual
budget, or all three?"

Once you have determined the answer to this question, you
can then ask, "How detailed should the budget be?" *This, too,
depends on the couple.*

*The key is to find a system that you both feel good about.
. . . Even if it means changing your pattern after twenty
years of marriage.*

This does not say that you should find a system of planning
that only one of you thinks is wise. It also does not say that you
are finished when you find a system that you both *think* is a
good one. The key is in the emotional response you have. You
need to find one that you both *feel* good about. A marriage is, as
you have undoubtedly come to appreciate, an emotional relationship, and you need to deal with your emotions as you are
redefining and refining your method of planning expenses.

Many couples have made the mistake of thinking that planning about money is entirely a rational process in which the most
important criteria are accuracy, accountability, logic, and effi-
ciency. If this has been your experience you have been planting
the seeds of economic success and marital failure. You need to
realize that, as important as these criteria are, the most important
criterion is the emotional reaction. An example of this comes
from a couple the authors know. The husband had coldly and
rationally decided there should be no money spent on Christmas
and birthdays one year, since the money was needed elsewhere.
From a logical and "wise" financial planning standpoint, the husband was probably correct, and he tried to stick with the plan.

The wife, however, felt he should have been named "Scrooge," and she had such an emotional reaction to the plan that the husband ended up spending as much for a marriage counselor as he had saved on his get-tough budget.

How do you plan your new budget? The first step is to identify your probable income. For some this is very easy, but those who have irregular sources of income have more difficulty. Whatever the case, you need to make some estimate of your income if you are to plan effectively. The next step in preparing a budget is to decide how much money should be spent in various areas. These projections can be fairly brief or they can be more detailed. The crucial consideration at this time is to evaluate your financial picture with your spouse so that your needs and your "feelings about your needs" can be assessed.

Her Business Too

Without doubt the most crucial financial adjustment (and subsequent marriage adjustment) occurred when we made the decision to go into business for ourselves. There were so many different things to consider, such as tight money, little job security, heavy time commitments, etc. We fasted and prayed and discussed this stepping-stone at great length. After we made the decision to proceed, it was exciting and a lot of sacrifice and hard work to budget and put it all together. As we have worked and watched the business grow from nothing, we have also been able to learn each other's dreams, ambitions, and qualities in many areas by working side by side. We've shared our frustrations, concerns, and successes, and in so doing have grown closer in our relationship.

It has always meant a great deal to me that my husband has confidence in my abilities to do things which help our business run more smoothly, for in so doing our marriage has also run more smoothly.

Remember, no plan is a plan—a plan for disaster.

THE ACTING PHASE OF THE CYCLE

The acting part of the management cycle is concerned with where you spend money for the things you need—where you actually put the money into savings accounts, pay bills, and make investments. In this step, *flexibility* is again the principle. Some couples have found a joint checking account a useful system. Others have found it best for the husband to have his checking account and the wife to have hers. One family known to the authors has about eight checking accounts, each for different purposes. Some couples prefer the "bottles in the cupboard" or "envelopes" system. In these systems, the paycheck is cashed (or the part of it which will not be paid out in checks) and the money is then put in the bottles or envelopes. When the husband or wife needs to buy something, they go to the envelopes or bottles for the funds. (In this system the source tends to dry up rapidly and unexpectedly unless the partners keep some kind of record of withdrawals and balances.) These systems are especially effective for many couples in the early months of marriage, when it is important to economize, when they have few categories of expenses, and when they want to work together.

Some couples find it effective for one partner to handle all the money while the other partner receives an "allowance." Other couples are so inept in handling money that they find it necessary to always work together to avoid making errors like forgetting to write something in the checkbook, writing down the wrong figures, adding or subtracting wrong figures, or forgetting certain bills. One couple known to the authors were so clumsy in this area that they had only two monthly statements on their checking account balance in the first fifteen years of their marriage. They relied on a "general impression" of how much money was in the bank. Their system was effective for them, but it was not accurate.

Several skills can be helpful in this phase of the management cycle. For example, being aware of when different products are on sale can help save money. Knowing how to shop efficiently for food and clothing can also help. Comparing prices before buying can result in considerable savings on items such as clothing, tools, automobiles, insurance, appliances, furniture, etc. Most importantly, we can follow the counsel of our prophet by living within our means so that we don't need to pay the costs of interest on loans or finance charges. While it is difficult to go without while we are putting the money away for something, in the long run we usually obtain what we desire and the financial savings are substantial as compared with going into debt for purchases.

THE RECORDING PHASE OF THE CYCLE

As you have undoubtedly experienced, there are many different ways to keep track of where your money is spent. Some prefer to keep a detailed set of books with journals and ledgers that help them know where everything is spent. One couple known to the authors keeps such books, and they know where every dollar in their marriage has gone. They enjoy their system and would be uncomfortable with less accountability. Other couples use other methods such as writing checks extensively and then using the returned checks to monitor how much is spent for various items. The cancelled checks are also useful as documentations of expenses in filling out deductions on income tax forms. Some couples save receipts to help them know where their money goes. A few couples rely on their memories and have an adequate system of knowing where their money is spent; but while this works for some, for most it would be like recording in the sand.

if you are a wise steward you will develop a system of keeping track that assists you in periodically evaluating what you have been doing with your funds. You then take these records into account in revising your budget plans and in knowing what you can and cannot afford. Those of you who decide not to take the extra few minutes to plan and record at all, have the benefit of freedom—you are free from the burdens of planning and recording. But unfortunately, this freedom is usually expensive, especially whenever financial resources don't go as far as they could. Without the help of any records, you must then decide which things you will have and which you will go without.*

* The ideas under the heading "The Management Cycle" were gleaned from Robert Bohn's *Budget Book*, Provo: BYU Press, 1976.

What About Indebtedness?

You may have experienced "credit nightmares," or you may have an established rule never to buy on credit. Actually, neither fire nor credit is inherently good or bad. It is what you do with them that is good or bad. You can do very effective things with fire, or you can be destroyed by it. It is the same with credit. If it is used wisely it can be useful, but if it is used unwisely it can be destructive.

As you may know, there are many different kinds of credit which can be grouped into two basic types, *open credit* and *installment credit.* In *open credit,* you receive a service or product and promise to pay for it at a later time. This is the kind of credit you get with bank cards such as VISA and Master Charge cards—if you pay the entire bill within a specified period. It is the kind of credit used by utility companies such as the telephone and gas companies. The biggest disadvantage of this type of credit is that some people cannot control their spending as easily when all they have to do is "charge it." The result is that many couples overspend.

But this type of credit can be very useful because receipts are provided for each transaction and it is easy to document where the money is spent. It is also convenient because many couples learn to pay their bills in a monthly or weekly cycle. Another advantage of this type of credit is that it can be helpful in minor emergencies. For example, having a bank card or credit card can be useful in traveling when unexpected expenses like automobile repairs or medical expenses are incurred. Those families who do not have a card or two should carry cash or travelers checks for these unexpected expenses.

With *installment credit* you purchase something on credit or get a loan and agree to pay a finance charge or interest for the privilege of paying the debt later. This is the type of credit you use in getting loans for major purchases such as automobiles, furniture, and a house. It is also the kind of credit you use when you charge more on a credit card than you can repay when the bill arrives. This type of credit is very expensive, and as you have surely come to know, the amount you pay for interest can be extremely high.

While a modest use of installment credit may be necessary, it is very easy to overuse it, because there are so many enticements to buy, buy, buy. And advertising makes things so attractive that it is easy to succumb and buy more than you need. Advertisements are designed, of course, to appeal to emotions rather than to intellect, and those who are easily persuaded need to be especially wary. An additional complication is that the unfamiliar and sometimes lengthy wording in contracts may leave the uninitiated with only a confused idea of the actual finance costs.

Most couples need to use an installment system to purchase a house, because there is seldom another feasible way. Installment credit is also useful in business transactions, because it can help you gain access to larger blocks of money or goods; and if you handle these wisely, you can pay the finance charge and still make money. Beyond these two uses, installment buying becomes very expensive.

The main point here is that it is tremendously expensive to use installment credit. With today's interest rates, you end up paying much more than the item is worth, at the same time keeping yourselves financially strapped as you pay the debt.

There are other good reasons to avoid this type of debt. One is that research has shown indebtedness to be correlated with marital miseries. Researchers are not sure whether indebtedness contributes to marital dissatisfaction or whether dissatisfaction contributes to installment buying. It is likely that the causality goes both ways. The important point is that they tend to go together, and this argues for avoiding indebtedness.

Another reason for avoiding installment buying is that the Church leaders have given very clear counsel regarding it. They have argued persuasively that Church members should avoid indebtedness except for the purchase of a house or for an emergency medical expense, etc. Typical of this advice are these admonitions:

> Avoid finance charges except for homes, education, and other vital investments. Buy consumer durables with cash. Avoid install-

ment credit and be careful with your use of credit cards. (Marvin
J. Ashton, *One for the Money,* [Salt Lake City: Deseret Book
Company, 1975], page 16.)

If you must incur debt to meet the reasonable necessities of life —
such as buying a house and furniture — then, I implore you, as you
value your solvency and happiness, buy within your means.
 So use credit wisely — to acquire an education, a farm, to own
a home. But resist the temptation to plunge into a property far
more pretentious or spacious than you really need. (Ezra Taft Ben-
son, *Speeches of the Year,* BYU Press, 1962.)

It is a rule of our financial and economic life in all the world that
interest is to be paid on borrowed money. May I say something
about interest? Interest never sleeps nor sickens nor dies; it never
goes to the hospital; it works on Sundays and holidays; it never
takes a vacation; it never visits nor travels; it takes no pleasure; it
is never laid off work nor discharged from employment; it never
works on reduced hours; it never has short crops nor droughts; it
never pays taxes; it buys no food; it wears no clothes; it is un-
housed and without home and so has no repairs, replacements, no
shingling, plumbing, painting, or whitewashing; it has neither wife,
children, father, mother, nor kinfolk to watch over and care for;
it has no love, no sympathy; it is as hard and soulless as a granite
cliff. Once in debt, interest is your companion every minute of the
day and night; you cannot shun it or slip away from it; you cannot
dismiss it; it yields neither to entreaties, demands, nor orders; and
whenever you get in its way or cross its course or fail to meet its
demands, it crushes you. (J. Reuben Clark, Jr., *Conference Report,*
1938, pages 102-103.)

HOW CAN YOU AVOID DEBT?

 You will likely agree that you should make every effort to
avoid indebtedness, but you may still find yourself making some
monthly payments on a loan or two . . . or three or four . . . or
five or six. You believe, but somehow you aren't able to attain
your ideal. There are several strategies that can help; four of
them are described below.
 Go slow. Those of you who are newlyweds should realize it
will take a few years to become established economically. You
need to acquire your house and furniture and cars slowly. Some
of you may think you need to set up your house on the same

economic level as your parents' home; after all, it is the style of life you are accustomed to. It is what you have known. You fail to realize that it took your parents twenty to twenty-five years to acquire what they have, and it ought also to take you a while. You need to realize that struggling together in the early years of married life can help build bonds and ties and love in a marital relationship. Working together for common causes and goals builds closeness. Obtaining your material possessions too rapidly by going into debt for them and then worrying about financial burdens has just the opposite effect. It is divisive and destructive. You are much better off getting by with an old clunker for a car and living with borrowed or used or handmade furniture while you save up to purchase your own. You are much worse off when you go into debt and start off "right," as you think, by getting all of the things you want. Actually it is just the opposite — this is starting off dead wrong.

Many of you in your middle age look back on the first few struggling years as the happiest years of your marriage. You "got by" with little, helped each other, and did without. Then, after you became established economically and had less mutual effort, you became more complacent, and your relationship may have lost a certain cohesion, radiance, and beauty. It is very different for couples in the first year or two of their marriage. Many of them are deeply in debt with car payments, furniture payments, house payments, and loan payments, and have a nice house, nice car, nice furniture, and nice clothing. They have the illusion that their quickly acquired and easily acquired material possessions will help their marriage. Unfortunately, they also have depressing times paying their bills and arguing about finances, while secretly blaming each other or someone else for their troubles. They have the Midas touch: they have turned their lives into material success, and *unknown to them*, it is destroying the things they care about most.

The wise go slowly in obtaining material possessions.

As the scripture says in another context (D&C 10:4), you should not try to run faster or labor more than you have means to do.

Pay yourselves second. Even though this may be a rerun for the forty-fifth time, the first thing a Latter-day Saint couple should do with income is set aside 10 percent as tithing. They should "pay the Lord first" and do so with a willing heart. Those of you who have the attitude of paying tithing because you want to, receive many blessings. You become more generous and kind and charitable. You also feel better about yourselves and thereby increase your self-esteem. The Lord has indicated that the windows of heaven are opened to bless you. As you have each found, your attitude toward your giving makes more difference than the giving, because when you give grudgingly you deprive yourselves of many of the blessings. (Moroni 7:6-8.)

The next thing you should do in refining your financial posture is to allocate money to a savings program. You ought to "pay yourselves" second, and 10 percent is a good figure to put aside in a savings program. It will allow you to build up and maintain enough savings that you can avoid installment credit, and many of you who are earning ordinary incomes can put part of the savings into an investment program that will gradually provide more and more income. If you can't take 10 percent out at the time, you ought to take 8 or 5 percent *but have a continuous substantial savings program.* If you first take out 10 percent for tithing and 10 percent for savings, you then need to adjust your standard of living so that you can live on the remaining 80 percent. This is a very different strategy from thinking 100 percent of your income is available to spend, and then taking out the tithing and savings last. Most couples who do this find that they don't pay tithing or accumulate savings.

Have specialized savings programs. Some couples have found it useful to have different savings programs. For example, they may have one account for investments such as stocks, bonds, land, or gold purchases. This can be used for income later or as part of a retirement program. They may also have an account for major expenses that occur infrequently, such as a savings account for Christmas and vacations. It is also a good idea to have a savings account of five hundred dollars or a thousand dollars that is for emergencies. Then, when the water heater goes out, the transmission on the car needs rebuilding, or you need a new refrigerator, rug, washer, TV, or whatever, you can use your emergency account. As you have probably found out, this usually saves 10 to 30 percent on the cost of the major item you are purchasing, as compared with taking out a loan.

Buy quality. When you are buying major items such as furniture, tools, appliances, and equipment, it is wise to purchase quality merchandise when you are ready to buy. Some couples learn this the hard way when they are first married. They see furniture store ads offering to "furnish three rooms for five hundred dollars" or get other "package" programs in which they seem to receive a lot of items for the money. These packages usually have the lowest quality possible. The goods are made to look attractive while they are new, but they wear out or break very quickly. Most of the time you would have been better off to accumulate a few items of good quality at a time, and live a little longer in a furnished apartment or with borrowed or hand-me-down items.

Buying Wisely

Many resources can help you be intelligent consumers. For example, you can take courses on money management. Also there are increasing numbers of television programs that describe effective and ineffective consumer skills. In addition, some literature can help. This includes periodicals such as *Consumer Reports.* It also includes pamphlets such as the series prepared by Household Finance.

The most important consumer skill is the ability to obtain information about alternatives and then evaluate the information in terms of your personal values, goals, interests, and tastes. This means that you need to be alert to trends and innovations, be informed, and be able to compare the advantages and disadvantages of different options.

Teach Your Children

It is important that you begin early to teach your children how to manage their money. In Elder Marvin J. Ashton's book

One for the Money he lists twelve points of successful money management, four of which deal with things you should do in teaching children. He suggests that you should:

1. Teach family members early the importance of working and earning.
2. Teach children to make money decisions in keeping with their capacities to comprehend.
3. Teach each family member to contribute to the total family welfare.
4. Teach family members to pay financial obligations promptly as part of integrity and honesty development.

Preschoolers can acquire many useful skills in handling money. For example, they can learn that choices need to be made among desirable things. You can't always get all the candy and movies you want and have money left over for birthday presents. Young children can be given allowances, or they can be hired for certain jobs by parents or neighbors. In addition, you can work out a system with your children wherein they pay a certain percentage of certain purchases. For example, when an elementary age child wants a bicycle, doll house or baseball glove, you can agree to pay for a certain percentage of the cost. The proportion should be adjusted to what the child can earn in a reasonable time. A seven-year-old may be able to pay 5 or 10 percent of a new bicycle, and a twelve-year-old may be able to pay 50 percent of a new stereo or desk. Learning to earn one's own way is important.

One effective system with young children is to use a group of containers for banks. Small bottles or cans with lids can be used. They can be labeled according to the categories you and your child find useful, such as Tithing, Savings, Presents, Free Spending (you have no say), and Supervised Spending (you and your child agree). Just as with the parents, there can be several bottles that are specialized savings accounts — one for a mission, one for a vacation, and one for special purchases.

Summary

This chapter has discussed the importance of and some of the skills associated with effective money management. The cycle of management was discussed — the process of planning, acting, and recording, repeated again and again. Skills in consumership were also discussed, as were the wise and unwise uses of credit. In addition, the importance of teaching children money management was also considered.

Even though many of you may have found this topic non-applicable, most couples can profit from a financial review in their marriage; hence the rationale for inclusion of this topic here.

Would you now walk out of your marital doors and consider the influence and impact others have on your marital relationship.

Therefore shall a man leave his
father and his mother, and shall
cleave unto his wife.
(Genesis 2:24.)

10

Friends are thieves of time.
(Francis Bacon.)

Surrounded by Significant Others

As you consider the title to this chapter, and then as you reflect upon the seemingly contradictory quotes above, perhaps you are asking yourself just what is the true message the authors are attempting to convey. If your interest is kindled and your ears are tickled, then read on.

Marriage does not exist in a social vacuum. It is a delicate social system that is closely tied to a larger network of other systems. For example, you interact as a married couple with relatives, schools, hospitals, employment, neighborhoods, and Church groups. Each of these outer systems has an influence on your marriage, as depicted in the following diagram. You can easily see that there are more forces influencing your marriage relationship than you may have previously considered. It is important not only to know these outside forces exist, but also to realize how much intrusion each (or all) of them can have upon your marital relationship.

As you consider these outside influences, perhaps you could label them (a) have to have, (b) nice to have, and (c) eternally essential to have. Quickly you begin to get the message. You know family is eternal, and that friendships also are lasting. You also know that you cannot conceivably divide yourself equally in all directions and hope to salvage any "emotional time" for your spouse. If you understand this, then what must you do to insure yourself against starving your marriage while interacting with these forces? Do you pick and choose and ignore some forces? No, that's really not possible. You don't have the freedom to ignore them, and you wouldn't want to if you could. These social networks or forces provide essential services, helping you attain your goals. *What you need to do is learn how these networks influence your marriage relationship and how you can interact effectively with them.* And thus you see the goal of this chapter.

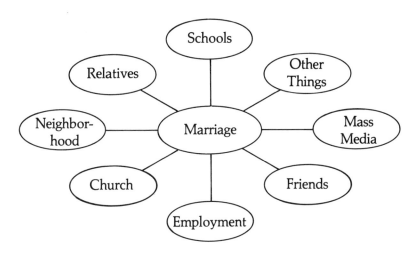

The Golden Mean

There is a general principle, discovered by Aristotle about two thousand years ago, that can help you in your quest for understanding how little or how much you should interact with these forces for the benefit of your marriage. Aristotle suggested that one crucial key to the good life is to avoid going to extremes; that too much or too little of certain things tend to be detrimental, and one is usually better off by staying with the middle of the road. He called it the "golden mean."

While it is obvious that you should not seek the golden mean in some areas of life (such as limiting your "honesty" to just so much, but no more), still you should do it in many areas. The authors feel that normally the golden mean is appropriate whenever a situation involves an investment of *time, effort, energy,* or *emphasis.* An example of this is the degree to which you interact with friends. It takes time and energy to interact with them, so moderation is wise.

The golden mean is very useful in your learning how to interact with the social networks around you. The general rule is that even though you need to be involved with each of the areas mentioned above, you need to discuss with your spouse the optimal amount and then not over-involve yourself in these areas. It is perhaps wise to understand that you should be involved with some of these areas more than others, and this will change as you move from one stage of life to another. For example, when you retire you will become less involved with employment, but during the years when your children are between six and eighteen you will be highly involved with education. You need to continually evaluate each of the separate areas to determine the golden mean in each of them.

It would be good now to look more closely at each of these areas to gain an additional insight into their nature and your relationship to them.

INTERACTION WITH RELATIVES

The scriptures provide a few guidelines as to how you ought to relate to your relatives. At the beginning of marriage the partners should leave their fathers and mothers and set up a separate home of their own. "Therefore shall a man leave his father and his mother, and shall cleave unto his wife: and they shall be one flesh." (Genesis 2:24.) President Spencer W. Kimball has elaborated on this teaching in discussing some of the ways you ought to cleave and not cleave:

> Sometimes in marriage there are other cleavings, in spite of the fact that the Lord said, "Thou shalt love thy wife with all thy heart, and shalt cleave unto her and none else" (D&C 42:22).
>
> This means just as completely that "thou shalt love thy *husband* with all thy heart and shall cleave unto *him* and none else." Frequently, people continue to cleave unto their mothers and their fathers and their friends. Sometimes mothers will not relinquish the hold they have had upon their children, and husbands as well as wives return to their mothers and fathers for advice and counsel and to confide; whereas cleaving should be to the wife or husband in the most things, and all intimacies should be kept in great secrecy and privacy from others.
>
> Couples do well to immediately find their own home, separate and apart from that of the in-laws on either side. The home may be very modest and unpretentious, but still it is an independent domicile. Their married life should become independent of her folks and his folks. The couple love their parents more than ever; they cherish their counsel; they appreciate their association; but they must live their own lives, being governed by their own decisions, by their own prayerful considerations after they have received the counsel from those who should give it. To cleave does not mean merely to occupy the same home; it means to adhere closely, to stick together. (*Marriage and Divorce*, pages 24-25.)

The intricate balance suggested here is beautiful. You ought to leave your parents and be independent from them—to stand on your own four feet as a couple; but it is not wise to become *too* independent. The principles of the patriarchal order still operate. You ought to seek counsel by asking your parents what they think about some of the major decisions you face in life. You ought to have the freedom to go against the advice if you wish, but their views should be taken into account as you make decisions.

As Malachi taught (Malachi 4:6), the hearts of fathers and mothers are to be turned to their children and the hearts of the children are to be turned to their fathers and mothers. This means that there should be strong bonds of family affection and love that last through the eternities. It means that parents and children should interact, visit, and do things together in ways that will promote good feelings and love and harmony. It does not mean that married couples need to spend all of their time with their relatives. It means that an optimal involvement is *some* interaction, *some* concern, and *some* attention, but not so much that it interferes with the other aspects of life that also compete for your attention, effort, and energy.

Cementing—By Becoming Unglued

My wife was not active in the Church until some years after we were married, and I feel the turning point came when we moved away from our families to the Midwest. Neither of us had any relatives in the new area, nor did we know anyone, so it was up to us for conversation, activity, and reliance for support. We truly became a family unit.

As I look back on this time, I recognize it was the breaking of family ties—ties that were so close they tied our marriage in continual knots—that gave us the impetus to get to know each other and to become active in the Church. After a period of time we returned to live in our home town, and then we had our spiritual life together, and we began a fresh and rewarding relationship with our families, knowing that keeping a little distance between us and those families only served to enrich our own marriage as well as our relationships with our parents and other family members.

Sometimes it is not relatives who prevent you from having a desirable type of interaction. The problem may be yourself or your spouse. For example, one of you may find it very difficult to cut the apron strings. You go to the family home regularly, depend on the opinions of your parents, or rely on them for affection and love. As you progress by dealing creatively with your problems, you must remember that different solutions work for different couples. For example, it may be that one individual remains overly dependent on his or her parents because the spouse does not meet important needs of affection, security, or tenderness. In other situations, making the break is merely a matter of forcing oneself to take the last step in growing up. A good way to do it would be to move a long distance away from one's parents to correct the problem. Each of you needs to determine where you are in this dimension of your life, what you need to do, and what will help you progress and grow.

THE WORLD OF WORK

Since very few people inherit enough wealth that they can go through life without an occupation, each marriage needs someone to provide economic necessities. The traditional pattern is for the husband to be the provider. Even so, you need to be careful not to underestimate the ways in which the wife has also been traditionally involved in providing economic necessities. A century ago the wife worked long hours to help with these necessities—spinning, canning, baking, tanning leathers, caring for animals such as chickens and cows to provide eggs and milk. She spent many hours each week washing and ironing clothes, sewing, mending, curing meats, tending gardens, and preparing meals for the hired help as well as the family. Most pioneer girls and women also found themselves in the fields helping with the work, especially in the planting and harvesting seasons.

Hence the traditional pattern was for the husband to be the main provider but for the wife to assist in many, many ways. This complemented the other division of labor wherein the wife had the primary responsibility for rearing the children and the husband assisted in that task in many, many ways.

As today's society has become industrialized and urbanized and has developed an advanced technology, there have been many important changes. The provider roles used to be carried out at home or close to the home, but now the home and the work place are generally separate. One leaves home to go to work, and the work world and home life seldom mix. This means that the typical father is away from the wife and children most of the time. Also, many of the things that used to be done in the home can now be done much more efficiently elsewhere. For example, home baking, quilting, canning, and sewing are fast becoming more expensive and inefficient than their commercial counterparts (though quality and nutrition may still be the determinants in some cases). This means such home activities may well become luxuries or hobbies which could actually drain economic resources rather than add to them. Such a situation makes it much more difficult for the wife to make significant economic contributions while also staying home where she can care for the children. (Despite such trends, the need for the skills in an emergency of course requires that they be acquired in normal times.)

What do all these changes mean?

What are their implications for your modern roles?

How can you effectively team up as husband and wife to provide the economic necessities, while you are also doing your most important task of rearing a family wisely?

The following five suggestions are offered:

1. *Keep your priorities straight.* Whatever you do in providing your economic necessities, you need to remember that there are several different roles that each of you must perform as a marriage partner. And you must perform all these roles at what is at least a minimal level of adequacy. You cannot afford to work so hard at one or two that the others are inadequately dealt with. Some *essential* roles are these:

1. You each need to seek first that spiritual level that will assure your *exaltation* in the kingdom of God.
2. You need to maintain a harmonious, loving, pleasant relationship in your *marriage.*
3. You need to rear your *children* so they will become good Saints and citizens, able to love others, earn a livelihood, and assume the responsibilities of adulthood.
4. You need to provide *service* to others by being involved in Church programs such as missionary, genealogy, and welfare work, and at the same time provide service in your neighborhood and community.
5. You need to provide the *economic necessities* for your family. This does not mean that you have to "keep up with the Joneses." "Necessities" means modest housing, comfortable clothing, nutritious food, adequate education, essential medical care, etc. They do not include luxuries such as fine carpets, TVs, stereos, newer cars, boats, cam-

pers, vacations, etc. Luxuries such as these are fine, but you should in any case not be concerned about them until the five essential roles are performed adequately.

Those who spend so much time in their provider roles that the other roles are inadequately performed need to rearrange their priorities. The father who works two or three jobs to provide things that are really luxuries is probably not adequately performing his husband or father role, since these other roles take a great deal of time, energy, commitment, and interaction. The father involved in a profession such as medicine, business, management, law, or teaching who works long hours or is away from home a great deal may be very successful financially, but he may discover years later that he was a failure in several other areas that ultimately count more.

If you keep your priorities in order, many of the following suggestions will take care of themselves.

2. *Avoid too much or too little time on the job.* Few people can provide for their family if they work less than full time — forty hours a week. Even so, many couples experience great stress when the husband has workaholic tendencies. If this is an issue in your marriage, then it would be well for you to sit down, discuss your feelings, and try to resolve your problem.

3. *Be creative in the way the wife assists in the provider role.* You need to be creative in evaluating your abilities, needs, personalities, and preferences and then work out the best arrangement for your family. In most homes, the best arrangement is to have the husband be the main provider and have the wife assist him, while she has the primary responsibility for the children, assisted by him.

How, though, should the wife assist?

Some wives assist in inappropriate ways. For example, the wife may spend a lot of time shopping to find the best bargains. She may spend two hours and three dollars worth of gasoline to save thirty-five cents on some green beans and sixty-five cents on fifty pounds of flour. Or she may spend a lot of time baking bread when the bread of the same quality can be bought less expensively at a store. Or the wife may can fruits and vegetables or make homemade quilts, when the economic gain might be as small as fifteen or twenty-five cents an hour for her work. *These would not be wise ways* to have the wife assist in the provider role. In other situations, these same behaviors might be economically wise, and you would be ahead by having the wife bake and sew and can; or you might feel that the better quality of the home product justifies the effort and expense. The answer is that you ought to examine these various activities rather than simply assume them to be natural roles for women. You need to examine them in terms of their economic value and the woman's personal interests and abilities (especially the ability and the equipment to perform these tasks in an emergency situation), and the family's tastes, ties and then decide together which roles are appropriate in your given circumstances.

In some homes, the best arrangement may be for the husband to become more involved in the housekeeping chores and for the wife to run a small business in the couple's home. In other situations, the temperament and abilities of the couple may be such that the husband should concentrate on being the provider and the wife should use the time not required for her homemaker, wife, and mother roles, in service activities that provide financial gain. In still other situations, the wife may make a financial contribution by the sale of literature or music she writes at home. Some couples may find it useful to have the wife work in a part-time job at a time when the husband can be at home caring for the children. Some couples can work out arrangements in which the wife can be highly involved in the provider role. For example, the husband and wife may each have a Ph.D. degree and the two of them may occupy one professorial position in a university. They can then arrange their roles so both teach and do research and both are involved in the parenting and housekeeping roles.

How creative are you? What innovations can you make?

We are limited only by ourselves.
The sky is the limit.

What you need to do is *keep your priorities in a proper order*, and then kick off the fetters of traditions that were appropriate for earlier and different times but are inappropriate for you. You can then be creative and innovative in arranging your unique patterns of providing for yourselves.

It is challenging to think of the innovative minds of the pioneer and early Church leaders. Joseph Smith inaugurated a women's organization in 1842. Brigham Young organized cities with wide and straight streets. The early Saints rebelled against some of the religious traditions of the time by promoting singing and dancing. The women in Utah Territory were the first women in the United States to vote. The early Saints were not afraid to innovate. They were creative and bold and faced their challenges with a willingness to "do things differently."

Even so, while you are being creative, you need to continually remember to keep your priorities straight. Your top priority should be your personal growth toward godhood, and your second should be to adequately perform your spouse and parental responsibilities. *Your creativity in arranging your provider roles should be directed toward helping you meet these eternal needs.*

4. *Have a back-up plan.* It is wise to have some well-designed plans for what to do if unusual emergencies were to arise. For example, what would you do if the husband were to become physically disabled, so that he couldn't provide a living? What would you do if the husband were to pass away? What would you do if sickness or accident were to keep the wife from making the financial contribution that you expect?

Women are encouraged to become educated and trained. This is wise, because then a wife will have an occupational skill she can fall back on if something happens to her husband. The advice fits in well with several other truths. Social sciences research indicates that marriages are usually better if the couple wait until they are well into their twenties before marrying. This gives both the man and the woman time to spend the first few years out of high school preparing for meaningful and rewarding occupational roles. The wife may not be active in this role while there are small children in the home, but she has the capability of doing it if needed.

5. *Be willing to rearrange your provider roles at different stages of the life cycle.* You have different needs at different

stages of your lives. Most people have a great need for financial resources when they are initially setting up a home and are raising their children. Needs are fewer after the children are gone. These changes provide the opportunity for you to have unusual methods of providing for yourselves. For example, you may want to have the husband and wife both work for several years after the children are reared, and then save the extra money. You may then both quit work for a period of time and do something different, such as go on a mission, travel, study, or develop artistic skills. Young couples will want to have both the husband and wife work until the first child arrives, and this helps them to acquire the resources for furniture or a down payment on a house. In this, however, there is a danger if you become accustomed to two incomes but need to cut back to one income after a child is born—you may find the cut very difficult. One way to avoid this problem is to have the second income earmarked exclusively for major purchases such as cars, housing, or furniture so you don't get used to "living on" the two incomes. Another possibility is to make provisions so that the wife can work inside the home after the child comes, if she desires. Even though you may be past this stage in your own marriage, it is sound advice for your children when they marry.

CHURCH ACTIVITY

The Church is another part of the social network, and it is imperative that you become involved and active in it. We are commanded to "meet together often" (D&C 20:75), and there we "teach one another" (D&C 88:118). In practical terms this means that families have several meetings on Sunday—priesthood meeting, Relief Society, Young Women, Primary, Sunday School, and sacrament meeting. In addition, one evening during the week may be set aside to attend other meetings. These include presidency meetings, planning meetings, Scout meetings, home teaching, visiting teaching, etc. If you are "seeking first the kingdom of God," you also become involved in a number of other religious activities. You involve yourself in missionary work, genealogical research, temple work, the welfare program, and firesides. You also study the scriptures regularly and "pray continually."

> *Is it possible that the golden mean should*
> *operate in the religious part of life too?*

> *Can you become too involved or too*
> *uninvolved in Church activities?*

In a sense we can say that the golden mean is involved in this area of married life, but there is a difference. We cannot plan service in the kingdom merely on a basis of preference or convenience, for example, as we can in the case of purely social activities. The Lord has indicated that we ought all to be "anxiously engaged in a good cause" (D&C 58:27). Some persons never become anxious or engaged enough, while others may be too anxious and too engaged to provide religious balance, at least in some areas. You need to exercise moderation, wisdom, and good judgment in continually monitoring how much you are and ought to be doing. This is one reason why Church members are being reoriented to spending more time and effort with their families.

Prior to the 1980 change in meeting schedules, many ward and stake leaders had the best intentions in leaving home early Sunday morning to be involved in Church activities all day. Unfortunately, many who did this were seriously abusing the Lord's instructions that his day is to be a day of rest. Some of the same people were then away from their homes so much during the week that they neglected their other responsibilities. Too often, a few years of excessive Church service drove a wedge between a husband and wife or between parents and children, and they were never able to recover. Unfortunately, it was usually family life that paid the highest prices when a person became too involved in Church activities. The husband-wife relationship withered, and the wife was left with more than her share of parental responsibilities.

If this pattern involved merely an occasional individual who got carried away, it could be mentioned in passing and few would need to be concerned. Unfortunately, however, it has become a common theme among Latter-day Saints — so common, for example, that jokes about the incorrigible "bishop's kids" are a normal part of LDS humor. The General Authorities have become so concerned about this that in 1978 they issued a number of directives to local leaders asking them to curtail the number of meetings held and to be more efficient in the ones that are held so that leaders will be able to fulfill their family and other responsibilities.

Later, in early 1980, a new Sunday meeting schedule was announced by the Church. The new schedule is designed to resolve some of the conflicting demands on members' time, and it is now easier to be more responsible for one's own stewardship of time and be better able to handle Church callings as well as family and other duties. It is still possible to be over-committed, however, and precautions are still necessary.

So . . . What can you do about it?

Here are several suggestions:

First: Evaluate. When you have evaluation and planning sessions for your marriage and family life (annual, monthly, or whatever), you ought to devote some time to this topic. You ought to determine how much you each are involved in the various aspects of Church activity and see whether you are too involved or too uninvolved in specific areas. For example, you may be overly busy in genealogical work or some other activity and not enough in something else. You ought also to look at the overall picture of your religious activity to determine if it is a desirable amount — whether it is too much or too little in the light of your family situation and other important needs.

Second: Listen to others. Sometimes you can get carried away and not realize it. Sometimes you can keep yourself more balanced if you ask for and then listen to someone else's opinion about how you are doing. Your spouse, your friends, and sometimes your children will see patterns that you don't, and if you are open to their suggestions, they may help.

Third: Learn to sacrifice but not overdo it. Your involvement in Church activities is different from employment. In the latter place you spend time so that you can *receive* something —

money; you get as well as give. But in religious activity, you can simply give without concerning yourself with getting. It is important that you lose yourself in the service of others, that you extend yourself, that you give (even until it hurts a little), that you sacrifice. Your sacrificing, however, needs to be monitored so that you don't neglect other important things such as your marriage or your children.

Fourth: Share information with presiding officials. Sometimes presiding officials such as bishops or stake presidents talk with you about assuming additional Church callings. The usual pattern is for the presiding officer, before extending a call, to ask how the person would feel about a particular calling. Such moments are very important in the management of this part of your life. The presiding official is seeking information about how you feel, what you think, what is going on in your home and life. If your response conceals crucial information, he may extend a call that is not good for you. For example, you may say something like, "Oh, things are going pretty well," or "I feel good about the jobs I have now"; while the truth of the matter is that one of the partners is not well, or that things are pretty hectic in the home and you are struggling to get everything done. This is unfair to your leader and is unwise management of the stewardship you have over your own life. You ought to explain how you really feel and what you really think, and if you think your marriage or family life is suffering from the demands you already have, you ought to say so. When you do share such information, it helps the presiding official make wise decisions about his stewardship, and he may or may not extend a call in these circumstances.

Fifth: What if you don't agree with the call? Sometimes you have heard that you should never say no to a Church call. It is interesting that this myth persists in the LDS culture even though it never appears in official Church publications and the General Authorities counsel against it. The counsel of the Brethren is that you ought to fast and pray about these decisions yourself and receive *your own answer* from the Lord about callings rather than always automatically accept a call. Fortunately, most of the time your feelings will be the same as those of the presiding official, and you will learn from your prayers that the call is what the Lord wants you to do. In some situations, however, for a variety of reasons, your answer may be different from that of your presiding authority. When this happens you ought to discuss your feelings with him and then perhaps fast and pray together, sharing your feelings honestly and openly. Most of the time these differences can be reconciled, and you will both feel good about the outcome. Only rarely will a difference persist. When it does, you are still the one who is responsible for your own life. Your life is *your* stewardship. It is not your leader's, and you ought to decide in accordance with the dictates of your conscience.

In summary, it is important that you manage the religious activity in your life. You need to monitor what you are doing and compare it with your beliefs as to what you ought to do. You should listen to the counsel of your loved ones to help you decide what to do, and you should be "anxiously" involved in building up the kingdom of God. Therefore you should do your part by being involved in considerable activity but not so much that other legitimate concerns suffer.

VOLUNTEER ORGANIZATIONS

There are many volunteer organizations that compete for your time, money, and participation. The following list identifies some of them:

— Service clubs (Lions, Sertoma, Rotary, Kiwanis, Elks, etc.)
— Labor unions
— The Red Cross
— Professional associations
— Political parties
— Boy Scouts and Girl Scouts
— YMCA and YWCA
— Leisure clubs like hiking, skiing, swimming, backpacking
— United Fund drive or specialized drives such as cancer or heart
— PTA
— Racquetball clubs
— Country clubs

—Missionary reunions
—Family organizations
—Little league
—Hobby clubs, such as model building, model trains
—Jogging clubs
—Health spas
—Fraternities or sororities

As in all other parts of the social network around marriage, it is easy to become too involved in some of these volunteer organizations. Sometimes you begin with a little activity in one of them and soon find yourself committing more and more of your time. You are elected to office and are then responsible for some of what occurs. Typically the office demands more time and energy than you thought it would, but you realize that it is important to a number of other people. Gradually you are swept into more and more involvement, until one day you realize that you are more involved than you really ought to be. You then cut back, painfully. Many go through this cycle over and over again by adjusting their activities, gradually becoming too involved again, and having to readjust to cutting back.

Others have a different challenge. They don't ever get involved in these organizations, but remain on the sidelines, isolated, lonely, and alienated. They need to become involved in some of these associations as part of being good citizens who are making contributions to others. This is a secondary benefit from the consolidated Church meeting schedule. Members are now more free to participate in community involvement.

The key is:

Establish an optimal amount of involvement in these activities—not too much, not too little; enough that you are involved in a helpful way, but not so much that it interferes with other important parts of your life.

FRIENDSHIPS

Most people have a network of close friends, and it is important to spend some time with them. Some are "couple" friendships, while others are men that the husband likes to associate with and women the wife enjoys as separate friends.

Parting . . . For Good

About six weeks after we were married, we were invited to a young marrieds' party. It was our first social as a married couple, so we were excited about going.

There were twelve couples attending the party, which began by our becoming acquainted over a superbly prepared candlelight dinner. As we finished eating, we casually made our way into the living room, all the while thoroughly enjoying the sharing with our new neighbors and friends.

Then it happened! One of the men told a "funny" story about his wife. It made her look very foolish, and she immediately flushed with embarrassment. Affected completely by what her husband had said in jest, this lady spent the rest of the evening without so much as even opening her mouth.

As could be expected, that story led to another by a second husband. Not to be outdone, he waded into a personally embarrassing experience that should have belonged solely to his wife. Her reaction was altogether different from that of the first wife, as she topped her husband with a degrading story about him. That was that, and the games were on for the rest of the evening. Each husband tried to outdo the others with stories proving his wife was more stupid than the last. The wives reacted in various ways—all negative.

We were stunned, to say the least. These were good people, happily married, and by all appearance of sterling quality. Without wanting to appear prudish we made several attempts to change the subject, or at least the mood, but to no avail. Finally, unable to endure more, we left.

As we left, we discussed the experience at length, deciding that we would try to avoid that kind of action toward each other. As the years have passed, we can happily say that in this we have succeeded. We have tried to compliment and build one another in front of others, including our children. Even our closest personal friends and co-workers have never heard anything about our personal conflicts or problems, or about things that may have annoyed one about the other.

This has helped us build a relationship of love and trust. We've had difficulties to work out and problems to solve, but we've done it together without outside interference. We've never had to worry about what others knew about us or our personal lives, and even more important, we have remained best friends.

Research on friendship networks has discovered several facts, one of which is consistent with the golden mean principle: You can have too many *or* too few friends. If you have too few, you tend to be lonely, and if you have too many, you tend to be strained and uncomfortable. You feel that you "can't get everything done" that you have to do.

The optimal number of friends is also related to the kind of relationship you have with your spouse. If you have a marital relationship in which your spouse is a close "friend," the optimal number of same-sex friends is lower than if you have less companionship with your spouse. It is as though there is a certain amount of *sociability* that all people need, and you can meet your socializing needs in several different ways.

Those who have a lot of companionate interaction in their marriage don't need as much interaction with friends. In fact, having a lot of friends would be a problem because they wouldn't have enough hours in the day to interact with both spouse and friends. Those who have less companionate interaction in the marriage usually feel a need to find someone outside of the marriage to be close to as a friend.

There is some evidence that these patterns change at different stages of the life cycle. Typically, newly married couples have highly companionate marriages. They spend a lot of time with each other, and friends tend to take a back seat in the relationship. Later, after a couple has several children and the marriage is stabilized, many couples have less companionate interaction with each other. Those who compensate for these changes by interacting more with friends remain happy with their marriage and their life situation in general. Those who do not seek out other ways of meeting their friendship needs tend to be less satisfied with their marriage and their life.

This illustrates that the golden mean applies to more than just the social networks outside of marriage. You need to evaluate how much energy, time, and interaction you have in your marital relationship and in your parental relationship as well as in the networks outside your family. Then, when you have a feeling for your total interests and demands, you can determine whether you are at the optimal mean for you.

The golden mean in your life . . . now.

All of this discussion about the golden mean and social networks is useful, but so far it has been all discussion and no action.

How can you use this information right now in your life?

AN ACTION PLAN

There are three things you can do, as a couple, to incorporate all of the ideas just discussed:

First, you can sit down alone or with your companion and write down some specific situations in which the golden mean can help you solve problems in your lives. As you do this, you can keep in mind the areas of relatives, employment, friends, schools, Church participation, etc.

Second, you can have a "couple home evening" by the fire and there evaluate your social involvements right now to determine how they are influencing you both and how satisfied you both are with them.

Third, if there are areas in which one or both partners are less than satisfied, you can discuss ways to bring the areas into a comfortable balance for you both.

Summary

The idea of being surrounded by many varied "significant others" has been introduced, in context with how these outside influences bear down upon your marriage. The golden mean concept developed by Aristotle was identified, and several ways of using it were then presented to you.

The bottom line for you to remember at this time is that you *must monitor your interaction with these outside forces* in a way that will allow your marriage relationship to grow rather than to be crowded out, wither, and ultimately die.

Would you now please tuck these ideas and issues into your marital pocket, with the expectation that they will be pulled out and evaluated from time to time.

You are now ready to turn a crucial corner in your reading experience and explore one of the most sacred areas in marriage —that is, the intimacy you are experiencing and the manner in which this intimacy is governed by and centered upon an eternal perspective.

And they shall be one
flesh.
(Genesis 2:24.)

11

Intimacy in an Eternal Perspective

Without question, one of the most vital spokes in the marriage wheel is that of physical intimacy. For this reason, and since many LDS couples find themselves groping in the clouds of misunderstanding that creep unknowingly into their homes, the authors feel that all Latter-day Saint married partners can benefit from a discussion of this nature.

As you reflect upon this area of *your* marriage, you have undoubtedly seen an increase in knowledge and understanding during the years you have been married, and therefore have crystallized many insights and notions. It is hoped that this discussion will deepen even further your insight into marital intimacy and then serve as an additional impetus to help you enjoy a mutually rewarding and fulfilling physical environment in which warmth and trust and acceptance flourish.

Perhaps a word could be said regarding the sensitive way in which you, as a married couple, should approach this subject. While it may be difficult for you to believe, many couples avoid *any* discussion of this part of their marriage for fear they are violating some moral or religious ethic. This is simply not so! As a married couple, you should feel free, even compelled, to reverently discuss marital intimacy with each other. Too many couples waltz through years of married life while each partner holds misconceptions, misunderstandings, and varied expectations of his or her own as well as of the other spouse's intimate behavior. It is the intent of the authors to sensitively explore this area, with the hopes that you, as a couple, will arrive at a consensus in this personal and sacred part of marriage.

Why Should You Discuss Intimacy Now?

While other reasons may exist, it appears to the authors that there are four primary reasons or justifications for discussing marital intimacy with couples who are married, regardless of how many years have passed since the honeymoon.

First: You are being bombarded with misinformation about sex which needs to be corrected.

Our society is passing through a unique historical period. During the Puritan and Victorian periods, it almost seems as if the existence of sex was often denied, and certainly some inappropriately repressive views about it were common. For example, the view prevailed that sexual intercourse is a necessary evil that should simply be "tolerated," and that it is the man's right and the woman's duty. The twentieth century has experienced a reaction against these excessive views. Unfortunately, this reaction has done more than just correct the errors of the past. Like a pendulum swinging too far, we have moved into a period of excessive permissiveness, where sex is flaunted and portrayed and abused. It is crucial that LDS couples stand fast and firm rather than allow themselves to be tossed to and fro with every wind of worldly beliefs and practices. We need to avoid the extreme views of the Puritan and Victorian eras, but we need to also avoid the hedonistic extremes of our own sexually "liberated" times. To do this we need to identify an eternal perspective on sexuality.

Second: Seek after that which is lovely and praiseworthy.

The thirteenth article of faith states that members should seek after that which is "virtuous, lovely, or of good report or praiseworthy." This is true in the sexual area as much as in any other part of life. Biological, medical, and social scientists have been discovering new information in many different areas of life, and just as these discoveries are welcomed when they deal with farming skills, management processes, technology, and so on, so we should receive them when they deal with the sexual part of life. You need to follow this article of faith, to look to the sciences for additional information about sexuality too, and then use that information *whenever it is consistent with revealed truths.*

Third: Avoid apostate beliefs concerning sexuality.

There are members of the Church who have naively accepted the belief that the physical part of the body is evil and debasing and should be shunned and avoided. This belief dates back to ancient philosophies, and continues to exist in several modern cultures. It springs from the concept that the mind or the spirit is the more pure or righteous part of man, and the physical body is the seat of evil things such as passions and corrupting influences. This has led people to want to enhance the mental or spiritual parts while avoiding physical pleasures. From this it was a short step to defining the sexual part of man as primarily a part of the physical body rather than of the spirit, thereby labeling sexuality as evil, carnal, and undesirable. This belief was incorporated into early Christian traditions and has unfortunately crept into the minds and hearts of some Latter-day Saints as well.

The debasing view that the physical body is something low and that sexuality in marriage is unholy or evil is incompatible with revealed truths about the nature of man. The restored gospel teaches that each of us is a temple (1 Corinthians 3:16-17), and that, since the physical body was made in the image of God, it is glorious and desirable. We are born innocent and pure. Then, as we grow up, we learn to do wrong and thereby become fallen. But evils in us are not confined to the physical body.

They arise in the heart and mind and spirit, and then our bodies may become victims of our unrighteousness rather than the source of it. In its mortal state, the physical body is subject to a variety of frailties and imperfections, but normal sexual drives and feelings are not in this category. The Lord gave us sexuality and commanded us to use it for his eternal purposes—and he called his work good (Genesis 1:31). Can we do any less? The Lord has cautioned us against viewing good things as evil: ". . . do not judge that which is evil to be of God, or that which is good and of God to be of the devil." (Moroni 7:14.)

Fourth: The sexual part of marriage is a crucial part.

A final reason we should deal with sexuality openly is that it is not a trivial area which you can ignore. It is a very important part of marriage. As Elder Hugh B. Brown has written:

> Many marriages have been wrecked on the dangerous rocks of ignorance and debased sex behavior, both before and after marriage. Gross ignorance on the part of newlyweds on the subject of the proper place and functioning of sex results in much unhappiness and many broken homes. (*You and Your Marriage* [Salt Lake City: Bookcraft, Inc., 1960], page 73.)

You will agree that it is important to learn about money management, how to get along with in-laws, child rearing, affection, and tenderness, because these are important areas of marriage. You will also agree that if you are inept or unskilled in these areas it can disrupt the marriage relationship. Is it any less so in the sexual area? Many marriage partners did not learn about the sexual aspect of life from their parents or peers. Many Church members are converts who grew up in undesirable settings and learned many unwholesome beliefs and practices about sexuality. In addition, everyone is exposed to horrible practices in the mass media in which the man is to be the agressor and the woman pursued, and the woman is to be sought for the gratification of the man. Almost all TV and movie scripts teach that seduction, hiding information about genuine feelings, exploitation, and partial truths are the best way to have physically intimate interaction. They also teach that all that is needed in marriage is for the man and woman to "be in love"; if they are in love, everything will turn out all right. These beliefs are so inaccurate, so unwise, in some cases so heinous, that it is no wonder the divorce rate has been skyrocketing.

You should deal with the sexual part of marriage openly, then, because that part makes so much difference in marriage, and because there is so much misinformation or lack of information about how to interact wisely and effectively. You must deal with this area carefully, tactfully, tastefully, and reverently, and you must do it in ways that are consistent with revealed truths, *but you must do it* if you are to be wise stewards over this area in your marriage.

An Eternal Perspective on Physical Intimacy

Now that you have explored the importance of knowing about and being sensitive to this sacred part of marriage, it is time to consider the eternal perspective on it. This discussion should properly start at the "beginning."

When your spirit body was organized in your premortal life, it was created according to natural laws by your being born to heavenly parents. As a spirit child you lived with these parents and were tutored by them. You recognized the differences between their glorified, immortal bodies and your limited spirit body, and you eagerly anticipated the day when you would be like them and possess the powers which were theirs. You were taught it would be necessary to leave your pleasant premortal surroundings — that you needed to be tried and tested and to grow by facing adversities, before you would be worthy of your heavenly parents' procreative powers. This process of living on an earth to prove one's worthiness and grow in worthiness is part of the plan of salvation, a plan designed to assist you in achieving your full potential by becoming like your heavenly parents.

There are many concepts in the plan of salvation. Three of them are as follows:

1. God's spirit children are to come to the earth and receive mortal, temporal bodies. While here, they are to have *free*

agency in their actions, in how they use these bodies. That is, they are stewards over their own behavior, and as such they will be held accountable for their actions and the way they use their bodies.
2. Through a proper use of this agency each is to prepare himself for an eternal companion and select that companion, in the process creating an eternal unit.
3. With that companion, and under the direction of the Holy Spirit, each is to participate in one of the most sacred experiences possible — that of procreation. This process permits spirits to come to the earth in physical bodies to experience their turn in mortality.

These procreative powers are central to the plan. It is the proper use of these powers within the marriage covenant that makes it possible to have that which your heavenly parents have — an eternal family. The wise use of these powers in this life make it possible for you to retain the reproductive powers and have them extended and expanded throughout the eternities. (D&C 131:4; 132:15-20.)

As Elder Boyd K. Packer has stated, the experience of procreation is in fact the *very key* to happiness, being central to the entire plan of salvation. ("Why Stay Morally Clean," *Ensign,* July 1972, page 113.) It is the way provided for spirit brothers and sisters to enter this life and thus prepare for an eternal life with a companion and with our Father in Heaven.

As Elder Packer also pointed out, this creative power that lies within each of us exhibits two significant features: it is both *strong* and *constant.* Knowing the difficulties encountered in rearing children, our Heavenly Father provided these features to motivate us to bring his children to the earth, since without these features many couples would be reluctant to accept the awesome responsibilities of parenthood.

The Lord also understood the elements of opposition facing his children in marriage, so he made this experience a bonding and unifying one for both men and women. You have no doubt found in your marriage that, since this power of procreation is constant, it has served as a medium for you to develop, express, and foster delicate and intimate love feelings.

Contrary to much that is in modern literature, the experience of procreation is not a self-oriented, personal gratification experience. Rather, within marriage it becomes one in which feelings of love, caring, and giving expand and grow. As a marriage partner, you can appreciate that when two people have this understanding, they experience the highest and most noble feelings of love and companionship. Then and only then can two really become one and thereby share in the depth of purpose of this experience — that is, to participate with our Heavenly Father in literally creating a body.

THESE DESIRES ARE INHERENTLY GOOD

Several man-made philosophies teach that the sexual aspects of man and woman are evil — that they are carnal and sensual and devilish. This view is an unfortunate and pernicious belief that distorts one of the most beautiful aspects of life. In the April 1974 General Conference, President Spencer W. Kimball quoted Billy Graham as follows:

> The Bible makes plain that evil, when related to sex, means not the use of something inherently corrupt but the *misuse* of something pure and good. It teaches clearly that sex can be a wonderful servant but a terrible master: that it can be a creative force more powerful than any other in fostering of a love, companionship, happiness, or can be the most destructive of all of life's forces. ("Guidelines to Carry Forth the Work of God in Cleanliness," *Ensign*, May 1974, pages 7-8. Hereafter referred to as "Guidelines.")

In sum, remember that this sacred power of procreation is the very key to exaltation in the celestial kingdom. It is a sobering thought to realize that only those who prepare for and then build an eternal relationship can participate in this sacred, life-creating act throughout the eternities as exalted *couples* — the only marriage partners to continue as husband and wife, father and mother, forever.

THE PURPOSES OF THE SEXUAL PART OF MARRIAGE

There are those of the Christian world who believe that the sexual part of marriage is only for the purpose of procreation. According to this belief, couples should engage in sexual intercourse only when their motive is to conceive. This idea differs markedly from the view that the sexual part of marriage has two major functions—*procreation* as well as *enhancement of the husband-wife relationship*. This difference is important because it leads to very different behavior in marriage. Those who believe that there are two purposes feel that sexual intercourse is desirable when couples have motives such as the expression of love, closeness, relaxation, making up, and tenderness. Those who believe that procreation is the only function of sex would not engage in intercourse at these times. They would also not have intercourse during pregnancy or at any other time when conception is not desired.

The issue is a sensitive one in the LDS community because some have publicly advocated one position while others have advocated the other. Apparently the Lord has not spoken on the matter, and so it is an issue regarding which differences of opinion are understandable. The authors think the belief that sex is only for procreation originated in the apostate concept that was discussed earlier (the idea that the body is evil while the mind and spirit are pure). This view was incorporated into Christian theology after the Apostasy and found its way into the thinking of some early Latter-day Saints because it was an assumed part of their culture before they were converted.

In the April 1974 General Conference, President Spencer W. Kimball quoted with approval the following statement from Billy Graham:

"... The Bible celebrates sex and its proper use, presenting it as God-created, God-oriented, God-blessed. It makes plain that God himself implanted the physical magnetism between the sexes for two reasons: for the propagation of the human race, and for the expression of that kind of love between man and wife that makes for true oneness. His command to the first man and woman to be 'one flesh' was as important as his command to 'be fruitful and multiply.' " ("Guidelines," page 7.)

Again, in 1975, President Kimball stated:

We know of no directive from the Lord that proper sexual experience between husbands and wives be limited totally to the procreation of children, but we find much evidence from Adam until

now that no provision was ever made by the Lord for indiscrimi-
nate sex. ("The Lord's Plan for Men and Women," *Ensign*, October
1975, page 4.)

Thus it is suggested that the sexual part of man and woman
was created for wise and noble reasons, to reproduce as well as
to unite, uplift, exalt, and glorify.

Summary

The purpose of this discussion has been to allow you to
pause for a moment in your marriage and see, as one might see a
beautiful forest, the magnitude of the blessing of marital intimacy
as created by our Heavenly Father. It now becomes appropriate
and timely to focus on and examine the individual timbers that
make up the forest fiber. As you do, it is hoped that you will
take advantage of your spiritual binoculars, so that what you
learn will be spiritually internalized as you continue your pursuit
of eternal happiness together.

All true love is grounded on a sensitive trust, a complete respect, and a concern for the mate every whit equal to the concern for self.
(Brenton G. Yorgason.)

12

Appropriate Responding in Intimacy

The Lord has indicated that to him all things are spiritual (D&C 29:34). This includes the sexual part of marriage. The physical union of a husband and wife can be a moment when they are partners with God in the creation of new life. It is the process which helps the Lord complete his plan by bringing his spirit children to their earthly existence.

Proper sexual interaction is also spiritual in the sense that it helps two people draw closer to each other in trust and affection. It is the most intimate type of giving and sharing, and it helps build bonds that can last forever. When used properly, it can also bring a couple closer to the Holy Spirit and expand their spiritual qualities. As Parley P. Pratt has written:

> The gift of the Holy Ghost adapts itself to all these organs or attributes [that man has which are possessed by God himself]. It

quickens all the intellectual faculties, increases, enlarges, expands, and purifies all the natural passions and affections, and adapts them, by the gift of wisdom, to their lawful use. (*Key to the Science of Theology*, 1883, page 101.)

Physical and Emotional Dimensions of Intimacy

While our discussion to this point has been centered around the eternal perspective of intimacy in marriage, it now becomes appropriate to move much closer to this part of marriage. As you read these pages, you will likely bring to the discussion additional insights from your own marriage experience. Notwithstanding that experience you have, the authors have felt compelled to examine marital intimacy in detail, if for no other reason than that a periodic review of this area as well as of all other dimensions of marriage can only serve to strengthen a marriage.

As you move through this discussion, it is hoped that you will keep in mind that the mortar used in marital intimacy as well as other areas of married life, consists of the Holy Ghost. It is hoped you will be guided by the Spirit as you examine, more closely perhaps than ever before, the dimensions of intimacy within marriage.

A Deepening Relationship

My husband owned a beautiful pharmacy in which we carried many lines of gift items as well. Twice a year we would attend the San Francisco gift show, and during those days we would make a special effort to have a romantic time together. We would make reservations in a nice motel, plan special dinners alone with each other, and then make sure we had time to enjoy several intimate evenings with each other, sharing and communicating, and in general deepening the sacred relationship that is ours.

THE CYCLE IN PHYSICAL INTIMACY

As you are undoubtedly aware, scientists today are learning at a record-breaking pace new things about the beauties and complexities of the human mind and body. They are learning enough about the body organs that doctors can repair many of them through operations, and can even transplant some of them from one person to another. They are learning enough about medicines and vaccines that they can prevent and cure illnesses that have plagued mankind since the beginning of time. Fortunately, some of the new discoveries can help you understand how your interaction with your spouse influences the physiological, mental, and emotional processes that occur within each of you. Such an understanding can indeed help you be wise in your sexual stewardship.

One of the insights gained about physical intimacy is that there is a cycle in the way a man and a woman become sexually fulfilled. This cycle has four stages, and each person experiences physiological, psychological, and emotional changes in each stage. The four stages are:

— The Excitement Stage
— The Plateau Stage
— The Orgasm Stage
— The Resolution Stage

The excitement stage. As you know, most of the time you are not experiencing sexual feelings. Your minds are occupied with other things such as studying, working, eating, cleaning your home, doing your Church work, etc. But every once in a while something happens that creates a slight sexual feeling. You may be holding hands at a special moment, or you may touch each other in just the right way, or your eyes may meet in a special glance. There are many circumstances that can create these initial feelings of intimate attraction.

Like any other emotion, sexual excitement begins as a very small feeling. Also, like any other emotion, this feeling can grow and expand until it becomes intense. If you are presently in a healthy, growing relationship, then you will appreciate that these feelings are natural for both you and your spouse and contribute to the depth of your relationship. In addition (as you have found), having intense feelings in marriage is good because when you allow yourself to be mentally and emotionally "swept away" by your feelings, a number of changes occur in both the husband's and the wife's bodies that help prepare for the sexual union.

This complex process of the mind, the emotions, and the anatomy all working together to prepare a couple for the act of love is sacred and beautiful, and it helps explain why the Lord created our bodies with these "strong" and "constant" drives and emotions. There are those who miss the extreme feelings of sexual fulfillment, beginning and completing the act as quickly as possible. These couples fail to recognize that the Lord placed the emotional and mental responses in them, and that these responses make the reproductive process more effective, natural, and enjoyable. The extensive loving and caressing that assist in creating the sexual excitement actually help prepare the bodies for the later stages of the sexual cycle.

The plateau stage. There is a plateau in the process of moving from the state of no sexual excitement to the most intense feelings. The participants usually experience more and more excitement until gradually they reach the plateau, when both the husband's and the wife's mental concerns are primarily with this intimate expression, and they experience a continual feeling of fairly intense elation and enjoyment.

You will already know that there is an important difference in the way the husband and the wife usually respond in the excitement and plateau stages. The husband usually moves through the excitement phase more quickly than the wife. When this occurs he is physiologically and emotionally ready to participate in the sexual act before his wife is. If the couple tries to complete the sexual union at that time, it can create several problems. The wife may not be physiologically ready, so at that time the act can be uncomfortable or even painful for her. She may not be emotionally ready and may therefore resent her husband's attempts to effect the union. If this pattern is repeated frequently and over a long period of time, it can build mutual resentment and frustration about the entire sexual part of marriage.

It is important, therefore, for married couples to periodically examine their ways of interacting. By doing this they will learn to love each other in ways that allow them to move through the natural cycle of becoming aroused and excited, thus preparing their bodies and emotions for the mating act. Perhaps the greatest shortcoming of couples who do not experience fulfillment is that they simply do not take the time to love and caress and enjoy each other, but rather rush into the experience and try to complete it in a short period of time. On the other hand, one should realize that it is not *always* important to have a long period of foreplay at the beginning of sexual intimacies. Most couples make a lengthy build-up their usual pattern but at times find it pleasant to have shorter love-making sessions. The important thing is for couples to communicate their feelings and needs and to respond sensitively to each other.

The orgasmic stage. As you will recognize, this is usually the shortest of the four phases, as it seldom lasts more than a few seconds. It is the brief period when the climax or peak of sexual excitement occurs. This climax has three components in the husband: (a) semi-involuntary muscular contractions in the entire abdominal area, (b) extremely intense and pleasant sensations, and (c) an ejaculation of semen containing life-producing chromosomes. While the ejaculated fluid is only about a half-teaspoon in quantity, it contains up to 500,000 sperm.

The climax for the wife has two components: (a) a series of semi-involuntary muscular contractions similar to the husband's and (b) the same type of intense and pleasant sensations. The wife's body does not experience anything comparable to the male ejaculation.

The resolution stage. The final phase of the sexual embrace is a period of gradual reduction in sexual excitement. The resolution in the male is involuntary and begins to occur within a few seconds after the ejaculation. The entire resolution phase for him may be over in a period as short as ten to thirty seconds. He then enters a period of sexual satiation, as his physiological and psychological ability to respond to restimulation is low for a period of time. As men grow older they find this satiation or refractory period gradually increases as their bodies require longer periods of time to recuperate. For the woman, however, there is no period of time needed to recuperate, and so the woman is capable of experiencing more than one orgasm during a single love-making session.

The wife moves through the resolution stage much more slowly than the husband, as she frequently experiences what is known as the "after-glow." This means that her interest in being physically close and romantic may take fifteen to thirty minutes to gradually subside. It is important that couples understand this natural difference between the husband and wife, because if it is ignored it can cause resentments. The husband may be inclined to "roll over and go to sleep," but he needs to learn how to continue to meet his wife's needs. He can at least be a pleasant conversationalist, and can also learn to enjoy being close and romantic, empathetic, and understanding during this time. The wife too needs to be understanding about the fact that his interest in sexual interaction has subsided more rapidly than hers.

Sharing Feelings

Our sexual experiences, our moments of sacred intimacy, have become even more fulfilling and meaningful as we talk to one another, expressing our feelings in words and relating what pleases us most. It has broadened the scope of our love to try to say verbally what lovemaking means to us, and what each of us means to the other.

EMOTIONS INFLUENCE WHAT HAPPENS

Sexual interaction is so delicate and sensitive that it is easily influenced by other emotions. When a couple has a relationship in which peace, harmony, unity, trust prevail, this helps the sexual interaction. It creates an atmosphere of trust and acceptance wherein husband and wife want to be close to each other and express their feelings of love and tenderness. On the other hand, when partners have unresolved disagreements that are bothering them, or if they feel resentment or animosity toward one another, these feelings interfere with the sensitive feelings they need for pleasant sexual interaction and fulfillment.

The sexual part of a marriage is therefore a good barometer of how well things are going in the relationship. When a couple is satisfied with their sexual relationship, this probably means that the other facets of their relationship are also very satisfying.

On the other hand, when a couple has problems in other areas of their marriage, their sexual fulfillment suffers as well. More often than not, the sexual problems are not at the root of a couple's problems; rather, a couple's sex life is usually the victim of their other problems.

Anxiety. There are two kinds of negative emotions that are particularly disruptive to sexual fulfillment. One of these consists of anxiety about the sexual part of marriage. When growing up, some people gained the impression that sexual intimacy is dirty or evil, or that sex is something to be endured rather than enjoyed. These beliefs tend to create anxiety as the person matures and begins to anticipate the sexual dimension of marriage. He or she feels tense, nervous, uncomfortable and ill at ease, and these feelings interfere with the spontaneity and freedom needed to achieve complete satisfaction and mutual fulfillment.

Feelings of anxiety can sometimes be especially disruptive for the wife. If she is anxious, the anxiety tends to make her tighten up inside. This keeps the muscles and tissues in the abdominal and pelvic area from relaxing in a normal way as she enters the excitement stage of the sexual response cycle. When this occurs, it makes the sexual experience difficult and uncomfortable—and ultimately undesirable.

What are some solutions if you have this problem?

First, you need to develop a healthy, positive attitude toward the sexual part of marriage. If you have been spending your marriage years feeling that sexual intimacy is dirty, evil, and unpleasant, or if you are suffering from some other negative feelings, then for "happiness' sake" allow yourself and your spouse to seek professional help. You may wish to talk to your bishop about your feelings, since they are ofttimes associated with guilt and feelings of inappropriateness about one's thoughts, desires, or behavior. You can also obtain medical assistance if necessary, or see a counselor who has been trained in this area (preferably a Church member or one with similar views on this subject).

Negative feelings. A second type of emotion that has a large effect on marital intimacy is negative feelings toward the other partner. Whenever you have negative feelings such as resentment, anger, fear, distrust, animosity, and hurt, these feelings interfere with the sexual part of marriage. This seems to be the case more for wives than husbands, but it occurs for both.

As you know, it is not a secret that all couples have problems and adjustments as they move through their married life. In addition, all couples experience negative feelings toward each other at times. If you have learned to resolve your problems and feelings so that you don't carry them around for long periods of time, then you have learned one of the keys to a rewarding and fulfilling married relationship. However, if you have not learned to resolve these problems or differences, then you know, just as surely as the night follows the day, that these feelings will eat away at the sexual part of your marriage.

Increasing Your Fulfillment

As you take this moment in time to pause and consider your sexual fulfillment as a couple, perhaps it will be refreshing to your relationship to discuss with each other the following "keys" to personal and couple sexual fulfillment.

BE LOVING

It is likely that loving behaviors influence a couple's sexual interaction and fulfillment as much as any other area, and maybe more. As you interact sexually, you need to remember to be patient, kind, and understanding. You need to avoid being puffed up and only caring about yourself. The Lord's admonitions about gentleness, compassion, tenderness, mercy, thoughtfulness, forgiveness, and concern for others ought to be the hallmark of your thoughts and feelings and actions at all times, and are especially important in sexual interaction. And, on the other hand, the ways of behaving that the Savior continually condemns are especially inappropriate in your intimate interaction with your spouse. Therefore, force, coercion, lack of consideration, arrogance, unrighteous dominion, deception, exploitation, half-truths, and selfishness ought to be expelled completely from your bedroom as well as from the rest of your home.

BECOME INVOLVED

Medical researchers have discovered that some individuals are sexually ineffective because they tend to be "spectators" as they participate in the sexual embrace. They remain a little aloof — they observe what is happening around them rather than becoming totally involved in the experience. One thing that can cause this is spending too much time thinking and reading about sexual techniques. Apparently too much academic involvement, like too little understanding, can be harmful.

As the sexual response cycle indicates, this intellectual analyzing is an unnatural way to behave, because the natural and wholesome thing is to gradually become totally immersed in the sexual experience and forget about other things. If you find that the sexual part of your marriage is not as fulfilling as you think it should be, you may want to examine whether you are remaining a spectator by not becoming fully involved emotionally.

There are a number of things you can do to promote total involvement. You can put a lock on your bedroom door and arrange the drapes so you will feel comfortable with total privacy. You can allow enough time in your busy lives for the moments of intimacy you both desire. As you know, the sexual feelings in most individuals cannot be turned on and off in a few minutes, so you need to devote time and attention and affection to become absorbed in making this a rewarding and fulfilling experience.

VERBALIZE

Perhaps one of the greatest hindrances to sexual fulfillment in marriage is the habit developed by many married partners of avoiding any conversations with each other about what they are experiencing. The authors know many couples, whom they have professionally counseled, who have lived with fears and anxieties and misunderstandings for years, when a simple conversation between the spouses would have allowed one partner to express his or her needs and feelings and the other partner to become sensitive to those needs and adjust his or her behavior accordingly. Without exception, each of these couples has experienced a breath of fresh air in the relationship as they have forced themselves, however uncomfortable it was at first, to explore each others' feelings and needs in open discussion. If you find yourself fidgeting with discomfort as you read this section, then the challenge is issued for you to select an appropriate time when the children are in bed, when you can be alone with each other, when you both have the emotional energy to communicate, and then just talk.

You have come to appreciate that the sexual embrace is for different purposes. Primary, of course, is the spiritual experience it becomes as a couple desires to create a new life. In addition, there are times when a couple desires a romantic experience, with each partner wanting to express feelings of love. This embrace may also be used to make up, to show support, for relaxation, for pleasure.

Even after years of marriage there are things you can learn about your spouse. How can you expect to know your spouse's needs and feelings and expectations if you don't talk about this important part of your lives?

You can't!

So . . . as a couple, you must talk, talk, talk, talk!

CREATE SECURITY

Researchers have found that feelings of security about one's spouse influence sexual interaction. You husbands will appreciate knowing that this is especially true for the wife. When your wife feels she can trust you to be faithful, when she can "count on" the stability of your mutual love, she feels free to invest herself more in the sexual experience. The result is that she enjoys the intimate moments more and is better able to attain sexual fulfillment. Take stock, husbands!

ENJOY PHYSICAL CONTACT

Researchers have also found that the enjoyment of sensory contact is an important part of physical interaction in marriage. If you feel good about your bodies, then as a couple you will likely enjoy a variety of physical contact. You will each probably feel pleasure when you are close to your spouse, and you will love to snuggle, hold hands, touch each other, and feel close to each other.

Such people usually are also sensitive to the pleasant *feelings* they have when they are thirsty and take a long cold drink of water—a sensory pleasure. They know that it *feels* good to take a rest after strong physical exertion—a sensory pleasure. At other times, such as when persons are waking up or are just going to sleep, they pause to soak up the pleasure of the moment. On a beautiful day people stop as they walk by a lovely garden just to let the *feeling* soak in. This habit of enjoying physical sensations of pleasure has many advantages. One advantage is that it helps a person be a responsive sex partner in marriage.

Some people are just the opposite. They do not like their physical bodies and do not think they should take pleasure in them. They may experience great joy from other things such as service, reading, music, or doing something well, but they avoid the feelings of pleasure that accompany their body. Perhaps they have been taught that bodily pleasures have a touch of evil to them. This pattern of avoiding or denying physical pleasures usually interferes with the sexual part of one's life. It may keep a person from being an effective sex partner with his spouse, at best depriving the couple of gratifications that are natural and proper, at worst raising physical roadblocks that make the sex act unsatisfying, uncomfortable, or even impossible. Either way the couple will miss out on a source of mutual tenderness and fulfillment that can be very beautiful and can promote feelings of love and attraction.

GET HELP WHEN YOU NEED IT

As you are aware by now, the sexual part of marriage is so intricate and complex that there are many things that can keep it from functioning properly. Physical abnormalities such as a growth or deformity in the reproductive organs can (and do, even many years into marriage) disrupt these processes. Emotional problems of any type can interefere with these delicate parts of marriage. In addition, there are a number of other psychological problems either the husband or the wife, or both may have that can disrupt normal sexual fulfillment. You are an unwise steward if you have problems such as these in the sexual part of your life and you decide to ignore them by not seeking help.

There are a number of different places you can turn to obtain help in correcting these problems. If your problem seems to be physical in nature, you would do well to get help from a medical doctor. An obstetrician or gynecologist, and many times a doctor in family practice, can be most helpful. If your problem deals with spiritual matters, you ought to seek help from your bishop or stake president. You may have feelings of guilt or unworthiness or inadequacy, and when these are corrected, your life will return to normal. If your problems concern your inter-action with your spouse, or your emotions, or if you are not sure what your problems are, there is a new specialty in the counseling profession that can be very helpful. Many counselors trained in the techniques of sex therapy are Latter-day Saints who are sensitive to the religious norms of this culture. They can help you determine what your problems are and how best to solve them.

As mentioned above, it is important for Latter-day Saint couples to know the background of the counselor selected. Many counselors who deal with sex problems differ a great deal in their sensitivity to LDS beliefs. In fact, some clinics offering sex therapy are very worldly organizations that advocate grossly immoral and unwise sexual practices. Some of them do not ap-preciate the LDS philosophy that the sexual part of life is a very private and personal area that should be revered; and they do not share the LDS belief that sexual interaction should be exclu-sively confined to the marriage. Fortunately, however, in many areas bishops and stake presidents have access to LDS counselors as well as to sympathetic non-LDS counselors who can assist you according to your beliefs.

This means that you need to be extremely careful in seeking professional assistance in this area. Many medical doctors have received no training to deal with sexual problems, and they are no more proficient than your next-door neighbor. In many states, counselors do not have to receive any training at all and they do not have to be licensed. You therefore need to be very cautious in obtaining professional assistance in this area.

Summary

By way of review then, this discussion has centered around the appropriate ways to respond sexually with your mate within an eternal perspective. While this discussion has been quite forthright, it is hoped you each have gained a further appreciation for your body, your emotions, and your personal responsibility in dealing with this area of your marriage.

While Satan has polluted the world so that it is difficult to know what is appropriate and what is not, as a Latter-day Saint, your protection must come, finally, from an earnest effort to allow the Holy Ghost to become operative in this part of your marriage. When you approach the sexual union with reverence and respect, and with a selfless desire to be concerned about your partner, then not only will your physical relationship grow and flourish but your entire relationship will experience satisfaction and fulfillment.

It is hoped that following this discussion you will now approach this area with a deeper respect and with a desire to communicate to your spouse your deepest feelings and expectations.

*The sacred books of the
ancient Persians say: If
you would be holy, instruct
your children, because all
the good acts they perform
will be imputed to you.
(Montesquieu.)*

13

Parenting Delights and Dilemmas

As you consider parenthood from the vantage point of *being
involved* with it, you no doubt find many varied emotions fluttering about in your mind and heart. Above all, you know
parenthood is work, it is fun, it is immensely rewarding, it is
equally frustrating, it is disappointing, and at times it is simply
painful. Being a parent seems to present an environment of
growth for both the parents and the children. And yet above all
it helps provide the joy that gives meaning and purpose to life (2
Nephi 2:25).

The Domestic Engineer

*Well, "body," get yourself up. It's time to make all of
those executive decisions. Do we have Cookie Crisp or Lucky*

Charms, or do we just have Cheerios for breakfast? Where are all those kids who eat oatmeal, eggs, and orange juice?

A reminder is needed for them to do their "chores" immediately. Now there's a word that has changed with the times. When I was a child it meant now, but today it roughly translates as "anytime I get around to it, if it doesn't interfere with any of my other plans." When I remind my child to hurry, what I get is a sigh. I've always wondered what that meant, exactly . . . a sigh.

Now I hear piano notes. Whoever said "practice makes perfect" did not have a ten-year-old taking piano lessons.

Again a reminder to get on with the chores. Now I hear muttering. I've never been a real fan of muttering. First, it never occurs close enough to hear what is said, and then if an encore is demanded, how can I make sure I get the whole mutter the second time around?

No one wants the bathroom in his list of chores, and frankly I don't blame any one of them.

I cannot believe how good this mattress feels!

Well, "body," get yourself up. It's Sunday; time for all those world-shattering decisions again . . .

While much of the world has been deceived, Latter-day Saints know parenthood to be an essential part of the plan of salvation. This is because only through parenthood can couples provide physical bodies for their spirit brothers and sisters, and only through parenthood can they receive and then pass on the guidance and assistance they need to become exalted. Obviously, then, parenthood is critical to the plan of salvation.

From the days of Adam we have been commanded to multiply and replenish the earth. The words of the Psalmist reflect in a profound and poignant way the value and blessing of having children:

Lo, children are an heritage of the Lord: and the fruit of the womb is his reward.

As arrows are in the hand of a mighty man; so are children of the youth.

Happy is the man that hath his quiver full of them. (Psalm 127: 3-5.)

For those who have been reserved to come forth in the latter days, the words ring out again and again from latter-day prophets. President David O. McKay stated it aptly:

> The very purpose of marriage is to rear a family and not for the mere gratification of man or woman. Keeping this thought uppermost in married life, we shall have fewer difficulties and more readily find content. (*Gospel Ideals,* [Salt Lake City: Improvement Era, 1953], page 467.)

This means that you should *want* to become parents — not just because everybody does it, and not just because the Lord has commanded it and the prophets have taught it. You should want parenthood because it can assist you in gaining your greatest fulfillment, your ultimate destiny, and the deepest feelings of joy and happiness life has to offer. For those who selfishly choose not to have children, there is no way to experience the growth, taste the depth of joy, or attain the exaltation of purpose that parenthood provides.

Our Quiver Is Filling

We had always planned on having a large family, and not being able to have children was a difficult realization to come to. After several years we were able to adopt one, and then another, and then another. Still, we felt incomplete as a family, so we petitioned our Heavenly Father for his guidance and his blessing.

Once again, our prayers were answered. Within the next four years we received five new children from various parts of the world. Now as we gather our eight children around us, we just marvel at these blessings, and we thank God for being personally involved as we have indeed filled our family quiver.

QUESTIONING YOUR QUIVER

While it is very true that husbands and fathers can stand easily and firmly on the parenthood soapbox exclaiming, "Oh, happy I am, for my quiver is full!" it is also true and much more sobering that children have a many-faceted impact upon wives and mothers, and subsequently upon the entire family stability. For this reason it is vital that you, as husband and wife, give much thought and prayer to actually know the contents of your personal quiver.

As married folk, you have at one time or another entertained the question of whether you should ever control conception. Those of you who already know what a quiver-full of loose nerve endings is like have undoubtedly come to appreciate that the obvious answer to this question is simply . . . yes. In fact, most Latter-day Saints would be counted as unwise stewards if they never controlled conception in any way. If a husband were to engage in the sex act with his wife only when she is physically capable of conceiving another child, then this intimacy would occur only every ten to fifteen months. Since the normal woman can bear children until she is well into her forties, this means that a couple could ultimately place as many as twenty to twenty-five children in their quiver. Obviously this is not what the Lord had in mind.

On April 14, 1969, the First Presidency sent to bishops and to stake and mission presidents the following letter which is reproduced here with permission:

> The First Presidency is being asked from time to time as to what the attitude of the Church is regarding birth control. In order that you may be informed on this subject and that you may be prepared to convey the proper information to the members of the Church under your jurisdiction, we have decided to give you the following statement:
>
> We seriously regret that there should exist a sentiment or feeling among any members of the Church to curtail the birth of their children. We have been commanded to multiply and replenish the earth that we may have joy and rejoicing in our posterity.
>
> Where husband and wife enjoy health and vigor and are free from impurities that would be entailed upon their posterity, it is contrary to the teachings of the Church artificially to curtail or prevent the birth of children. We believe that those who practice birth control will reap disappointment by and by.
>
> However, we feel that men must be considerate of their wives who bear the greater responsibility not only of bearing children, but of caring for them through childhood. To this end the mother's

health and strength should be conserved and the husband's consideration for his wife is his first duty, and self-control a dominant factor in all their relationships.

It is our further feeling that married couples should seek inspiration and wisdom from the Lord that they may exercise discretion in solving their marital problems, and that they may be permitted to rear their children in accordance with the teachings of the gospel.

This letter will help you realize that you should use self-control and think and pray and plan carefully in this area of your marriage. Just as it would be unwise for a farmer to plant field after field of crops without ever thinking about whether he could take care of them, it would be unwise for couples to have child after child after child without thinking about whether they could take care of them. Consider for a moment the issues raised by the First Presidency of concern for the *health, vigor,* and *strength* of the parents.

Health. Of utmost concern in deciding whether to conceive a child is the physical health of the mother. For example, if she has given birth to several children in rapid succession, it may be that she will need a number of months (or even years) to fully regain the health necessary for an additional pregnancy. Less obviously, this also refers to the mental, emotional, or psychological health of both the father and the mother. The authors know of one couple who has triplets aged four, twins aged two, and a baby. Obviously, this couple need to be and are concerned for their health, and especially for the health of the mother.

Vigor. Webster defines vigor as one's active strength or force, one's energetic activity or one's intensity. This factor has little to do with the process of conception and little to do with pregnancy. Couples can conceive and give birth to children with but little vigor. It *does* become important though when you think of the energy that is demanded in answering the endless questions of the four-year-old, mediating the sibling squabbles of school-age children, and reasoning with teenagers who have learned to think for themselves. It comes into play when the mother is trying to be a mother, chauffeur, shopper, dietician, cook, housekeeper, lover, daughter, genealogist, neighbor, Saint, wife, and confidant for her children—all at once! Fortunately, most mothers have the vigor needed for parenthood. Even so, there may be some who have but a limited supply of vigor, and so should avoid the problems that come with too many children.

Strength. The dictionary defines strength as bodily or muscular power, mental power, force or vigor; and moral power, firmness, or courage. Again, even though it takes some strength to bear children, the great demands on one's strength come with the *rearing* of the children.

Some women, such as a neighbor of one of the authors, have large and powerful bodies and are able to work long and strenuous hours day after day. This neighbor has fifteen children and handles them very well. Her laundry room could be mistaken for a laundromat, her kitchen for a cafeteria, her car for a bus. She is undoubtedly at one end of a continuum as one who is nearly indefatigable in her capacity to manage a home. Her husband is able to cope as well and to provide a six-thousand square-foot home and enough food, clothing, etc., for the family's needs. He doesn't make enough money for his family to have as many luxuries as they could have had with a smaller family, but they also couldn't be more happy.

On the other end of the continuum are those women whose physical and mental health would never allow them to have even half as many children as the neighbor mentioned. Are these women to be viewed as less or more righteous than the woman with fifteen children? Certainly not. Mothers will be judged by how they use their talents they have been given, their potentials, and the intent of their hearts.

Whenever you decide, as parents, to limit the number of children you are going to have, you should make this decision by carefully and prayerfully evaluating your motives. If you convince yourselves that you want to prevent children from coming into your home because of physical or emotional health when in reality it is because of your selfishness and unwillingness to sacrifice your time and material wants, then you are in fact setting yourselves up for a loss of blessings as well as judgment from our Heavenly Father. President Spencer W. Kimball says:

> . . . do not limit your family as the world does. I am wondering now where I might have been had my parents decided arbitrarily

that one or two children would be enough, or that three or four would be all they could support, or that even five would be the limit; for I was the sixth of eleven children. Don't think you will love the later ones less or have fewer material things for them. Perhaps, like Jacob, you might love the eleventh one most. Young people, have your family, love them, sacrifice for them, teach them righteousness, and you will be blessed and happy all the days of your eternal lives. (*Marriage*, pages 22-23.)

As you can see, the counsel has been consistent and unchanging over the years. Latter-day Saints have a solemn obligation to bear and rear children if possible. It is also interesting that many who are now on the earth, born in homes that gave them a chance to understand the gospel, may not have been here if their ancestors had not listened to the counsel of these Brethren. The Lord does, however, make allowances for individual circumstances, and the ultimate decision as to how many children should arrive (and when) should be made by the husband and wife subject to confirmation by the Lord. This point is beautifully illustrated in a discussion of these issues by Dr. Homer Ellsworth in the August 1979 issue of the *Ensign*. He wrote:

> I recall a President of the Church, now deceased, who visited his daughter in the hospital following a miscarriage.
> She was the mother of eight children and was in her early forties. She asked, "Father, may I quit now?" His response was, "Don't ask me. That decision is between you, your husband, and your Father in Heaven. If you two can face him with a good conscience and can say you have done the best you could, that you have really tried, then you may quit. But that is between you and him. I have enough problems of my own to talk over with him when we meet!" So it is clear to me that the decisions regarding our children, when to have them, their number, and all related matters and questions can only be made after real discussion between the marriage partners and after prayer.

Some couples have a desire to turn to Church leaders for detailed answers about what they ought to do, but they should accept more of the responsibility of discovering the mind and will of the Lord for themselves through fasting and prayer. Some people want to be like sheep, led around in everything they do.

They want the burden of responsibility lifted by being told by their leaders what they should or should not do. It is doubtful that this will ever happen, for they have been told that it is a slothful and unwise steward that must be commanded in all things. They are given general instructions and guidelines and then left on their own to apply these principles to their personal marriages.

For example, the wife of one of the authors has only one kidney and was told by a competent physician that she should consider adoption instead of trying to bear children. Try as they might to find scriptural guidance for mothers with only one kidney, they found nothing. They also found nothing in the counsels of the Brethren, nor was any local leader willing to take on their responsibility by telling them what they should do. Making these kinds of decisions with the help of the Lord is what the test upon the earth is all about. Sensing this, this couple felt grateful for personal revelation and prepared themselves to be worthy to receive the help promised to those who are willing to ask for it; at last count, they had received seven "answers."

The First Presidency's letter also teaches members *how* they should approach the decision of whether to prevent conception. They emphasize that they should "seek inspiration and wisdom from the Lord" to help them "exercise discretion." This is probably the most important point in the entire process of making this decision. Each couple needs to seek inspiration or revelation about their unique situation and rely upon such inspiration in making their decision. They have the general commandment that they should multiply and replenish the earth, that they might have joy and rejoicing in their posterity. They also have the guidelines of health, vigor, strength, and genetic makeup to help them evaluate what they should do. These, however, are merely general guidelines. They provide guidance and a sense of direction, but they do not tell a specific couple what is best for them at a given time in their relationship. Each couple therefore needs to think about their unique situation, seek guidance from the Holy Spirit as to what is best for them, and then act upon the promptings they receive.

How Can You Facilitate Conception?

THE RHYTHM METHOD OF FACILITATING CONCEPTION

It is possible to monitor the processes that occur in the female to determine when ovulation occurs. This permits couples to plan when to have intercourse so that it will increase the chances of conception. This is called the rhythm method; it can substantially increase the likelihood of conception. The key to the rhythm method is that menstruation usually begins twelve to fourteen days after ovulation. If a woman has the usual twenty-eight days between her menstrual periods, and if she is fairly regular in this cycle, a couple can determine fairly closely when she will ovulate. It will be fourteen to sixteen days after the previous period began. The couple can abstain from intercourse for a period of time before ovulation to attain the highest possible sperm count in the male's semen and then have intercourse frequently at the time of ovulation and immediately after it.

Some women have more than the usual twenty-eight days between periods. These couples need to determine when the cycle of ovulation occurs, and it will be twelve to fourteen days after that before the next menstrual cycle will begin. If the woman's usual cycle is thirty-five days, ovulation will usually occur twenty-one to twenty-three days after the previous period began. If her cycle is forty days, ovulation is usually about twenty-six to twenty-eight days after the previous period. It is important to emphasize the word *usually* in these descriptions because there are usual patterns and there are also many exceptions.

The rhythm method can also be used to prevent conception. The couple can determine when ovulation is likely and avoid intercourse during those parts of the month. They can then have intercourse at other times, during the "safe period." Since the sperm may live for several days in the woman and ovulation may vary a little in the cycle, it is usually wise to avoid intercourse for a week to ten days if the couple is serious about avoiding conception.

THE BBT METHOD OF FACILITATING CONCEPTION

Most women experience a slight change in what is called their basal body temperature (BBT) at the time of ovulation. The BBT is the temperature taken immediately upon waking in the morning, before the woman gets out of bed or has anything to eat or drink. As soon as she gets up and has any type of physical activity, her temperature rises slightly, usually about one half of a degree just after ovulation. It is thought that estrogen secreted by the growing follicle is a temperature depressant which causes a decrease in BBT as ovulation is approaching. The lowest point is reached usually just before ovulation occurs. The progesterone secreted by the corpus luteum causes the BBT to rise. The temperature then remains at the higher level until the time of menstruation, and if pregnancy occurs, it remains relatively high.

The BBT method is helpful for some couples, but it involves many complexities and is not always reliable. There are many other factors that influence body temperature, and they in turn make the BBT records difficult to interpret. There is also a lot of variation in some women in a series of cycles, and no patterns can be detected in them. In other situations, the changes in BBT and in ovulation do not always coincide. (Edmond J. Farris, *Human Ovulation and Fertility* [Philadelphia: Lippincott, 1956].) Conception has been recorded in one situation where intercourse occurred ten days before the change in temperature, and in other cases where intercourse took place more than two days before the change. (Rafael Garcia-Bunnel, "New and Experimental Methods of Fertility Control," *Current Medical Digest,* vol. 33, no. 6 [1966], pp. 889-899.) This method is therefore one thing that can be done to help conception occur, but it is not a cure-all.

How Can You Prevent Conception?

There are some circumstances in which it is righteous and wise to prevent conception. When these conditions occur, you need information about which methods are moral and immoral, and which are effective and ineffective. Again, a comment in Ellsworth's article in the August 1979 *Ensign* can help you understand these issues:

> If for certain personal reasons a couple prayerfully decides that having another child immediately is unwise, the method of spacing children—discounting possible medical or physical effects—makes little difference. Abstinence, of course, is also a form of contraception, and like any other method it has side effects, some of which are harmful to the marriage relationship.

While it is not a method of preventing conception, we should say here that abortion is an undesirable method of preventing birth. Abortion is the process of killing the embryo or fetus so that it will not be born; it is a grossly immoral practice that is only practiced in a degenerate society. It is ironic that our modern society is upset about the slaughter of six million innocent people in the concentration camps of World War II, yet it calmly accepts the slaughter of many millions unborn children each year!

The LDS position on abortion is made very clear by the First Presidency. They have stated:

> The Church opposes abortion and counsels its members not to submit to, be a party to, or perform an abortion except in rare cases where, in the opinion of competent medical counsel, the life or health of the woman is seriously endangered or where the pregnancy was caused by incest or forcible rape. Even then it should be done only after counseling with the local bishop or branch president and after receiving divine confirmation through prayer. (Personal correspondence.)

Abortion is clearly an immoral method of birth control, except when it is used as a medical emergency. It should not be used or condoned.

What about other methods? Are any of them moral and desirable? The First Presidency has not issued an additional statement about the other methods, and as the following comment by President Hugh B. Brown suggests, they do not think it necessary to do so:

> I'm speaking now for myself, and I think the Brethren would agree, we feel that we'd better not make any sweeping pronounce-

ments such, for instance, as the Catholic Church has made, because of the difficulties which result. There are so many different conditions in the homes, different people to deal with, that this whole question of birth control becomes very much involved and very complex. But, as a general rule, we say to our young people, the purpose of your marriage is to have children. If you wish to regulate or space those children, that's up to you. We're not going to follow anybody into their bedroom. I think freedom in this matter ought to be understood. . . . I think as man and wife we owe it to each other to take a reverent view of all these matters, and then act accordingly. (Eugene E. Campbell and Richard D. Poll, *Hugh B. Brown: His Life and Thought* [Salt Lake City: Bookcraft, Inc., 1975], p. 288.)

Thus decisions about which methods of controlling conception are desirable and undesirable are part of the stewardship of each couple. When married partners are faced with a situation in which it is desirable to prevent conception, they each need to become informed about the options that are available and the various advantages and disadvantages. In becoming informed, it is useful for them to seek advice and counsel of medical doctors to learn the physical and medical advantages and disadvantages of the various methods. In addition, when they have concerns about the moral propriety of the methods, they can pray and seek counsel with their bishop. Then, in the last analysis, each couple must determine what is best for them.

Summary

The focus of this discussion has been of a different nature; not the *hows* and *whys* of rearing children, but the hows and whys of bearing them. Because this issue is one which involves all LDS couples at one time or another, it is hoped that the discussion has been of help and a positive enlightenment — and that as married partners you will pay the price to determine *by the Spirit* what our Heavenly Father expects of you and your personal family system.

Would you now put on a pair of patriarchal glasses, gaze intently through those lenses, and determine how this eternal system of operations helps you achieve unity in your marital relationship.

*No power or influence can or
ought to be maintained by virtue
of the priesthood, only by
persuasion, by long-suffering,
by gentleness and meekness, and
by love unfeigned.
(D&C 121:41.)*

14

Achieving Unity Within the Patriarchal Order

Think for a moment, if you will, of your marriage and your home being an island which is surrounded on all sides by the swift and changing polluted waters of the world. As you know, many of your parents' and your grandparents' notions (regardless of their religious persuasion) are now being questioned or discarded by the world. You can find evidence of these changes in the waning tide of virtue as marital sexual attitudes and behavior deteriorate. In addition, many women (even in the Church) are reexamining traditional roles they have been given and are finding them no longer acceptable or fulfilling.

Statements by well-known feminists challenge the traditional role of wife and mother, suggesting that women do not have equal opportunities for education or jobs and that marriage and family are instruments of women's oppression. They speak of the beauty and sacredness of motherhood as archaic and being an inappropriate concept.

After being bombarded daily with statements like these, Latter-day Saint women then listen to conference addresses and hear statements such as the following by President Spencer W. Kimball:

> When men come home to their families and women devote themselves to their children, the concept will return; that to be a mother is her greatest vocation in life. She is a partner with God. No being has a position of such power and influence. She holds in her hand the destiny of nations, for to her comes the responsibility and opportunity of molding the nation's citizens. ("Why Call Me Lord, Lord, and Do Not the Things Which I Say?" *Ensign,* May 1975, page 7.)

As you can see, Latter-day Saints are caught in the middle of a very real and emotional tug of war to determine how they should think and act as men and women and how they lead and follow and create equality in marriage. Hopefully, this discussion will assist you as you resolve some of these pressures, and then as you walk confidently through the rest of your married life knowing that your course has been set in truth and with heavenly assistance.

An Eternal Perspective

Perhaps the first step you can take to assist you in resolving these conflicts is *backward,* as you purposefully back away and make sure that your basic perspective is correct. If it is not, you may be like the four blind men who were feeling the elephant to determine what elephants were like. As one felt the leg, another felt the ear, another the tail, and another felt the side, they each came up with very different conclusions, not one of which was accurate and complete. As with the blind men, you need to gain an overall view if you are to make sure of a correct perspective so that you can make wise decisions about both you and your spouse's roles in your marriage.

Two opposing perspectives about male-female roles dominate the current controversy. One is well-intentioned and partly true. Unfortunately, it is also short-sighted and partly false. It can be called the "earthly" perspective. It assumes that social roles are created only by earthly conditions such as economic systems, traditions, migration patterns, and a gradual evolution over time. It also assumes that there is no limit to the ways roles can be modified and rearranged whenever circumstances change — for example, whether one is living in a rural or an urban environment.

The second perspective is quite different. An "eternal" perspective asserts that earthly life is only a part of the eternal experience and that pre-earthly as well as post-earthly lives have an influence on the roles men and women should have. This perspective affirms that social conditions should justify some changes in roles, *but there are limits to the amount of change that should be made.* Some roles should not change at all, and some can change only within certain previously established limits.

These two incompatible perspectives lead to very different views of male-female roles. The earthly perspective allows people to rearrange such roles according to temporary conditions. Those who adopt this perspective see nothing wrong with radical changes, such as eliminating distinctions between men's and women's roles in a highly industrialized society.

People in both groups can learn something from the other. Those with an earthly perspective would be better off if they were to recognize pre-earthly and post-earthly conditions, and in the long run they will make some foolish mistakes if these conditions don't influence what they do in their roles. Even so, two wrongs don't make a right; and some of those who have the eternal perspective have been more rigid than the eternal truths justify. They have sometimes forced men and women into roles and have mistakenly thought them to be eternal. LDS couples need to recognize that there are many ways in which male-female roles can change according to customs and cultures, and then feel free to make the appropriate changes.

Dishpan Hands and a Green Thumb

As anyone in our neighborhood can tell you, my wife has the "proverbial green thumb." She has boned up on everything there is to know about shrubs, flowers, lawn care, and yard maintenance — she literally thrives on working in the yard, and as a consequence we have the best groomed yard in our area.

I enjoy working with her in the yard, but I also enjoy cooking, and have done my fair share of the dishes. I personally enjoy cooking breakfast, especially on Christmas or other holiday mornings when all of our family can be at our home. I, like most men, enjoy broiling steaks and hamburgers on the patio, too.

Now, I want to make it perfectly clear that I am neither a male chauvinist nor a supporter of ERA, but would like to think that I'm a real he-man, and the fact that I do participate with my wife in cooking, doing dishes, and other housework, while she loves to keep our yard manicured, has only served to increase our satisfaction with each other.

> Woman was made from the rib of man.
> She was not made from his head, to top him.
> Nor from his feet, to be stepped upon.
> She was made —
> > From his side, to be equal with him;
> > From beneath his arm, to be protected by him;
> > Near his heart, to be loved by him.

(Author unknown.)

The Patriarchal Order

The next step in recognizing the roles men and women ought to have in marriage is to have an accurate understanding of the patriarchal order. The underlying purpose of the patriarchal order is to *create order*, not to elevate one spouse above the other or to encourage servant/master roles in marriage. To create order, the patriarchal system specifies a division of re-

sponsibility between the marriage partners. Each spouse has a
specific stewardship, assigned by law and appointment, and it
cannot rightfully be abdicated to the other. In this manner, both
the husband and the wife can feel they have a place and a purpose in an eternal plan.

When properly administered, the patriarchal family order is
one of equality between the marriage partners. President Marion
G. Romney emphasizes this point:

> They [husband and wife] should be one in harmony, respect,
> and mutual consideration. Neither should plan or follow an inde-
> pendent course of action. They should consult, pray, and decide
> together. . . . Remember that neither the wife nor the husband is
> the slave of the other. Husbands and wives are equal partners,
> particularly Latter-day Saint husbands and wives. They should so
> consider themselves and so treat each other in this life, and then
> they will do so throughout eternity. ("In the Image of God,"
> *Ensign,* April 1978, pages 2, 4.)

This statement emphasizes the equality of the marriage partners; it is not a doctrine of "sameness." It is very different from
the worldly view that there are few, if any, inherent psychological and emotional differences between the sexes; that all
differences are learned from our culture. Though many roles can
be given as well to men as to women, there are some basic differences that should not be ignored. Elder Boyd K. Packer has
provided some unique insights into these differences:

> "We recognize men and women as equally important before
> the Lord, but with differences biologically, emotionally, and in
> other ways." [First Presidency Statement on the ERA, October 22,
> 1976.]

> We cannot eliminate, through any pattern of legislation or regu-
> lation, the differences between men and women.
> There are basic things that a man needs that a woman does
> not need. There are things that a man feels that a woman never
> does feel.
> There are basic things that a woman needs that a man never
> needs, and there are things that a woman feels that a man never
> feels, nor should he.
> These differences make women, in basic needs, literally opposite
> from men.

A man, for instance, needs to feel protective, and yes dominant, if you will, in leading his family. A woman needs to feel protected, in the bearing of children and in the nurturing of them.

Have you ever thought what life would be like if the needs of
men and women were naturally precisely the same?

What would it be like if they both naturally needed to feel
dominant all of the time, or both naturally needed to feel protected
all of the time?

How disturbed and intolerable things would be.

When God created male and female, He gave each important
differences in physical attributes, in emotional composition, in family responsibility. We must protect and honor the vital differences
in the roles of men and women, especially in respect to the family.
("The Equal Rights Amendment," *Ensign,* March 1977, pages 6, 7-8.)

Many in the world disagree with Elder Packer. Even so, there
are many in the scientific community who agree with him. One
such is John H. Crook:

The biological roots of human sexual behavior are different in the
two sexes and likely to be fundamental determinants in the dif-
ferentiation of mature personality. . . . The naive idea of a psychological "equality" of the two sexes and of their total interchange-
ability in the performance of social roles has gained support from
certain studies purporting to demonstrate that gender role is determined simply through developmental conditioning. This view ig-
nores totally the significance of genetic and physiological differences between the sexes that in current research are shown to exert
profound effects during the behavioral maturation of the growing
organism. . . .

Those concerned with Women's Liberation would be wise to
ponder the biological and psychological complementarity of the
two sexes and their deep emotional needs for partnership as a
counter to the notion of a poorly defined equality. (John H. Crook,
The Evolution of Human Consciousness [Oxford: Clarendon Press,
1980], page 242.)

While we may not yet understand in every instance which of
the many differences between men and women are inherent and
which are created by our cultures, it would be very unwise and
premature to conclude that they do not exist.

THE HUSBAND'S ROLE IN THE PATRIARCHAL ORDER

In a pamphlet dated 1973, the Church has provided some

specific guidance as to the duties included in the role of husband/
father:

> Fatherhood is leadership, the most important kind of leadership.
> It *has* always been so; it always will be so. Father, with the assis-
> tance and counsel and encouragement of your eternal companion,
> you preside in the home. It is not a matter of whether you are most
> worthy or best qualified, but it is a matter of law and appointment.
> You preside at the meal table, at family prayer. You preside at
> family home evening, and as guided by the Spirit of the Lord, you
> see that your children are taught correct principles. It is your place
> to give direction relating to all of family life.
>
> You give father's blessings. You take an active part in establish-
> ing family rules and discipline. As a leader in your home you plan
> and sacrifice to achieve the blessings of a unified and happy family.
> To do all of this requires that you live a family-centered life.
> (*Father, Consider Your Ways,* pages 4-5.)

This statement does not mean that the husband is to make all
of the decisions for the family. It means that the husband is to
direct the process. We need to keep in mind President Romney's
statement that neither the husband nor the wife is to plan or
follow an independent course of action. They are to consult,
pray, and decide together, and neither is the slave of the other.
To preside does not mean to dominate and dictate but to coordi-
nate and to guide.

Patience Prevails

*Sometimes a wife needs to wait for her husband until he
is ready to preside in their home, rather than nagging at him
to do so.*

*I had worried for many weeks about our family prayers.
We had prayed together each night as a couple, but we had
not had family prayers. Both of us had been reared in families that had prayed together. Our little children were getting
old enough to join us in family prayers and so I suggested
that we begin having them. My husband agreed that it was a
good idea, but didn't follow through. I really questioned
whether I should nag him about it for the children's sake, but
decided that it was not my role to do so. To this day I am*

grateful that I didn't nag my husband into family prayer because when he was ready, he started a family prayer program. I can cheerfully support him now, realizing that I did not jeopardize our loving relationship by imposing my wishes upon him.

While keeping these truths in mind, you should also remember that the Lord occasionally intervenes by revealing his will. This occurs in many ways, but usually through revelation to one or both spouses. When the revelation comes to only one spouse, it is important that the other spouse be willing to comply. Sometimes the revelation comes to the husband. An example of this was when the Lord spoke to father Lehi in a dream, directing him to leave Jerusalem. Even though Sariah was not enthusiastic about leaving her home at Jerusalem, still she followed the direction given to her husband. At other times the revelation may come to the wife, as when Rebekah was told why she was expecting two sons when she had previously been barren (Genesis 25:22-23.) In this instance, the husband was supportive of the revelation the wife received.

A Presidency — Together

What makes our marriage "go"? Three words: love, selflessness, together. Our love for each other and for the Lord has helped us to develop an attitude of selflessness and a desire to be and to do together.

One of the greatest "together" experiences we have is weekly temple attendance. I seldom feel closer to my husband than I do when I'm sitting on the opposite side of the room at the temple. The opportunity there to re-examine the depth of my commitment to my husband and to know that he is doing the same brings a great strength to our marriage.

Weekly temple attendance didn't just happen — it is something we planned together. One day many years ago, I brought home from a Relief Society Mother Education lesson the idea of holding a "family presidency" meeting. My sweetheart liked the idea and improved upon it. Why not prepare ourselves for that important meeting by going to the temple? And so our plan developed: Each Tuesday morning, we attended a temple session, then drove home, had a kneeling prayer together and began our presidency meeting. On our agenda were such things as the progress of our eldest son in his Cub Scout work, preparing our second son for his baptism, budgeting for dance lessons for our daughter, and how to help the three older children not make fun of their little brother. We also planned the family schedule so that we could all participate in a family morning devotional, before school and work separated us for the day. A friend of mine teaches her children, "Satan uses real bullets, kids, so you'd better have your armor on." We've tried to "arm" our family each morning with fifteen minutes of scripture study and private prayer, and then as we all gather at the breakfast table we report to each other about the chapter or verses we've studied. This morning, for example, we heard about King Benjamin (Mosiah 2), General Moroni (Alma 49), the miracle of the loaves and fishes (Luke 9 and Matthew 15), the death of Saul and Jonathan (1 Samuel 31), and the opening of the seven seals in the book of Revelation. That is good preparation for our family prayer, and for the day.

The plans for that kind of daily experience were laid in our presidency meeting. Other items on the agenda might include plans for next summer's vacation, family night assignments and who might need help on them, the calendar for the coming week, and anything else we need to talk about — including how we feel about each other, our relationship and what we could do to strengthen it physically, emotionally, and spiritually.

Doing together has been the hallmark of our marriage. We attend Education Week together and this year we have devoted several home evenings to a review of the things learned there and what our family would do to implement what we learned. We share the writing of letters to our sons in the mission field and our daughter in Israel; and we see this example taking root in their lives as they not only write us faithfully, but also correspond with grandparents, aunts and uncles, neighbors and friends. Our missionaries say that none of their companions ever had letters from their fathers so faithfully as they did.

Domestic chores (both inside the home and out) are usually done together. We make the bed together, prepare breakfast as a team, do dishes together, pull weeds, plant garden, shop for groceries and for Christmas together. Oh, we do some things separately too. For instance, he doesn't sew, and I don't tune the car. But wherever we can help each other and enjoy being side by side, we like to be together. We even planned the writing of this article together.

Prayer has always been an important part of our marriage. Indeed, it was prominent in our courtship too. We have found that not only private and family prayers are important, but the times when just the two of us kneel together. One of the nicest compliments I ever received from my husband came in a Sunday School class at the BYU ward where he was bishop. The lesson was about love, and the teacher asked the class, "How can you tell you are loved?" There were many different responses: "He spends time with me"; "We're comfortable together without having to talk"; "She does special things for me." Then the teacher asked, "Bishop, how do you know your wife loves you?" He answered, "I can tell by the way that she prays for me."

In the simplest possible terms, our marriage involves a triangle: husband, wife and the Lord, together. That is the strategy that works for us.

THE WIFE

One of the questions often asked by women in the Church is, "If the husband is to preside over and lead the family, can the wife really be considered an equal? If so, how?"

The answer has at least partially already been presented in this discussion. From Elder Packer: "We recognize men and women as equally important before the Lord, but with differences biologically, emotionally, and in other ways." From President Romney: "Husbands and wives are equal partners." A further quotation from an apostle will help determine just how we can be equal even though one presides:

> Woman does not hold the Priesthood, but she is a partaker of the blessings of the priesthood. That is, the man holds the Priesthood, performs the priestly duties of the Church, but his wife enjoys with him every other privilege derived from the possession of the Priesthood. This is made clear, as an example, in the Temple service of the Church. The ordinances of the Temple are distinctly of Priesthood character, yet women have access to all of them, and the highest blessings of the Temple are conferred only upon the man and his wife jointly.
>
> The Prophet Joseph Smith made this relationship clear. He spoke of delivering the keys of the Priesthood to the Church, and said that the faithful members of the Relief Society should receive them with their husbands, . . .
>
> This division of responsibility is for a wise and noble purpose. Our Father in Heaven has bestowed upon His daughters a gift of equal importance and power, which gift, if exercised in its fulness, will occupy their entire life on earth so that they can have no possible longing for that which they do not possess. The "gift" referred to is that of motherhood — the noblest, most soul-satisfying of all earthly experiences. If this power is exercised righteously, woman has no time nor desire for anything greater, for there is nothing greater on earth! This does not mean that women may not use to the full their special gifts, for . . . the more woman exercises her innate qualifications the greater is her power for motherhood. Woman may claim other activity, but motherhood should take precedence in her entire scheme of life. (John A. Widtsoe, *Priesthood and Church Government,* Deseret Book Company, 1939, pages 83, 84.)

Without man's leadership role, he would be stripped of much of his purpose and identity. Thus there is complementarity in roles rather than similarity, coordination rather than duplication, and order rather than confusion.

Following in Righteousness

As a wife, I believe I can receive inspiration and revelation on my own in response to prayerful study of a certain situation or problem. Quite often (or often enough that it is an issue) my husband and I disagree on the solution to a problem, and as a result I frequently find myself on my knees pleading with my Father in Heaven to inspire and direct my husband, and help me that I might be able to follow his counsel and example. In addition, I pray that the Lord will confirm to me that my husband's decision is right for us so that I may follow him and be obedient to him as he is to the Lord.

ACCOUNTABILITY

Within the family all members have an accountability for their stewardships or assigned roles. You have undoubtedly worked out an accountability format for your home. Regarding priesthood accountability, the apostle Paul explains in 1 Corinthians 11:3: "But I would have you know, that the head of every man is Christ; and the head of woman is the man; and the head of Christ is God." This can be diagramed as follows:

God ◄   Christ ◄   Man ◄   Woman

From this it can be seen that the husband is not excluded from having to submit to someone who has a stewardship over him. The husband is commanded to submit himself in righteousness to the will of the Savior, and the wife is counseled to submit herself to her husband as he obeys the Son, who in turn obeys the will of the Father.

There is, however, an important qualification for submission within the patriarchal order—that of *righteousness*. The husband should have no qualms about submitting his will to the Savior's will, as Jesus Christ is always consistent and is perfect in his love and administrations, as is the Father. The wife however (and you wives will smile as you read this, knowing how true it is) is required to submit to a mortal man who is but a god in embryo, a novice who is trying to become perfect—who has not yet arrived. This point was disputed once by a young woman student who had been married only one week. By the end of the semester, however, she also agreed that her husband had, in fact, not yet arrived at perfection. It is interesting to note that the

Hebrew word for husband is *baal*, which has two meanings: (a) lord and master, and (b) *false god*. The latter meaning is probably closer to the truth much of the time.

In the meantime, what does the woman do who marries an egotistical, lord-and-master type who is in fact a spiritual midget? Of course it would have been best not to marry him in the first place. It has been said that individuals should go into marriage with both eyes wide open. If, however, it's too late for that, a woman can choose to keep both eyes half closed. If a husband is striving for perfection despite his many shortcomings, the wife has an obligation to help him grow spiritually. On the other hand, Brigham Young offers the following counsel:

> It is not my general practice to counsel the sisters to disobey their husbands, but my counsel is — obey your husbands; and I am sanguine and most emphatic on that subject. But I never counselled a woman to follow her husband to the Devil. If a man is determined to expose the lives of his friends, let that man go to the Devil and to destruction alone. (*Discourses of Brigham Young*, comp. John A. Widtsoe [Salt Lake City: Deseret Book Company, 1954], pages 200-201.)

Slavery, oppression, inequality, and unrighteous dominion have no part in the patriarchal order. A woman is not obligated to suffer this type of oppression. As to when enough is enough, that will have to be prayerfully considered as the problem arises.

> No power or influence can or ought to be maintained by virtue of the priesthood, only by persuasion, by long-suffering, by gentleness and meekness, and by love unfeigned. (D&C 121:41.)

PRESIDING IN RIGHTEOUSNESS

For those of you husbands who desire to preside in righteousness and yet are unsure as to what that entails, the best guide is found in the above section of the Doctrine and Covenants, including the verses that follow verse 41. From these words of the Prophet Joseph it becomes evident that most men do *not* automatically and innately know how to preside correctly. Presiding is a skill that must be learned. Fortunately the Prophet Joseph was not impressed to conclude that most bearers of the priesthood cannot lead in righteousness. He said there are basically ten ways men can lead properly in the patriarchal order and in other priesthood roles. Consider, if you will, the authors' interpretation of these concepts below, and then consider, if you will, the manner in which these traits are made manifest in *your* home:

1. *Persuasion.* This is likely the chief tool of priesthood leadership. It means an attempt to convince one's spouse and family through the presentation of ideas and concepts. It is the opposite of force or tyranny. It is talking and reasoning — without raising one's voice or threatening. It is sharing ideas to show others the wisdom in what one desires. Whenever one *persuades,* the other person is free to agree or to disagree according to his free agency.

2. *Long-suffering.* Patience and a willingness to overlook imperfections in one's mate are an important part of priesthood leadership. This is the opposite of impatience, fault-finding, and expecting perfection.

3. *Gentleness.* A gentle husband is one who respects his wife and considers her his equal. A gentle husband is sensitive to his wife's needs, both emotional and physical, and is never guilty of forcing his own desires upon her.

4. *Meekness.* To be meek is to be teachable and willing to conform to the gospel standards and thus submit one's will to the Lord's will. The meek husband is not a law unto himself. He cares about others' feelings and is willing to be taught by them.

5. *Love unfeigned.* An unfeigned love is one that is sincere, not counterfeit or hypocritical. It is genuine. Under this principle we do not love our mates simply for what they can do for us; we love them as persons of unique worth in and of themselves. Their lives are as important to us as are our own lives.

6. *Kindness.* Kindness is an attitude which should moderate the actions of priesthood leadership at all times. It is the opposite of cruelty, revenge, and being nonforgiving. Perhaps the highest form of kindness we can show others is to forgive them completely.

7. *Pure knowledge.* To preside with pure knowledge is to lead one's family by revelation and inspiration. Pure knowledge comes from God and is undefiled and unpolluted by the theories

of men. How fortunate is the family that has a patriarch at its head who is able to use this gift to bless his family!

8. *No hypocrisy.* The father-husband within the patriarchal order should not be guilty of requiring his wife and family to sacrifice, work, go the extra mile, do without wants or necessities, forego recreation or hobbies, etc., if he himself is not willing to live by the same rules. There cannot be two codes of conduct based on the assumption that the one spouse has an inherent right to more privileges than the others.

9. *No guile.* To lead guilefully is to lead with deceitful cunning, by duplicity (or doubleness) of thought, speech, or action. There is no place for this type of presiding within a true patriarchal order. To see as we are seen and know as we are known is to be without guile and to be completely genuine.

10. *Charity.* Charity is the pure love of Christ. It is an essential character trait of the patriarchal leader. Couples who manifest charity are promised confidence, understanding, the constant companionship of the Holy Ghost, and an everlasting dominion of righteousness and truth. (D&C 121:45-56.)

LEAD WITH GENTLENESS

A beautiful example of how a husband is to preside was given by Spencer W. Kimball. In at least one situation where he was presiding over a meeting in the temple, rather than telling the others that he would give the prayer, he asked, "Is it all right if I give the prayer?" (From Personal Correspondence with authors.) He phrased it like a question to those over whom he presided, rather than just telling them. It was more like a gentle request than an instruction or order. The difference between gentleness and force, between softness and coercion, may be small in words, yet it is great in effect. How often did the Lord speak of being merciful, kind, peacemaking, forgiving, gentle, and loving? How much should a partner in marriage act in these ways, either in presiding or supporting?

As in other areas of marriage, each couple probably will have a style of their own for presiding and following in the home. In your style you ought to adopt the components advocated by the Savior—patience, mercy, kindness, love unfeigned, and gentleness. This will create an atmosphere of joy and peace in your home.

ALLOW FOR AGENCY

One of the most difficult challenges for a husband as he presides is to find the proper balance between the interests of each family member and the family as a whole. Each family member should be able to exercise his own free agency, yet he cannot have complete freedom because excessive freedom may interfere with the rights of others. This can be demonstrated in families where several teenagers as well as the parents have needs for the family automobile. All need to show consideration, with each member sharing any inconvenience that might appear.

When children are small, they are given little freedom, simply because they lack wisdom and experience. They are told what time to go to bed, what time to get up, what to eat, how to act at the table, and so on. As these children grow up, two things change. They are allowed more and more freedom, and the parents gradually learn to change the methods they use to obtain compliance. The parents learn to ask more and tell less. They learn to make suggestions and give advice, and the children are gradually allowed enough freedom and independence that they can choose to accept or reject suggestions and advice.

Allowing for agency is more complex in a marriage relationship, because both partners are adults. They both deserve and desire certain freedoms and independence, and occasionally they even want freedoms that interfere with their marriage or family life.

What do you do then?

There are no simple solutions to this dilemma, but there are several things that are good to remember. First, both extremes are unhealthy. You can have too little or too much freedom. Second, most individuals in our modern culture err in allowing too little freedom to those around them. They want them to do things *their* way. They want too much control over what the other spouse and the other children do. Every adult needs to recognize that *each person* in the family needs to make choices and learn by the good and bad decisions he makes.

Summary

This discussion has centered around the fundamental parts of the patriarchal order and has described several things each spouse can do to use this system of family government wisely. The patriarchal order provides a division of labor wherein the man is to preside in the family and the woman is to give birth to the children and have the primary responsibility for rearing them. In both areas the other spouse is to assist. This creates a harmonious complementarity that does not elevate one sex above the other. Both have crucial responsibilities. This provides order and equality, but not sameness.

There is considerable freedom in the way a couple can administer the patriarchal order in their home. The presiding member is to *direct the process* in the home rather than always have his way. He is to make sure that things get done, and the best way to accomplish this is to be a gentle leader who seeks consensus from family members about decisions, who makes assignments, who delegates responsibilities, and who monitors what is happening to determine when new decisions need to be made. He is therefore a steward, a servant, and a manager rather than a drill sergeant or dictator. Assisted by his wife, a husband/father employs methods of leading which include persuasion, kindness, love, encouragement, affection, and gentleness.

It is now time to consider a final matter which affects the journey of your marriage relationship. Whether you have been married one year or fifty years this discussion will be of value, as it seeks to nurture the feelings of love and fulfillment you have for each other—in anticipation of an eternity together.

*As one string upon another
  builds a rope to anchor
  the mightiest ship,*

*One loving act upon another
  builds ties that bind
  beyond the grave.
  (Author unknown.)*

15

*Those Passing Years
—With Pleasure*

Reflect, if you will, back in time to the period of your engagement. To do this perhaps it would be enjoyable to lay this book in your lap, lean back, take a deep breath, and close your eyes. As you do this, think back to the day you became engaged and experience again the excitement and fluttering sensation in your heart as you thought of spending eternity with your chosen sweetheart. Take three or four minutes to just bask in the sensation of what you then felt for your fiancé(e).

Now then, wasn't that an enjoyable experience? As you considered marriage, one of the feelings you undoubtedly had was that of "bondedness" with your companion. That is, you had developed some very significant, deep *ties* with your sweetheart that served to motivate you both to want to share your eternity with each other. Perhaps your feelings and desires were similar to those expressed as follows by a couple as they prepared for marriage: "We want to be a close-knit couple, to be very much involved with each other, to feel like a team instead of just two people who are married. We'd be lost without each other."

While it is true that bonds of love exist prior to marriage, and in fact serve to propel a couple toward matrimony, they continue to deepen and strengthen as a couple progresses "in righteousness" through the milieu of married life. Consider the words of a husband who is entering his golden years, as he reflects upon his marriage:

"When we were first married we thought we were more in love than anyone else and there was no way our love could be better. It's funny. We look back now and realize that what we had was fine, but it was shallow. It was exciting and thrilling and made our hearts beat and made us tingle, but it was so superficial, so surface. The love we have now is so much deeper, so much more rich. We're so intertwined now and mean so much more to each other that there is no comparison. It's as different as a small sparkling spring with fresh, clear water bouncing down a hill, and then later a deep, wide river with strength, majesty, and security. I wouldn't trade what we have now for what we had then — not for anything."

Wouldn't it be fantastic for all couples (especially Latter-day Saint couples who have the highest ideals known to man) to be able to speak of their marriage as this husband has? It is apparent that this couple had nurtured their relationship, deepened their bonds of love, and paid the price for happiness in their relationship.

Surprise Company
or
Preventive Maintenance

I told my family Thursday that we were having special company Monday. The only clue I gave them was that the company were the most special people we could have come to dinner at our home.

Monday came and I wasn't feeling very well and was half tempted to call the whole thing off, but I decided to go through with it. It turned out to be the best medicine. I became so busy preparing the dinner that I didn't have time to feel sick. I made a chocolate torte—a too rich one for Allen. I had been waiting for a special occasion to make one. The children helped me make four Raggedy Ann salads. They kept eating the raisins off them, but I wasn't upset.

We set the table for four adults in the dining room. I said the children could eat in the kitchen (to carry out our surprise). We used our green lace tablecloth and best dishes. Allen helped me dress the children in their Sunday best and I dressed in my favorite long green dress—I hadn't worn it for a long time. I thought as I was changing that dressing up for dinner takes such little effort but makes the occasion so special.

I lit the candle and then informed everyone that they were my special company. (I tried first to have them guess who was coming by giving them clues of each person's special qualities, but they were more interested in eating.) Katie kept asking, "Isn't anyone else coming?" (She loves company with children to play with.)

It was a most enjoyable dinner, as I wasn't as nervous as I am with other company. I wanted it to be a special treat for Allen too, and fix it all myself. He made the garlic bread and vacuumed up a bit and helped set the table, though. Afterwards he gave me a special thank-you hug and kiss. (That made everything worthwhile.)

Later when I was getting ready for bed, I noticed an extra clean towel and washcloth hanging in the bathroom. I said, "Allen, what are these for." He said, "Those are for our company."

Unfortunately, not all couples have a "preventive maintenance" program implemented in their marrige to insure the preservation of these bonds and the fulfillment they provide. Perhaps you can identify with the words of the following wife, who, after years of marriage, has found herself groping frantically in the fog of unfulfillment that has gradually enveloped her marriage:

"Are all marriages like ours? Do they just fizzle out? We started out with a great thing going, but it has just disappeared. We were madly in love. Now, we just live together. We don't share anything anymore. We're just married, and I guess we'll stay that way, but it's sure not what I thought it would be."

Or perhaps you can identify with the following wife, who after several years of marriage has more or less drifted into a pattern of marriage that is much like a flat tire, it just doesn't have much life to it, and is not really going anywhere:

"Judging by the way it was when we were first married, say the first five years or so, things are pretty matter-of-fact now — even dull. They're dull between *us*, I mean. The children are a lot of fun, keep us pretty busy, and there are lots of outside things — like Little League and PTA and the swim club, and even the company parties aren't always so bad. But I mean where Bob and I are concerned — if you followed us around you'd wonder why we ever got married. We take each other for granted. We laugh at the same things sometimes, but we don't really laugh together — the way we used to. But as he said to me the other night, 'You know, you're still a little fun now and then.'

"I don't say this to complain, not in the least. There's a cycle to life. There are things you do in high school, and different things you do in college. There you're a young adult. And then you're middle-aged. That's where we are at. I'll admit that I do yearn for the old days when sex was a big thing and going out was fun and I hung onto everything he said about his work and his ideas as if they were coming from a genius or something. But then you get the children and other responsibilities. I have the home and Bob has a tremendous burden of responsibility at the office. He is completely responsible for setting up the new branch now. You have to adjust to these things and we both try to gracefully. Anniversaries though do sometimes remind you kind of hard."

Although everyone would hope for fulfillment to the extent that was expressed by the first wife, still that is no doubt the ideal rather than the norm, and couples find themselves experiencing periods of disenchantment and disillusionment after the honeymoon is over, either soon or later.

Most LDS couples consider themselves well insulated against the demon of divorce that enters into such a large percentage of American homes today. Simply saying it, however, does not necessarily make it so. As President Spencer W. Kimball stated, one survey revealed that one out of ten temple marriages had ended in divorce. (*Marriage and Divorce*, page 11.) This 10 percent were the couples who decided to terminate their relationship; it does *not* take into account those LDS couples who have resigned themselves to a lifetime of unfulfillment, while abhoring the thought of dissolving their marriage through divorce.

Perhaps the bottom line here is the vulnerability of Latter-day Saint couples to dissatisfaction in their marriages, which has been observed to be the trend in marriages throughout the United States. Studies conducted among Latter-day Saint couples find that most couples experience a gradual decrease in their satisfaction over the first fifteen to twenty years of their marriage, followed by a slight increase in the later years of life.

You can appreciate the fact that this dissatisfaction and disenchantment does not just happen. It takes place when marriage partners begin to find fault with each other, when they spend less *quality* time with each other, and when they spend less effort communicating and sharing feelings with each other. In other words, when an LDS husband and wife continue to court each other and remain interested and involved in each others' lives, then their happiness and fulfillment should continue.

Ways to Enrich Your Marriage

To assist you in your quest for fulfillment in your marriage, the following considerations are shared.

CONTINUE COURTSHIP

Prophets agree that it is wise to continue to court after marriage. President Spencer W. Kimball has said:

Love is like a flower, and, like the body, it needs constant feeding. The mortal body would soon be emaciated and die if there were not frequent feedings. The tender flower would wither and die without food and water. And so love, also, cannot be expected to last forever unless it is continually fed with portions of love, the manifestation of esteem and admiration, the expressions of gratitude, and the consideration of unselfishness.

. . . If each spouse is forever seeking the interest, comforts, and happiness of the other, the love found in courtship and cemented in marriage will grow into mighty proportions. Many couples permit their marriages to become stale and their love to grow cold like old bread or worn-out jokes or cold gravy. Certainly the foods most vital for love are consideration, kindness, thoughtfulness, concern, expressions of affection, embraces of appreciation, admiration, pride, companionship, confidence, faith, partnership, equality, and dependence. (*Marriage and Divorce,* pages 22-23.)

The following was taken from a sermon given in the Congregational Church of Jaffrey, New Hampshire, on August 10, 1947, by a substitute preacher, an engineer, William E. Wickenden.

Two Miles of Marriage

Then there are the two miles of marriage and family life. How quickly the glamour of courtship, the exaltation of the wedding ceremony and the new-found intimacies of the honeymoon descend to the drudgery of earning and economizing, the drab routine of cooking and dishwashing or of furnace-tending and lawn-mowing, and the difficult or even exasperating process of mutual adjustment, on a lifetime rather than a weekend basis. How quickly the experience of parenthood, with its unique expansion of the ego, descends to the plane of slavery, to bottles and formulas, of midnight feedings, of diapers and washtubs, of staying in nights and of doing without generally.

Just about the time the mile of marital compulsion begins to seem endless, the young couple discover that a successful marriage is not a lucky break, or, for that matter, a heavensent boon, but is rather one of the most exacting of human achievements and one of the most rigorous of personal disciplines. The simple truth is that the finest human product cannot be achieved in isolation nor by an unlimited exaltation of individual selfhood, but through the merged personality of a man and woman who are willing to pay the price . . . by going the second mile.

"And whosoever shall compel thee to go a mile, go with him twain." (Matthew 5:41.)

President David O. McKay also commented on the importance of continuing to court after marriage:

Remember that consideration after the ceremony is just as appropriate and necessary and beautiful as gentleness and consideration before the wedding. (*Gospel Ideals,* page 471.)

Next to loyalty as contributive to a happy home, I should like to urge *continued courtship,* and apply this to grown people. Too many couples have come to the altar of marriage looking upon the marriage ceremony as the end of courtship instead of the beginning of an eternal courtship. Let us not forget that during the burdens of home life—and they come—that tender words of appreciation, courteous acts are even more appreciated than during those sweet days and months of courtship. (*Improvement Era,* June 1956, page 396.)

Spice and variety. The aspect of courtship that has just been discussed deals with basic processes in our relationships, such as courtesy, assistance, emotional support, kindness, and companionship. These are tremendously important in that they are the bread or staff of life of loving relationships. There is also a different aspect of courtship that you can use to enhance your marriage. It is more like the seasoning or spice in cooking or the frosting on a cake. It is that marriages can become very dull and drab if a little novelty and variety isn't added to them.

The Sixty-dollar Weekend

Last spring, after surviving a long and difficult winter with four small children, heavy financial pressures, and a new baby just three weeks away, we took our sixty-dollar cure. Greg's secretary agreed to stay with the kids, and we were off for one night in a small yet not too distant community.

It wasn't where we went or what we did that was memorable, but the opportunity that we had to get away and to communicate—nonstop. This break in our everyday routine seemed to manicure the frayed edges of a relationship that had gone on unattended.

We have found this to be the case many times. We need to make the effort to continue the courtship that was started several years ago — and which we hope will continue on into the eternities.

One author has written several best-selling paperbacks that have capitalized on this part of marriage. Marabel Morgan's books *Total Woman* and *Total Joy* explain hundreds of ways to "put a little kick" into marriage, and the advice has been so needed in modern American marriages that she has sold millions of copies of her books. She discusses such nutty ideas as the wife greeting her husband in pajamas when he comes home and then having an oriental dinner on the living room floor. The husband can do such things as wrap up a candy bar as a present and tie it in an obvious place in the kitchen with a note that it can't be opened for several days.

It would be easy to overdo the spice and romance and silliness, and it would also be unfortunate if a marriage were based on these superficial frills rather than on the more basic aspects of life. On the other hand, too many couples ignore the humorous, spontaneous, light aspects of marriage.

If you were to overdo the spice and romance, it would be like putting too much butter on a piece of bread or too much salt in the cooked cereal. It would become distasteful and objectionable. On the other hand . . .

What is the oatmeal like when we forget the salt?

What is the bread like when we run out of butter?

What would pizza be like without a little oregano?

What would a car look like without any chrome?

What would marriage be like without a little spice and variety?

What are some specifics? The following list identifies a number of things that you can do to continue to court. Some of the suggestions deal with the basic aspects of your relationship, such as trust, concern, appreciation, courtesy, and charity. Others deal with the more superficial aspects of fun, novelty, spice, and romance. You may want to implement different combinations of these, and surely you can add some creative ideas to this list. The bottom line is to be aware of the importance of this part of marriage and court each other a little.

Ways to Make Marriage Exciting

What a husband can do:

1. Kiss the back of your wife's neck often.
2. Don't think you always have to keep your chin up. Cry a little—she'll love mothering you.
3. Bring her flowers while she can still smell them.
4. Use the same good manners with your wife that you would with a business client.
5. Bring home some phonograph "golden oldie" songs you both remember fondly.
6. Even if you've been married a long time, compliment her cooking.
7. Ask your wife's advice on business problems and sometimes take it.
8. Don't think tenderness is sissified; it's really strength.
9. Send presents to your wife for no reason at all.
10. Give her what you know she wants instead of what you think she should have.
11. Never say, "I had that for lunch today."
12. When she is telling a story, don't give away the punch line.
13. Learn some new jokes for the sake of your wife, who has heard the old ones so often.
14. Bring home a flower once in a while.
15. Leave parties when your wife wants to—within half an hour or so.
16. Never ask her, "What have you done all day, dear?" Say, "Tell me about your day."
17. Kiss her in public. She may look embarrassed and sound sore, but most wives love it.
18. When you have finished reading this sentence walk over to her and tell her you are glad you married her and that you would do it all over again.
19. Take her out to lunch once in a while.

What a wife can do:
20. Tell the neighbors you're happily married—it will get back to your husband and please him.
21. Don't tell him your problems until you've fed him.
22. Treat your husband with at least the same attention and love you give your children or your dog.
23. Buy a new negligee and wear it.
24. Learn to translate your husband properly. "You look okay" may mean "Darling, you look wonderful tonight."
25. Write him a love note once in a while.
26. Have a comfortable home where he can relax.
27. Don't make him the family "meany." Don't say to the children, "Just wait until your father gets home" or "I want to let you, but Daddy says no."
28. Remember the things you said and did to land him and try them again.
29. Don't shush your husband if he sings at parties or acts the clown.
30. Don't keep telling him he's too old to do some of the things he wants to do.
31. Don't be on the telephone when he comes home, and don't start talking on the phone until after he leaves in the morning.
32. And be home when he gets there.
33. No pincurls when he's in sight.
34. Put on your cold cream in the daytime.
35. Find some place to keep the bobby pins, all of them.
36. If he's usually amorous and aggressive, turn the tables once in a while.
37. Watch him shave, as Queen Victoria did Prince Albert.
38. Pay cash for his presents—don't buy him a gift and then charge it to him.
39. When he brings home a mess of fish—no matter how unappetizing—clean them, cook them to the best of your ability, and eat them.
40. Don't keep asking him, "Do you love me?"
41. Believe him when he says that he does.
42. Sometimes *you* take the babysitter home.

43. Don't borrow his razor.
44. Don't give him surprise parties.

What you both can do:
45. Treat each other occasionally as though you were meeting for the first time.
46. Don't address each other as Mother and Father. Use first names or terms of endearment.
47. Go to an auction together.
48. Never sleep on a problem without a solution or some agreement.
49. If you offer prayer together before you go to sleep, you'll have your thoughts on something higher than your problems.
50. Do genealogical work together.
51. After years of marriage, some husbands and wives get to look and sound alike. Don't.
52. Take up a daring sport that you can do together—like skin diving, water skiing, or mountain climbing.
53. Stop keeping up with the Joneses.
54. Drop friends who are always bickering.
55. If one of you puts the first dent in the new car, laugh about it—even if it kills you.
56. Don't live all your life by the clock—don't condemn the other if he/she is a little late.
57. Avoid both getting mad at the same time.
58. Respect each other's privacy.
59. Contribute to the support of a foster child and correspond with the child.
60. Don't sacrifice all your fun today for what you think may be security tomorrow.
61. Take a walk in the rain together.
62. Brainstorm problems with the whole family.
63. Toss out all the furniture that irks you.
64. Spend the night at a hotel together.
65. Make a family picture album together.
66. Have one night out alone together at least once a month.
67. Switch off the TV and talk.

68.   Always have some project going for the future—something to do, build, or buy.
69.   If you have relatives living with you, see if they can visit someone else occasionally.
70.   Seldom use the words *I, me,* and *mine.* Use *we, us,* and *ours* more.
71.   Build up each other in public. Don't try to compete.
72.   If you must take medicine regularly, keep it out of sight.
73.   Have a fireplace built in your bedroom.
74.   Go on a diet together.
75.   Never begin a sentence with "It seems to me a good husband would . . ." or "A good wife would . . ." or "After all I've done for you. . . ."
76.   Stop going to parties you don't want to go to.

(Adapted from John and June Robbins, "84 Ways to Make Your Marriage More Exciting," *McCall's,* October 1958, pages 50, 147-148. Appreciation is expressed to them.)

Unsaid Words

There is no song that larks can sing,
No perfume roses shed,
That takes the place within our lives
Of loving words, unsaid.
                        (Zara Sabin.)

VIEW MARRIAGE AS A DEVELOPMENTAL PROCESS

Another thing that can help the quality of marriage go up rather than down is to view life and everything in it from a developmental perspective. One way to do this is to view life as a long journey, an eternal journey. Your journey didn't ever begin and it won't ever end. And your journey will be as pleasant as you make it. You will have many companions on your trip, but the one person who will be with you the most is your husband or wife. *The essence of living is to make your journey as pleasant as possible, to create joy for yourselves and those who journey with you.*

The earthly part of your journey is a unique part of this trip. It is a time when you generally travel through a mist or a fog.

You can't see very far, and you can't see very clearly. You also have a temporary amnesia because you can't remember anything about the earlier parts of your journey. This means that you have to learn all over again how to take care of yourself; and you have to learn how to interact with your traveling companion. You also have to learn again what the journey is all about.

It goes without saying that traveling brings new experiences. One encounters problems, joys, sorrows, new faces, new challenges, and new ways of thinking. And that is the way marriage is. It begins in early adulthood, and many think that they will then stop traveling and settle down to a relatively unchanging, stable situation. They have just finished the hectic years of growing up when everything was changing and they were different each year, and they can hardly wait for the stability of adulthood. These people fail to realize that adulthood is not different as regards change. It is just the next part of the journey of life.

Surprisingly, this new part of the journey has just as many changes, surprises, challenges, and new experiences as any other part. This means that you will be changing as individuals. You will develop new beliefs and opinions. Some of the things that are important at age twenty-five will not be important at age thirty. The challenges at age eighteen are very different from the challenges at age twenty-eight or forty-eight or sixty-eight.

So what does this mean for your marriage? It means that you ought to view marriage as a dynamic, growing, changing process. The courting period of single life contains a lot of entertainment, discovery, excitement, intense love, optimism, and hope. Gradually, the hectic process of raising a family crowds out some of these parts of life, and if they are not replaced by other things that pull you together, you grow apart. There are many things that you can have only after a few years of marriage, and they can replace the attractions of courtship and early marriage. Things such as the security that can be felt only after a relationship has lasted a few years—trust, stability, reliance, strength of character in times of difficulty, sacrifice, assistance when it is difficult but needed, and sharing the joys and sorrows of life—such things can gradually change the nature of your marriage.

It is amazing how much a person changes in adulthood, how much one must adapt, how much two people face as a couple. The young mother who wants to have a dozen children finds that having the responsibility of several young children has changed her opinions. The young executive realizes that he doesn't want to pay the price or doesn't have the skills it takes to become the president. He then has to change to a different type of occupation and needs the support and assistance of an understanding wife. The young couple who have three lovely children discover that the mother has a serious illness, such as multiple sclerosis. They then need to completely rewrite their script of what it means to be successful and happy in life. The woman who has been taught that she ought to be a good mother discovers that her temperament and personality are just not very compatible with the demands of motherhood. The husband who has several failures in his occupation is so devastated that he loses confidence in himself and becomes chronically depressed. The person who wants to be a loving parent has feelings of dislike for his child. The wife has a spouse who becomes disillusioned with the Church and falls into inactivity.

Those persons who recognize that marriage is a changing, flexible, and evolving process will be able to anticipate changes and adjust to them wisely. It is the hope of the authors that you will catch this vision, for these insights can truly help you find ways to develop and grow in desirable ways.

Perfecting yourself is a gradual and uneven process. When you view marriage as a developmental experience, you should recognize that perfecting yourself is a very slow and gradual process. While accepting the commandment from the Lord to become "perfect, even as your Father which is in Heaven is perfect" (Matthew 5:48), you should recognize that it can't be done overnight. In fact, if you work too hard at perfecting yourself, sometimes your anxiety about your inadequacies will actually get in the way and slow you down. The proper perspective therefore is to recognize the potential that you have and gradually improve yourself in a line-upon-line, precept-upon-precept manner. As you are able to live some of the laws correctly, you can rejoice in these accomplishments and gradually improve in other areas.

Growing Pains

We were an ordinary, likeable LDS family. We had what seemed to be a good marriage, fine children, and a future that looked bright. Stan had always been an ambitious, hard worker who provided us with a better than average life-style, and was a loving and helpful husband and father. I was dedicated to my challenges as a wife and mother and worked hard to make our home pleasant and took good care of our children. Our young family had grown rapidly to four children in less than eight years, and we enjoyed the privilege of having these delightful little people in our home. We lived in a comfortable home in a growing neighborhood with other families who shared many of the same experiences in rearing young children and trying to make ends meet in these times of high inflation.

We had been lucky and had accumulated wealth from business investments and planned soon to build a dream home. Stan and I spent hours discussing and formulating plans for the new house. It was an exciting new adventure for us.

During this time we also had to face some tremendous challenges. One of these was a business investment that was going into a serious slump that would eventually cause us to lose the money we had invested and also money that had been invested by trusting family members. Stan gave his all and more to save what had been invested. He was gone a good deal, and when he was present he was noticeably nervous and seemed unable to relax. The time we needed as a couple and as a family was infringed upon because of his work, and we found that we could not handle the additional stress. We both began to feel resentful and trapped into a situation over which we had no control. The same responsibilities we had handled before with relative ease seemed more burdensome. Our communication had diminished greatly, which seemed to create more misunderstandings and the resulting hurt feelings. Then we found ourselves subtly and purposely trying to hurt one another to get back at the other for the hurt each felt. We began to question the love that had bound us together for so long, and we began to feel confused and disillusioned. Heaven even seemed to have closed up on us. Most of all, a terrible dread and hopelessness loomed over us that was literally painful to bear. We felt ashamed that a good LDS couple like us was having a "marriage problem," and we felt vulnerable to the talk of the neighborhood. We withdrew into ourselves and didn't want to talk about our problems for fear we would be misunderstood and talked about. It was great comfort at this time to know that we did have friends and relatives who cared about us, however.

I feel it was inspiration that caused me to think of counseling. I desperately wanted to preserve what love was left in our relationship. I longed for a trusting, loving relationship where we could share and conquer life's problems together without having to put one another down.

Stan was reluctant to go for counseling, still thinking things would eventually work out by themselves. He didn't want to believe that our problems were that serious. He ended up going for counseling sessions mainly because I wanted him to.

Those first sessions were painful ones. We were embarrassed to be there in the first place, and when we brought up issues it seemed as if we were digging up long-abandoned garbage, and bringing it to the surface again to view the ugliness and experience the stench of years of decay. Later we grew more used to it, but it was still a time of strain and discomfort. I believe a good deal of it was because of our preconceived ideas that marriage counseling was for people with "something wrong" psychologically. We struggled with feelings of guilt, inadequacy, and resentment, but we also found that once we aired these feelings and talked about them openly and frankly, we began to have a more complete picture of where we were and where we could go from here. Both of us agree now that the counseling was what helped us to get on a good course again by following advice given to us by a caring, experienced marriage counselor who was trained to help couples cope with their problems in a positive manner.

Also, we now realize how important it was for both of us to remain faithful to each other throughout the crisis. It was the glue that must have acted in keeping us cemented together even when our foundation was cracking.

We have learned too, that great stress has its effect on almost everything a couple is involved in. When the burdens become lighter, things seem to normalize, with stress decreasing proportionately.

We're thankful for the fact that we have made it through a difficult time together and feel closer to each other and more understanding of each other because of this experience. We seem to have needed it to grow. We hope that we will be able to meet whatever trials come our way by remaining true and continuing to seek growth in life's experiences.

This awareness—that perfecting takes a long time—can add an important dimension to a marital relationship. It means that as a couple you can help each other work on areas that need improvement, while realizing the importance of encouragement and praise as you each make progress. It also means that you ought not to demand perfection of your spouse or be disappointed or nagging if he or she is less than perfect in a variety of ways. You too are imperfect, and the marital relationship can help you both slowly grow and improve. This changes the emphasis from being harsh toward faults and critical when the other person makes mistakes, to recognizing that it will take a long time to become perfect, and then toward slowly and consistently helping each other.

Second, you perfect yourself in an *uneven* way. You are each better in some things than others. For example, one of you may be fairly good—close to perfection—with regard to patience and kindness, but not be able to worship or meditate well. Another may have a quick temper but a heart of gold. Each of you ought to recognize the areas in which you and your spouse are fairly good and rejoice in these areas of proficiency. You should also recognize the areas where you are each less than proficient and gradually work on the ones you can improve, without rejection from your spouse or unwanted nagging or pressure. You can lean on your spouse for help in constructive ways.

JOINT SOCIAL NETWORKS

There is one final idea that can help you enrich your marriage as the years pass. Those who use this principle find themselves growing together, and those who ignore it find themselves growing apart. The general idea is this:

The more we associate with a group, the more we tend to become like the people in that group.

The application of this principle in this situation is fairly obvious. A husband will become like the members of the groups he associates with, and a wife will become like those in the groups she associates with. If these groups are different, the husband and wife will gradually lose the similarities they shared at the time they were married.

Consider, for example, the following couple:

Sue and Harry had a lot in common when they were dating. He sang in the choir she directed, and she loved to watch him play on the intramural teams. They were both majoring in chemistry, and they helped each other in their studies. After their marriage, she was too occupied as a mother to do much with chemistry. Gradually, their interests became a little different. He became more involved in sports, and she became more involved in music.

They've now been married ten years, and Harry has become a sports nut. They have two television sets, and he turns both of them on when more than one game is being broadcast. He used to play in the city softball league until his age slowed him down too much. Since then he has been coaching in the Little League in the summers and the church league in the winters. When he's not coaching, he's refereeing. He's happy when he can talk, read, watch live athletics.

Sue's leisure time is spent with the arts. She loves music, and she's on the board of directors of the local symphony. She leads a group of singers who put on programs, and she writes original music for them.

Harry loves to associate with his sports-minded friends, but he finds arty friends a little more stuffy each year. Sue thinks Harry's buddies are too loud and they never take anything seriously except sports.

What is happening to Sue and Harry? They are finding that the groups of people they are associating with are more different as the years pass. If the above idea is true, they will also become more and more different from each other as the years pass. And, having less and less in common, they will experience less unity, less interaction, less companionship, more differences, and will probably be less satisfied with their marriage.

So what should they do?

Should they do everything together?

The accompanying circles show three different degrees of "overlap" in the social networks of couples. Condition A is where a couple participates in virtually all of their networks together. They belong to the same clubs, have no friends that are not mutual friends, visit relatives together, interact together with the people at the office, etc. Condition B is where most of the people they interact with are the same, but there are a few areas where they lead separate lives. Condition C is like Harry and Sue. A few of their associations are together, but most of them are different.

Which is best? It will be different for different couples, but there are a few guidelines. Couples like Sue and Harry will grow apart over the years, so you should avoid that much separateness. You should have a sizeable part of your associations in common. You can also err in the opposite direction by having so much in common that you would be stifled and lose too much individuality and freedom. This is another situation where the golden mean operates, where too much or too little is unwise and there is an optimal place in the middle. Within the optimal levels, there is probably still a lot of room for differences between couples.

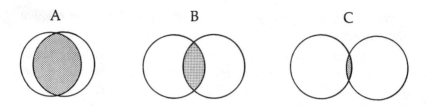

Some of you may even want different patterns at different times in your lives. It may be that you will also find a slight ebb or flow in this, in that you may gradually drift a little too far apart and then have to make slight adjustments. Or you may find that you have a lot of interaction together but one individual wants to be alone a little more. As long as the substantial "core" of your associations are common ones, you can make these changes without creating any problems.

In summary, this is another aspect of the marital system that you need to monitor periodically. You should notice what is happening, because it can gradually influence precious things in desirable or undesirable ways. As long as you have a sizeable part of your social networks in common, you can just notice what is happening and then forget it until your next "check-up." If your periodic check-up reveals that you are having fewer and fewer common associations, you ought to seriously evaluate what you are doing and how it will probably affect your marriage over the years. You may find that your "separateness" is temporary and that you needn't worry about it. Or you may find that you have drifted in separate directions and that you ought to try to find new ways to combine your associations.

This poem, written by a husband who had recently lost his wife, teaches a beautiful message about strengthening marriage as the years pass.

ONE ROSE

You surely recall youth's sweet moments:
The stars and the moon shone so bright
As you wined her and dined her to music
With a bouquet of roses each night.

It was, oh, such a beautiful courtship;
You kissed her full lips and pink cheek
    And sighed in her ear,
    "I love you, my dear."
There were orchids or roses each week.

The honeymoon deepened your romance
As you pledged your true troth once again.
    This bond would not sever;
    You'd love her forever.
There were pansies and pinks now and then.

Then came babies, the bottles, the budget;
And things just didn't seem to go right:
    But don't you suppose
    She still needed a rose
And a kiss on a Saturday night?

There was cooking, and sewing, and cleaning,
While time itself seemed to take flight.
    The work's never done:
    Still she longs for some fun
And one rose on a Saturday night.

You declare love with gifts when expected—
Anniversaries and each Christmas Night—
    But some people say
    There's a much better way:
Try a rose on a Saturday night.

As the years pass, we all grow neglectful:
Hold her hand; touch her lips; hold her tight.
    As life ebbs to a close,
    She still longs for a rose.
Bring a fresh one this Saturday night.

One day when your sweetheart has left you,
You will have God's own word she's all right.
    When the spring breezes stir
    Fragrant memories of her,
Crush a rose to your lips every night.

                    (Alvin R. Barlow.)

Summary

All marriages start out happily, with bonds of affection motivating couples to form a lasting relationship. As married partners begin their life together, they do so with love for each other and with total optimism toward their future.

Unfortunately, in most marriages the luster gradually fades and the relationship becomes less desirable than the partners would like. As the love and warmth and companionship begin to fade, the partners begin to drift apart. At the same time the faults of each begin to surface and to grate like sandpaper against the grain of the relationship. Yes, the gate to marital mediocrity is wide, and many find it and find themselves enticed to pass through it.

Even so, Latter-day Saint couples need to keep in mind that there is another gate. It is the gate to marital growth and joy, and, like the gate to heaven, is more narrow and strait, and fewer there be that find it. Those who keep the commandments, who remain unselfish, and who continually "invest" in their relationship through courting, communicating, and trusting, are those who will experience joy and happiness in their marriage.

It is the sincere hope of the authors that you will have profited and grown, both individually and as a couple, from the issues discussed in this book. Our Heavenly Father *will* guide you, and *will* direct you toward an eternal relationship—if you but do your share. An eternity of happiness and companionship certainly makes the investment in this life worthwhile.

God bless you both in this quest.

Index